A PLACE FOR YOU

A
Place for You

Psychology and Religion

PAUL TOURNIER

SCM PRESS LTD
LONDON

Translated by Edwin Hudson from the French
L'homme et son lieu
Editions Delachaux et Niestlé,
Neuchâtel and Paris, 1966

SBN 334 01263 5

First published in English 1968
by SCM Press Ltd
56 Bloomsbury Street London WC1
Second impression 1970

© SCM Press Ltd 1968

Printed in Great Britain by
Fletcher & Son Ltd, Norwich

CONTENTS

PART ONE

The Place

I

"Somewhere to be"

THE WORDS were those of a young student with whom I had formed a deep friendship. He was sitting by my fireside, telling me of his difficulties, of the anxiety that never left him, and which at times turned to panic and to flight. He was trying to look objectively at what was going on inside himself and to understand it. Then, as if summing up his thoughts, he looked up at me and said: "Basically, I'm always looking for a place—for somewhere to be."

It sometimes happens that a remark unexpectedly strikes an answering note in our minds and hearts; and that is what happened with me that day. The remark set going a whole new train of thought in my mind. I should like in this book to gather these thoughts together, because I feel that they have helped me to a better understanding of some of the fundamental needs of men and women, and of the distress that besets large numbers of them.

Of course, it was because I knew something of my friend's life-story that I found his remark so striking. He had been an only child in a strictly religious family. He vividly remembered his grandfather, an austere old man, invested with all the prestige and authority of a patriarch. But his parents did not get on well together. Disharmony between parents always has a harmful effect on children, and the anxiety it causes is made much worse when the tradition of the family is one of high moral standards, so that there is a marked contrast between violent acts and professed beliefs.

There is no need for me to go into great detail. The situation has been described by all the psychologists. At first the child struggles vainly to reconcile his parents. When he was a little older this young man had taken his mother's side out of pity for her, and had become antagonistic to his father. This had only made matters worse. In situations of this sort the child intuitively senses that his mother

is trying to find in him some emotional compensation for her unhappiness, and this makes it impossible for him to respond freely to
her love. He thus lacks any sound emotional relationship with
either of his parents. The ambivalence of his attitude to his mother,
the tension in his mind between contradictory feelings of sympathy
and antipathy towards her, are no doubt more harmful to him than
his open hostility towards his father.

The boy's anxiety state had become acute at the time of his
parent's divorce, and the remarriage of his father. He remained cut
off from his father, and powerless in the face of his mother's distress. He went up to university. He hesitated, and then changed to
another course of study, and did badly in his examinations. He
soon found himself paralysed by an inability to concentrate on his
work. And so that young man—highly intelligent, sensitive, and
idealistic—sees the months and years slipping away, while his life
is wasted in this complete blockage.

His is a case of failure neurosis, in which powerful unconscious
forces themselves prevent the sufferer from realizing his dearest
ambitions. He makes solemn resolutions, but has not the will-
power to carry them out, school himself as he may. He cannot bring
himself to work. He tries religion, going every morning and evening
into various churches to pray. I too try to help him. I know well
that exhortation and advice are of no avail in such cases. What is
required is the release of the negative forces lying buried deep in
his mind. We uncover hundreds of painful memories. We analyse
his dreams, and oddities in his behaviour which surprise even him.
He has great confidence in me. I love him, and believe I understand
him. And yet we achieve no decisive result.

On a visit to Assisi, he had a sudden strong feeling of fellowship with St. Francis, and felt that now everything would be different. But back in his little room at home with his books, he sees
that nothing has changed. He is torn between two worlds—the ideal
world, that of Pascal, in which he is passionately interested, and the
world of reality, the "everyday" world, as it is called—and there is
absolutely no communication between them.

I sent him to a foreign colleague, who received him with great
affection, but also with a firmness which is not part of my nature.
"You are floating in the clouds," my colleague said; "a tree, if it is
to raise its branches high, must have its roots sunk deep into the
ground." (The ground, you will notice—the place!) "When you

have passed your exams.,", my colleague added, "you will be able to have useful discussions about Pascal with Dr. Tournier. But the first thing is to work." And so our student stayed in his room, and opened his books in front of him, so as to look as if he were working should the doctor happen to come. But he was not working.

The ground, a place! That was what he had been looking for through all those dark years. He had looked for it first in the Church, but without ever becoming fully integrated into its life. Disappointed with the Church, he had turned to militant Communism, only to be disappointed once again. Then he had associated with existentialist groups, and then with unruly leather-jacket gangs. Always he was looking for a community to which he could attach himself, and every time he was disappointed. He wandered like a shadow or an automaton from one group to another, always with the feeling that he did not belong. On rare occasions, in some small smoky bar, he had felt himself "in", but the feeling was only a fleeting impression.

The whole of society seemed to him so false! His parents and their friends put up a pretence of middle-class respectability, affecting empty conventionalism, and a façade of moral principles. They indulged in mutual flattery, and formed alliances or fought one another as the occasion demanded to achieve their ends and enrich themselves. Even the academic world of the university was imprisoned in its conventions and shot through with intrigue and jerrymandering. The communists, too, were playing their own game in their own fashion. And as for all the young people with whom he associated, his brothers in distress, rootless like himself, in revolt against society, were they not all looking for an excuse for their heavy scepticism? They too were acting a part, playing a role of the rebel, and sometimes the cynic. And when he looked at himself he observed that he too was imitating them, and without much conviction.

His best friend had committed suicide, and that had been a great shock to him. Is not suicide, for many young people, one more way of looking for a place which they have sought in vain on earth, a protest against life for having shut them out? We must try to understand these disillusioned young people of today, who haunt the coffee-bars. They read Camus,[1] who declares that life is meaningless,

[1] Albert Camus, *The Myth of Sisyphus*, translated by Justin O'Brien, Hamish Hamilton, London, 1955.

and Sartre[2] with his indictment of idealism, of those who serve principles which they claim are absolute, when in reality they have chosen them arbitrarily solely in order to escape from the anguish of nothingness.

"I'm always looking for a place," he said.

What he was looking for, and had not found, was a genuine community into which he could really fit. One feels, however, that his failure has less to do with his superficial disappointment than with a powerful internal blockage. What we have here may be termed a non-engagement complex. One has a definite feeling that there is an internal determinism compelling him to wander ceaselessly, blocking the road to that social adaptation which he longs to achieve.

The ideal place for the child is the family. When I questioned him on the subject, my student friend told me that he had happy memories of his childhood and youth. But upon analysis all his happy memories proved to be situated outside his home. When the family is such that the child cannot fit himself into it properly, he looks everywhere for some other place, leading a wandering existence, incapable of settling down anywhere. His tragedy is that he carries about within himself this fundamental incapacity for any real attachment. He bears about with him his constant, increasing, and unsatisfied nostalgia. He feels he is repulsed, excluded, or ignored. His contacts with others are merely conventional and impersonal.

The child who has been able to grow up harmoniously in a healthy home finds a welcome everywhere. In infancy all he needs is a stick placed across two chairs to make himself a house, in which he feels quite at home. Later on, wherever he goes, he will be able to make any place his own, without any effort on his part. For him it will not be a matter of seeking, but of choosing.

There is, then, a kind of law, which recalls Christ's thoroughly realistic words: "To him who has will more be given, and he will have abundance; but from him who has not, even what he has will be taken away" (Matt. 13.12). He who has once had the experience of belonging in a place, always finds a place for himself afterwards; whereas he who has been deprived of it, searches everywhere in vain. I have shown elsewhere that the same applies to the sense of

---

[2] Jean-Paul Sartre, *Existentialism and Humanism*, translated by Philip Mairet, Methuen, London, 1948.

the person, the ability to achieve personal relationships. He who has been brought up in an impersonal atmosphere finds himself in an entirely impersonal world. Even people are just things to him. On the other hand, he who has once experienced the dialogue of person with person engages in it again with all he meets—even with brother wolf and brother sun, like St. Francis, with animals and things, plants and stones. They all become persons for him.

There are two worlds, the impersonal world and the world of persons; not so much a world of things and a world of men, as a personal and an impersonal view of both men and things. Between these two worlds there is an invisible frontier which is within ourselves, and it is very difficult to cross. This is what Martin Buber meant,[3] when he contrasted the "I-Thou" relationship with the "I-It" relationship. He himself took the example of a tree which is only an "It", a thing, so long as I admire or examine it from the outside only, but which becomes a "Thou" if I have the faculty of entering into personal communion with it. Buber underlines in this way the contrast between the self-commitment of the "I-Thou" relationship and the indifference of the "I-It". In his terms, we may say that there are "It-places" and "Thou-places", according to whether we remain strangers to the place we are in, or integrate ourselves into it.

It was, of course, a "Thou-place"—a real community—that my young friend was looking for. Martin Buber feels keenly the tragic solitude of modern man, and sees him in search of God, often without realizing it. "In each Thou," he says, "we address the eternal Thou." And in this connection he quotes the magnificent invocation which Simeon the New Theologian addresses to God: "Come, lonely One, to him who is alone!" Martin Buber has re-awakened in us the sense of community, which our modern civilization, and even our churches, have tended to forget. Community is the place where we meet God. "We are waiting," writes Buber, "for a theophany about which we know nothing except its place, and that place is called community." And again, "Whether he likes it or not, whether he takes it seriously or not, the human person is part of the community into which he is born or in which he happens to live."

But Buber also formulated a law, that the personal relationship

[3] Martin Buber, *I and Thou*, translated by R. Gregor Smith, T. & T. Clark, Edinburgh, 1966.

is fragile and fugitive, that the "Thou" quickly degenerates to an "It", and that the "I-Thou" relationship must constantly be revitalized and even rediscovered. For example, even the relationship between husband and wife can become commonplace as soon as they think they know each other. They become things to each other unless there takes place a deeper and costly self-revelation, which will rekindle the spark of true communion.

I sometimes wonder whether the relationship of people with places is not more stable than that with their fellow human beings. For instance, we often find it difficult to remember a face, even if it is someone we have known well and loved. The face may come into our dreams with all the clarity of a photograph, whereas in the waking state we can summon up only a vague and imprecise picture of it. But when, on the other hand, a person is telling me the story of his life, he readily gives me a precise and detailed description of the various places which form the background of his experiences.

All our experiences, emotions, and feelings are indissolubly linked in our memories with places. "There are places we admire," wrote La Bruyère; "and there are others which affect us, and in which we should like to live. It seems to me that we depend on places for our thoughts, humours, passions, tastes, and sentiments." Man is not a pure spirit, and he has part in the places in which he has lived and experienced joy or sadness. He is bound up with matter, with things, with the ground he lives on. Our place is our link with the world. All the places we have lived in remain with us, like the pegs in a vast storehouse, on which our memories are hung. They symbolize all the states of mind through which we have lived, with all their varied shades of feeling.

"My place is my bed, in which I have so often wept," a woman patient told me. We all have places which mean more to us than others, because of the particular experiences with which they are connected. For my wife and me, for instance, our car is one such place, because in it we have had many a heart-to-heart talk, while on the road and out of reach of the telephone and such-like interruptions. Or there is a certain stretch of seashore, or a clearing in the forest, because they were the scene of decisive turning-points in our lives.

Any of the places in our past lives may be recalled in our dreams, evoking on their appearance the emotions we felt in them at the time. The background of a dream is as significant as the action that takes place against it. A dream conveys a message even in the places which it chooses, and which carry us back into a specific emotional atmosphere. It uses the places of the past to reveal to us our present feelings. At every moment of our lives an ineffaceable network of correlations is being set up between our inner world and the external world. One will always recall the other to mind.

Places of singing and places of crying, places of menace and places of reassurance, places of hurt and places of consolation—we preserve them all within us. The place of the first declaration, and the first kiss; the place of a great testing, a great decision, a struggle, or an important encounter; the quite ordinary place, perhaps, which has been the scene of a very minor event—this place, for example, in which I am writing these lines, and which will for ever be associated in my mind with this book I am starting here; and the place where you are as you read it—I do not know where that is, but with this book I am reaching out to join you there. Nothing happens in pure abstraction.

My place consists also of all the things I incorporate into my person—the suit in which I feel at ease, or that other one that makes me feel uncomfortable, or the tie given to me by a friend. For a woman, there is the dress that flatters her figure, or the other one that gives a false impression of the sort of person she is; her rings, her bracelets, and her necklaces. There is the brooch or the handkerchief my wife chooses before she comes out with me. A woman's handbag and a man's pockets are places that belong to their real lives! Then there is my typewriter, a favourite book, or the pictures I have hung on my walls, and which each have their special memories. There is the vase of flowers my wife has put on my desk.

It is, of course, quite legitimate to use the word "place" in a figurative sense. Our country, our church, a political party, a philosophy of life, a career—all are places in which our person is situated. We take our stand under all sorts of banners, both in order to follow them and in order to assure ourselves of a place in society. What my student friend's remark brought home to me, however, was the extreme importance of the place he occupied, in the quite literal and material meaning of the word.

Abstractions such as country or church are too big for us to grasp. What really counts for us is the familiar view, a reflection in the

lake, a street-corner, a tree, a fountain, a flag on a church tower; or
our favourite pew in the cathedral, where we have sat hundreds of
times, opposite a certain pillar in the nave, our gaze never tiring of
wandering over every stone and every curve of the capital. And now
the Church is something more than cathedrals and shrines—it is
work camps, evangelical courses, and all the places in which we
have been to lay retreats and conferences. For many of us such
places are remembered as the scene of a decisive experience of both
human and divine fellowship.

In order to understand a man, we must follow him into all the
detailed places of his life as he describes them to us. We must re-
live in them with him. Listening to such accounts, I have in
imagination shared the lives of many, many people, in places that
have become as personal to me as those of my own life, so that real
human fellowship has grown between us. A castle in Sweden, an
island in the ocean—a paradise for the angler, the swimmer, the
yachtsman, the horseman or the hunter, a little rose-garden in
which each bush has its own story. Some of these places have
been on an even smaller scale—a certain corner in an attic, a particular armchair, a stair that squeaked to betray the child whose
foot had trodden on it, or a secret hiding-place.

This is why it is so important for husband and wife each to visit
the places where the childhood of the other has been spent. To
understand St. Francis, and enter into communion with him, it is
not sufficient to visit the magnificent basilica which has been built
at Assisi. You must go up to the Hermitage in the hills, where he
lived. Thus it is that the house where an author, an artist, or other
famous man was born is presented, and sometimes turned into a
museum; or else the room where they worked is left exactly as it was
when death took them. Their trace can be found in these places that
were familiar to them, just as surely as it can be found in their
works.

I might refer here to all those novelists who make us know and
love the characters in their books through loving descriptions of the
places they live in, and of the close bonds that exist between person
and place. And even more, to all those autobiographies in which the
author introduces his readers into the delicate and poetic intimacy
of the places in his life, especially those of his childhood. There is,
for example, a charming record[4] in which Jean-Pierre Chabrol tells

---

[4] *Jean-Pierre Chabrol raconte*, a Barclay record, No. 80.257 A.

of how he went back to the mountain village where he had been brought up by his grandmother. The path to the main road, which had seemed so long then, how short it was! How low the walls of his grandmother's farm, which once had seemed so high! Then he speaks of that place *par excellence*, the village, with its church or its chapel, its square, its bakery, its carpenter's shop and its smithy. "I think a man needs a place to belong to," he says in his deep voice with the attractive accent of the Cévennes highlands.

I remember a talk by Professor J. H. van den Berg, the pioneer of phenomenological psychology, which I heard a few years ago in Holland. He too was telling of how he had come back to his native village. He had been a little disappointed at finding so little he could recognize, civilization had brought so many changes in the interval. He had, however, followed the road he had once taken daily on his way to school. At one point there was a wall, which was still there, and running along it was a crack into which as a child he used to put his finger. Now he had to bend down to put his finger once more into the crevice; but as he did so the whole world of his childhood was with him again, as if his finger were the stylus of a pick-up bringing to life music that had been recorded long before. That little crack in the wall was a place that was for ever attached to his person.

And now a personal memory. I have told elsewhere of how I was three months old when my father died, and how my mother died when I was six. My mother's death was without doubt the most important event in my childhood. On the day she died, a maid took my sister and me to live with an uncle and aunt. To reach their home from the Place Neuve where we had lived with my mother, it was necessary only to go through the Jardin des Bastions, in which stands the University of Geneva, and where the international monument to the Calvinist Reformation has since been erected.

I have a precise memory of stopping at a particular spot in the garden, near a statue of David, by Pradier, and asking the young woman who was taking us: "Shall we never be going back to the Place Neuve?" I was realizing at that moment that life was irreversible. And it was in terms of place that I expressed the one-way movement of time. The Place Neuve was my childhood, the world of my parents, which we were now leaving behind. I realized that the stages in our life, to which one after another we must say a last good-bye, are marked out by places.

This Place Neuve, the New Square, is so called because at the
time of the demolition of the walls of Old Geneva it was formed on
the site of the New Gate. It was the New Gate which the Duke of
Savoy had hoped to blast open with his petard in order to take the
city at the time of his notorious Escalade, in 1602, which had failed
so ignominiously. And it was also at this New Gate that, one evening more than a century later, a young apprentice-engraver called
Jean-Jacques Rousseau[5] had presented himself too late, because he
had spent too long meditating in the countryside. He also had lost
his mother, and his father had had to go into exile.

He was extremely sensitive to the language of things and places.
The two uprights of the raised drawbridge seemed to him like index
fingers threatening him. So great was his emotion that he felt as if
his native town were rejecting him, and he decided to leave it. His
wandering life had begun. He too was to say later that he was for
ever looking for "a place to live".[6] True, he was happy at Les
Charmettes, under Mme. de Warens' protective wing, and with a
good post she had found for him with a geometrician. But he was
giving up all that, to become a wanderer for the rest of his life. Because he thought himself rejected, he was in fact to find himself rejected everywhere he went, and to become the victim of an inextri-
cable mixture of real and imagined persecutions.

His last consolation was to be Nature. But Nature herself is a
place which takes on a particular colouring in accordance with the
state of mind of the beholder. Jean Starobinski, in his excellent
study of Rousseau,[7] brings out very clearly the importance of the
incident at Bossey, six years before he left Geneva, when the young
Rousseau was unjustly accused of a minor irregularity. Appearances
were so strongly against him that he was unable to prove his innocence, and this plunged him into a sudden and extreme distress.

The interesting thing for us here is Rousseau's reaction at that
time. He felt as if all at once a veil had been cast over the countryside he loved. He had suddenly lost the wonderful feeling that a
child has of the transparency of places, of direct, total, and natural
communion with them, and also with people. Reading Starobinski's

[5] *The Confessions of Jean-Jacques Rousseau*, translated by J. M. Cohen,
Penguin Classics, London, 1953.

[6] "A Discourse: What is the Origin of Inequality among Men?" translated
by G. D. H. Cole in *The Social Contract. Discourses*, Everyman Edition,
London, 1913, reprinted 1955.

[7] *Jean-Jacques Rousseau, la transparence et l'obstacle*, Plon, Paris, 1957.

book, one realizes that the whole of Rousseau's wandering life was to be nothing but a passionate and nostalgic search—doomed always to disappointment—for that lost transparency. "He established his dwelling in truth," writes Starobinski, "and for that reason he was to become a homeless person, a man fleeing from refuge to refuge, from retreat to retreat, on the periphery of a society which has obscured the original nature of man and distorted all communication between one mind and another. . . . Rousseau's solitude was a return to sincerity."

In his *Letter to Malesherbes*, Rousseau speaks of this quest for an ideal place: "I was walking quietly along, looking for some wild spot in the forest, some solitary place where no trace of the hand of man would remind me of servitude and domination." Clearly, his writings themselves spring from the unhappy experience of his childhood, conceiving as he did of a primitive Golden Age which has been destroyed for us by civilization and the injustice of men. He was thus seeing the history of the whole human race in terms of his own personal history.

But Rousseau's great innovatory contribution to literary style was to proceed from the same overpowering urge to rediscover the sincerity that had been lost: for the first time in history he was to attempt to describe himself "after nature";[8] he was to say "I", and address his reader as "Thou". He was anxious by his openness to establish with him the personal "I-Thou" relationship which Martin Buber has described. He did not only put ideas and theories —sometimes doubtful ones!—into his writings, but laid bare his very self. That is what gave his books their seductive power. No matter that he was wrong, and increasingly so, in his view of himself: he gave himself in person as he saw himself. His readers sensed this; and it explains the enthusiastic devotion which the people showed towards Rousseau on the eve of the French Revolution and of the American Declaration of Independence.

I myself feel close to him, although I hardly ever agree with his ideas, because I find in him the disquiet which was to become one of the hallmarks of our modern age, the unquenchable longing for real personal contact from which we have been cut off by our individualist and technical civilization. Perhaps also because I am a fellow-citizen of his. Rousseau the wanderer always retained his attachment to his little fatherland. He was to dedicate to it his

[8] *The Confessions.*

Discours sur l'origine et les fondements de l'inégalité parmi les hommes. It was only much later that he reluctantly relinquished his title of Citizen of Geneva, when his *Emile* was publicly burned in his native city. And still later he was to relate how his father, watching the population naïvely fraternizing with the soldiers in the street one day, had taken him in his arms and said, trembling with emotion: "Jean-Jacques, love your country!"

I too love my country. I can indeed, in this book about "man's place", speak of my love for my native city, as also of my love for my Swiss fatherland, whose ally the Republic of Geneva had been for centuries before it united its destiny with that of the Confederation, drawn towards it by the passion for liberty they both shared. The history of my country lives in me. Patriotism is the indestructible bond between man and his place. It does not prevent us from loving other nations. Rather does it give us a firm base for the wider love. This seems to have been a somewhat paradoxical characteristic of Geneva—to be turned in upon itself at the same time as being turned out towards the world; arousing in the hearts of its inhabitants a passionate love for their city, but at the same time awakening in them an equally passionate interest in the world at large.

We find this double love, close and distant, in those men whose actions have counted for most in the history of Geneva. In Calvin, who, though not born there, was so closely identified with the town that it is called Calvin's City; and yet his thought and ministry were universal. In Rousseau, whom I have just mentioned. In Pictet de Rochemont, who, even before Geneva joined the Swiss Confederation, made the nations of Europe recognize Swiss neutrality, and understand that its true destiny was to promote international peace. In Henri Dunant, in General Dufour, and Moynier, and all those others who in founding the Red Cross gave the world one of its most universal institutions. They all display the same firm attachment to their homeland, joined to thought and action going infinitely beyond it. This is the same law of the place that I described earlier: to have strong roots in one's own place is to be the more able to enter into real communion with all the other places in the world.

Countries themselves all have their own sacred places. When my wife and I were in the United States we did not miss going to see the "Independence Bell", in Philadelphia, and the austere room in which the Declaration of Independence was drawn up. In Washington also, we went to see the George Washington Monument, and the impressive memorial to Abraham Lincoln. In the same way, one cannot properly understand Switzerland without going up to the Meadow of Grütli, where the first Confederates swore before God mutual fidelity and brotherly aid. We took our children there when they were quite young, and in their turn our grandchildren were taken there by their parents.

In the summer of 1940, after the fall of France, when Switzerland found itself entirely encircled by the armies of Hitler and Mussolini, a wind of defeatism blew across my country. "What's the good of trying to defend ourselves? No one can stand up any longer to the new masters of Europe!" Then General Guisan, the commander-in-chief of the Swiss army, carried out his plan for a National Redoubt. In the heart of the mountains a Redoubt would be fortified, and from it the army would be able to offer effective resistance to the enemy, even if the greater part of the country had had to be given up. The sacrifice envisaged was a hard one. It was necessary to explain it to the troops and to the nation, and so, on that same Grütli Meadow, near the shore of the Lake of Lucerne, General Guisan on 25 July, 1940, solemnly called together all the senior officers of the army, so that they could renew the old oath of resistance to the death against all invaders, made in 1291 by the founders of the Confederation. In choosing that symbolic spot, the General was touching the soul of the whole nation and restoring its confidence and its resolve.

Yes, man needs a place, needs to attach himself to a place. The wider his horizon is, the greater is that need. Abraham is called by God to leave his place (Gen. 12.1–3), the fully-developed urban civilization of Ur of the Chaldees. He takes up once again the nomadic life of his distant forbears. God promises that his destiny is to be a universal one: in him all the nations of the world will be blessed; he will become the father of the faithful. He sets off on the great adventure of faith. But when he arrives in Canaan his first act is to buy a field (Gen. 23), the field of Ephron, so as to have a place in which to bury his wife. The owner wants to make a present of it to him, but the patriarch insists on buying it, so as to have a place that is really his own.

Thus, burials provide the most important archaeological evidence of ancient civilization. They bear the mark of even the most primitive man's need for a place, of his need to attach himself both to a place and to the line of his ancestors.

The hearth, the home, has also been throughout the ages the place of human fellowship, in family, tribe, and society as a whole. It is no accident that we say of a young couple that they are going to set up a home. Marriage is not only love, it is also the choice of a place which will from then on be common to both husband and wife, and to which they can invite those whom they wish to admit into their intimacy.

This is why when people come to see me in order to get to know and understand themselves better I interview them at my fireside. In their letters they often allude to the fire beside which we have sat and talked. For all of us the fire in the hearth is a powerful symbol, full of poetic meaning: it gives warmth, it is alive, it dies down and burns up again, it must be stirred, it is fascinating; it is a focus, a radiant centre. The Rev. Vernon Sproxton, of the B.B.C., understood this well when he came with his cameras and television lights into my consulting-room, to show me to British viewers sitting by the fireside where I follow my profession of conversing with men and women.

Nevertheless there is a limit. In order to be able to welcome others, husband and wife must also preserve their own intimate life together, as well as the intimacy they owe their children. I always remember with pain two of my patients with whom I failed. Both, on widely separated occasions, asked me the same favour, that they might come and live with us for a while as one of the family. Neither of them was able to accept the refusal I had to give.

And for a couple their choice of a house—when the property market allows them any choice at all!—is no less important. "It is better," writes Dr. Theo Bovet,[9] "to sleep on the bare floor and sit on old packing-cases than ... to go to live with in-laws." But when the young couple are able to go on to the furnishing of their home, the choice of curtains and furniture, of whether the style is to be traditional or modern, will all be the occasion for a fruitful interchange, in which they will learn how to give and take generously, how to recognize each other's different tastes, habits and personalities without one riding roughshod over the other.

The place is a sort of mirror of the person. One privilege which

[9] T. Bovet, *A Handbook to Marriage and Marriage Guidance*, English translation, Longmans, London, 1958, p. 108.

the family doctor enjoys, and which is almost unknown to the specialist, is that of visiting his patients in their homes. A glance around the house tells as much about its inhabitants as any number of confidences and psychological tests. I remember once being called urgently to visit a husband and wife who were at odds with one another, and found the interior of their very nice flat in indescribable disorder. There were heaps of dirty clothes, ash-trays filled to overflowing, things left lying about everywhere, the kitchen table piled high with dirty dishes, and not a single unencumbered chair to sit on. I felt that the husband, seeing me looking around at the state the flat was in, expected me to side with him, and to pity him for being the victim of such an untidy wife. But I thought to myself: "This woman must be unhappy, to let things go like this!" So there is always a close connection between a human being and his place. Each place has a symbolic significance for each individual.

This individual symbolism, however, forms part of a universal symbolism which springs from the collective unconscious of the human race. One is aware of this in every page of the excellent book by Gaston Bachelard on the "poetry of space".[10] It is noteworthy that a philosopher, more especially a scientific one, should strike out in this way beyond the rational world of science and philosophy, to understand and express so sensitively the lyricism of places.

We all carry about within us the images he evokes, such as the little cottage, cosy and warm amid the darkness of the night and the snowstorm, a symbol of the need of every man to be welcomed and protected. In the cottage window shines a lamp: "By its distant light, the house sees, watches, guides, and waits." He asks himself: "How is it that these images, which are so rare in actual life, have such a powerful hold on the imagination?" There is also the image of the "dream-house", big or small: "Each of us has his cottage moments and his palace moments." A remark which reminds me of what a young woman said to me recently: "My husband needs a small, cosy, intimate house, but I need a palace."

I can quote only a few of the striking images mentioned by Bachelard. There is the dark cellar, which recalls the obscure depths in our minds; and the stairs, of which he remarks: "The cellar stairs, always *down*... the stairs to the bedroom—we go up them and down as well... And lastly the attic stairs, steeper and rougher,

10 G. Bachelard, *La poétique de l'espace*, Presses Universitaires de France, 1960.

always *up*." He speaks of intimate corners, the drawers and chests in which secret treasures are kept. And the symbolism of the door, with its key and its handle: "In the realm of values, the key locks rather than unlocks. The handle opens rather than closes." What insight, what poetry there is in all this! The whole life of man is expressed in the mythology of places.

2

Deprivation

MAN NEEDS a place, and this need is vital to him. Where, then, does the need come from? I believe that in fact it is a manifestation of a need to live, to exist, to have a place in life. Life is not an abstraction. To exist is to occupy a particular living-space to which one has a right. This is true even of animals. The zoologist, Professor Portmann, of Basle, pointed out to me that the seagulls on the railings along the quay-side always stand at least twelve inches apart. If another gull comes down between them, they fly away at once. All respect the law, that each has a right to a minimum living-space.

Architects and sociologists ought to give thought to this, because man is less conscious of his vital needs, and more ready to disregard them. He allows himself to be herded into compact masses, without realizing that he loses his individuality as a person in a society that is too compact. To exist is to have a place, a space that is recognized and respected by others. Even in early infancy the great thing—on which one's whole future life will depend—is the dawning consciousness of oneself as a person. This process depends very largely upon the respect which the child's parents, brothers, and sisters have for his personal place: if not a room, at least a small corner he can call his own, where he can leave an unfinished game without someone coming and tidying it away; if not a cupboard, at least a drawer in which he can keep his treasures.

When a couple come into a restaurant and glance round the empty tables there is always a certain uneasy feeling in the air. The head waiter approaches, tactfully. Those who already have places at tables look at the newcomers coldly, as if they had no business to be there. Are they going to find a table they like? There! The one

they would like is reserved. Their mortification seems greater than
the importance of the matter would warrant. The fact is that it has
its roots deep in a particular anxiety that is never far from every
man's heart: Will I find my place in the world? Or will I feel out of
place? Will I be accepted, or rejected as an intruder?

Or else you arrive at a conference and report to the office to get
your card and find out where your accommodation will be. The girl
secretary is sweet and charming, but inexperienced. She hastily runs
through the lists, asks you to repeat your name, and finally asks:
"Are you quite certain you sent in your application form?" The
anxious thought crosses your mind—can they have missed you out?
But, happily, the secretary finds your name there, on another list.
You are expected after all; you have your place; the Conference is
counting on you.

It is readily understandable that to be denied a place is to suffer a
serious moral trauma. It is a sort of denial of one's humanity. Deprived of the place that belongs to him, man is no more than a thing,
to be treated by everybody without the respect due to a person. It
should be clear that in speaking of the deprivation of place I am not
denying the seriousness of the deprivation of love, of which the
psychoanalysts talk. There can be no gainsaying the decisive
demonstration they have made of man's vital need of love, especially in the case of the child, who is thrust defenceless into the world.
Nor can one deny the tragic consequences of deprivation of love.
All this is, in fact, quite in accord with the biblical revelation, of
which modern psychology has provided striking confirmation.

Deprivation of love and deprivation of place overlap; they have
a cumulative rather than a counteractive effect. Deprivation of love
is certainly the more serious. In stressing the importance of deprivation of place, I am really describing one particular aspect of the
tragedy of deprivation of love. I referred just now to my mother's
death, and the question I put to the maid: "Shall we never be going
back to the Place Neuve?" It was an indirect, veiled, diffident way
of putting that other question which without doubt I did not dare to
formulate: "Shall I never be seeing my mother again?" The
essential fact was the rupture of the emotional bond that tied me to
my mother—without any doubt all the more closely since my
father's death.

My question, however, was put in terms of place because the
deprivation of maternal love was accomplished by the loss of the

place in which my childhood had been spent, with all it meant for me of happiness and security at my mother's side. It was in fact this aspect of my misfortune which I felt first. To speak of deprivation of love is to describe a purely psychological effective event. The human person is more than a psychological mechanism, his life is more than his emotional psychic life. Deprivation of place makes us feel the materiality, the incarnateness of all the events of our lives.

Moreover, love itself, starting with maternal love—as the psychologists have clearly shown—is more than an effective relationship. It is expressed and experienced in kisses, embraces, caresses, in corporal manifestations. Mlle. Suzanne Fouché has described how she was asked to visit a model nursery. All the nurses wore masks like those worn by surgeons in the operating theatre. "Take all those masks off at once!" she exclaimed. "But what about the germs?" they replied. "Aren't you afraid of germs getting at these little babies?" "There are many other dangers besides germs!" she said. "These babies have never seen a human face, a human smile!"

The face is the place of the smile, where the message of love is read. We perceive the world, with its smiles and its threats, not in the abstract, but in faces with expressions on them, in things and in places. Simone Weil, who had a profound feeling and understanding for human distress, writing of the roots that every human being has in the things of the world, declares: "Affliction is the tearing up of these roots."[1]

Uprooting: the word expresses at the same time both the effect of being torn away from the love of one's fellows and the loss of one's place in the world. What I am describing is the state of mind of the person who is without roots—uprooted from his natural soil, he does not succeed in putting down new roots anywhere. A young man has suddenly broken off his engagement, though his relationship with his fiancée was harmonious and happy. He realizes he has acted stupidly. He has no serious complaints against the girl. He is spoiling his great chance of growing roots. But the impulse was too strong for him. He panicked at the thought of the commitment involved in marriage.

All orphans have had their roots torn up. Some suffer unconsciously because of it. Others are quite well aware of the fact. Such

[1] Simone Weil, *Waiting on God*, Collins Fontana Books, London, 1959, p. 134.

a one was a woman who told me of the feeling of rebellion against God that had filled her heart since her mother's death thirty years before. But for all it is something more than a broken emotional tie; it is also a material event affecting their whole person; it is a break with the past, with the place which has been the scene and the symbol of a past that is gone for ever.

Uprooted too are all the children of parents who are in conflict or divorced—like the student of whom I spoke at the beginning of this book. More exactly, I ought to describe them as rootless, for it is their misfortune never to have had any roots, never to have found any soil favourable to the growth of roots. The place they occupy is constantly shaken, as the soil of a volcanic region is constantly shaken by earthquakes. Their situation is even more injurious to them than is that of orphans, since deceased parents may come to be treated by their children as private tutelary divinities, as happened in my case with my father and mother. One does not enter into conflict with the departed; they have only good qualities, and no faults; they can be admired without reservation; they become ideal, a superego that is at once severe and benevolent, whereas the superego is usually so cruel a taskmaster.

Living parents, on the other hand, have their weaknesses and their faults which hinder the rooting process in the child. Take, for example, a woman patient whom I had been tending for a long time, not without success, although progress was always precarious and interrupted by relapses. We had often talked about the painful scenes that were always taking place between her parents, about the brutality of her father and her mother's attempts at suicide—both of them ill, without doubt. But one day, embarrassed and upset, she began to tell me about the frightful filth of the home in which she had grown up, about the bugs and the lice, and the revulsion she felt at the sight of her slatternly and shameless mother.

Such memories are terribly hard to speak about, but bringing them out into the open meant a much more real liberation for my patient. She at once began to take a keen interest in looking after her flat, having urgent repairs done, instead of constantly postponing them as she had been doing, buying and installing a handsome mirror, and putting up pretty curtains. One could see her taking root and growing. She was transforming the place she occupied, and taking pleasure in living and working in it. Now at last her social and professional integration was beginning to take place. She took up a course of study which she had never thought she would be able to do. Of course it had first been necessary to analyse the emotional factors contributing to the blocking that had taken place; but this quite material and physical aspect of her problem, her repugnance with regard to her place, we had never explored until then. It illustrated clearly the importance of place and of roots in a person's life.

On the other hand, one sometimes comes across people who retain such wonderful memories of the places of their childhood, that they cannot come to terms with the fact that they have left them. They avoid that part of the town, so painful is it to them to see their old haunts occupied by strangers, perhaps even altered or demolished. They too are people without roots.

There are French-Swiss whose work has compelled them to settle in Zurich or Basle, and who spend many years there feeling like exiles, even though they are in their own country. They find it impossible to assimilate themselves into their new canton, to learn its language properly, or to make friends with any but other French-Swiss people. One also sees women who have married a foreigner, but have not married his country. They remain rootless, incapable of integrating themselves into their new country, and sometimes end up by bringing their husbands to the place of their own childhood, making them rootless in their turn.

When husband and wife belong to two different cultures, when, for example, one is Slav and the other Latin, or one Moslem and the other Christian, their children can suffer from the effects of rootlessness, even where the parents live in harmony. A girl whose mother is a Jewess and her father a Catholic is not slow to feel the reticence between the two families, caused on each side by their prejudices towards each other. She goes to see her grandmother, and hears the latter whispering to a friend who has complimented her on her grand-daughter: "Yes, she is pretty, but her mother is Jewish, you know. Such a pity." And so the little girl pictures the world as being divided into three kinds of people: Jews and Catholics, who can both be loved completely, and the "half-and-halves", as she calls them, who can never be more than half loved!

I remember a young woman whose mother was Arab, and her father Jewish. The age-old hatred between these brother races is well known. The child had felt it keenly. She still remembered with pain how her mother had said to her once: "I curse you!" She had gone to a plastic surgeon to have the shape of her nose altered, but was dissatisfied with the result of the operation, and felt that her nose still betrayed her paternal heredity. The surgeon then realized that this was not a case he could deal with, and sent her to me.

The girl had soon confided in me her keen preoccupation with religious matters. She had rejected the Judaism and the Islam of her parents. She was engaged to a Roman Catholic whom she hesitated to marry. She was assiduously reading the writings of the Indian sages, and going to Christian Science meetings. She too was looking for a place! I have often quoted her as an example of how the doctor must avoid any suspicion of proselytizing: if I had tried to teach her my Genevan Calvinism, I should only have been making matters worse for her. Now she is happily married to her Catholic fiancé, and has adopted his religion.

"I have always felt myself to be a foreigner," a friend once said to me. "First in Italy when I was quite small, because I was a Jew; later on in German Switzerland, because I was an Italian; and now here in Geneva, because I come from German Switzerland!" All those whom the changes and chances of life have shuttled from one country to another are people without roots; so too are political exiles, refugees, and stateless persons. They can all echo the words of the poet: "To depart is to die a little." I worked for the Red Cross after the First World War, and before the League of Nations created the "Nansen Passport". I saw then what a terrible misfortune it is no longer to have any country to recognize and protect you.

After the Second World War, and following upon various other political events, the number of refugees increased enormously. The United Nations Organization had in its turn to come to their rescue, and a High Commissioner for Refugees was appointed. For refugees, in addition to being uprooted, there is the feeling that no one wants them anywhere, even sometimes in their own country. Small numbers of refugees, as happened after the Hungarian rising, may be given a warm welcome, and even treated as heroes. But when the influx is considerable, as was that into West Germany from the eastern Zone, or from Algeria into France, they may be met with hostility. A German doctor once told me that in the little town where he lived there were more refugees than original inhabitants. One can understand that the latter should react in self-defence against such a flood of invaders. Even in church the refugees had to take back seat because the regular congregation refused to give way to them. They tried to keep their unfortunate brethren segregated from them.

The exile of the Israelites in the time of Isaiah, Jeremiah, and Ezekiel, furnishes a good illustration of the great distress caused by deportation. Many of the Psalms and passages in the books of the prophets re-echo the heart-rending grief of the exiles. They utter their obsessive nostalgia for Jerusalem, for the Temple, for their ravaged homeland. In moving poetry they sing of past happiness. They beg Yahweh "to hear the groans of the prisoners" (Ps. 102. 20). They announce that his help will come when he chooses to send it: "I will bring you back to the place from which I sent you into exile" (Jer. 29.14). Such texts have universal value. They speak of man's attachment to his place, his grief at being torn from it, and his tenacious hope.

It is not difficult, however, to find among the refugees some who quickly form roots in the new soil, wherever they may be, while others remain passive and broken. This shows that the most important determining factor in their fate does not lie in eternal constraints or events, but in their own make-up. It is more serious to be affected by the psychological complex of rootlessness than to be rootless in fact. I do not mean to minimize the suffering of exile. That is in fact the theme of this book. But far worse is to carry about in oneself an invisible and powerful impediment to the growth of any new roots.

As always in psychology, we have to go back to the events of early childhood, which have repercussions throughout the whole of life. One man has had a mental attitude of rootlessness since his youth because of the emotional conditions under which he has been brought up. He will be broken by exile, where another would be able to stand up to the test, and even grow in stature through it, because he has had a secure place in his childhood. Healthy, strong, and united parents will give their children a sense of security that will be strong enough for them to withstand even exile without serious harm, and enable them to integrate themselves easily into their new surroundings. On the other hand, however, there are cases which suggest a hereditary complex of rootlessness; cases in which parents have communicated to their children a feeling of family inferiority which prevents them from feeling at home wherever they may be.

There are also many who are spiritually rootless, those who have

rejected the faith, the ideals, and the outlook on life of their childhood. They are frequently the children of very religious, very in-
tolerant parents, confident that they have a monopoly of the truth.
Every child, of course, must pass through a phase of rebellion
against his parents on the way to the attainment of spiritual adulthood and the adoption of a truly personal faith. But in fact if the
psychological climate of the home has been liberal and healthy, the
child will be able to choose his faith and take root in it—and it
will often be nearer that of his parents than he supposes.

Really serious—and I have seen it happen too often—is a rebellion that comes to nothing, a purely negative attitude of revolt,
which tosses a person about at the mercy of the most contradictory
spiritual influences, without his being able really to commit himself to any. It is in such cases that one can speak of a psychological
complex of rootlessness, characterized by an obsessive and nostalgic
search for a spiritual home, together with a tragic inability to adopt
one. The sufferer argues endlessly with representatives of every
kind of religion. But argument is an intellectual place, not a
spiritual one. A spiritual place is one in which one encounters God,
and it is very rare for him to be encountered in argument. It should
be understood, however, that this is not the person's fault. He is the
victim of some distant moral trauma which must be uncovered. He
may even become an enthusiastic missionary for one quite different
belief after another, and still find no real peace.

Even in the quite different case of conversions which take place
as the result of serious conviction, determined not by rebellion but
by clear-minded adhesion to the new belief, it is possible to observe
in the convert symptoms of anxiety which arise from the uprooting
that is involved. It is a delicate subject. A man has taken a courageous and honest decision to detach himself from one church and
join another, and he has accepted in advance that he will have to
pay the price. But his decision may turn out to be more costly than
he thought, in the first fervour of his conversion. One may find him
adopting an aggressive and over-critical attitude towards the church
he has left, as if he still needed to justify his action in leaving it. Or
he may become a zealous supporter of ecumenical activities, as if he
hoped that by bringing the various churches closer together he will
feel less torn inside himself.

Throughout the Protestant world there seems to be an unconscious complex that might well derive from the fact that it broke

away. This was of course not the intention of the Reformers, who wished only to reform the Church, and organized their followers in churches only because they were rejected by Rome. Nevertheless it was the Church of Rome which, over the centuries, had transmitted the Gospel to them, and they were still its spiritual heirs. Calvin makes frequent quotations from the Fathers of the Church. A painful uprooting has certainly taken place. And Luther's famous words, "I can do no other!" express his sincerity and his courage, but also his suffering.

A vague nostalgia caused by the feeling of having been cut off from the parent body may well account for the compensatory assertiveness of many of the Protestant sects. This, I think, is the psychological explanation of the proliferation of such sects. They all lay claim to greater fidelity to the Gospel, in a sort of compensatory attempt to outbid the rest. We see people going from one sect to another tossed and torn between opposing teachings, hesitating, unable to come to rest. I always used to look upon them as the victims of the proselytizing of the various sects that were trying to win them over. But closer study reveals that they are restless, anxiety-ridden souls who already bear within themselves an intense longing to know the truth as far as possible, and to belong to a community as nearly perfect as possible, as well as a tragic incapacity to take root anywhere. They are continually disappointed, and cannot overcome their disappointment.

Thus the complex of rootlessness always goes along with a vagabond complex. A person who has this unconscious obstacle in his own make-up wanders from one place to another, from one job to another, from one social circle to another, from one philosophy to another, from one church to another, without ever experiencing any lasting peace, any full satisfaction, any complete and stable integration. Can such observations help us to a better understanding, not only of the sick, but also of the human condition of all of us? Some of my readers must be thinking that I am the victim of my professional failing—that most of those who come to see me are ill, or at least worried, and that I am too inclined to generalize on the basis of those particular cases.

I think, on the contrary, that the sick reveal to us the existence of universal problems with which those who are well manage somehow to come to terms, without finding real solutions to them. I always think of the sick as a sort of magnifying-glass which shows up an anxiety which we all have within us, more or less unconsciously. Proof of this is to be found in the dreams which we all have, whether we are ill or well.

The dreamer sees himself in movement, going somewhere. He must catch a train, without knowing why, nor where it is to take him, but he knows that it is imperative for him to catch it. There is no argument about that. He starts running, he makes desperate efforts, encumbered by his luggage, terrified that he is going to miss his train. And in fact the train often goes by just in front of him. Sometimes he is lucky enough to be able to jump on to the step after it has already started, and he realizes that it is the wrong train, or that there is no room for him inside. Generally the dream comes to an end before the traveller reaches his destination, or before he has been able to recognize the strange and inhospitable place where he must get out of the train.

There are innumerable variations on this theme of the anxious journey. The striking thing is the extreme frequency with which it occurs. Where can all those people be going, as they rush off on foot, on horseback, on skis, in cars, trains, ships, and soon in space rockets? In the light of all these dreams, the whole human race seems to be inexorably engaged in a frantic race, the race of life. The dreamer must follow a dark, narrow corridor, he encounters monsters which he must fight, iron doors which he must open with a key he does not possess, and behind each door there is another, and another.

Where has he come from? Where is he going? He does not know. He knows only that he must at all costs go forward, overcoming obstacles, jumping on to trains, driving madly along the edges of precipices. Is not that what the human race is like? Dreams always tell the truth. That dream tells the truth about the man who is talking to me about it; but it also tells the truth about me: it proclaims a universal truth.

Our patients always expect us to interpret their dreams for them. But to do so would be to take up an aloof attitude, a scientific rather than a human attitude. I am much more concerned to get inside the dream I am being told about, to feel it, to appropriate it to myself, to make the places and events in it my own, than to make an academic interpretation of it. In this way the telling of a dream creates real fellowship between my patient and me. The doctor needs to be a poet.

This is admirably expressed by Gaston Bachelard in the book I have already quoted. He is, I think, sometimes a little unfair to psychoanalysis, since the cold objectivity of its technique is in fact an indispensable therapeutic weapon in the treatment of certain conditions. This is indeed why I prefer to send some patients to a Freudian psychoanalyst rather than to a Jungian, who would be much more sensitive to the poetry of dream images. But I think Bachelard is right when he says that "his technique is such that inevitably the psychoanalyst intellectualizes the image". And again, "poetry manifests itself at every point in psychoanalysis".

He insists on the priority of the imagination: "The image comes before the thought." "The image emerges into the conscious mind as a direct product of the heart, the self, the being of a man as he really is." This being of a man as he really is, is what I call the person. A patient comes to me avowing himself to be a rationalist and utilitarian. Apparently nothing matters to him unless it can be weighed and measured, and demonstrated by logic. He seems to have no feeling for the poetry of the world and of life. When he tells me one of his dreams, however, I discover to my great surprise that it consists of images full of delicate light and shade, colourful and sensitive—images of extraordinary beauty. All this poetic side of his person, which he has repressed in his realist life, comes to the surface in the dream, and he reveals himself to be quite different from what he seemed. Even he himself is astonished at it. He discovers what Minkowski, in contrast to rational causality, calls *retentissement* (reverberation).[2]

For, as Bachelard says, it is "dream values which are communicated poetically from one soul to another". This is what creates between that man and me a personal contact which rational discussion and intellectual analysis would be incapable of producing. This is another example of the distinction I have often pointed out between the comprehension of a "case" and the comprehension of the "person". The comprehension of a case is a technical matter, calling for the exercise of my technical ability. The comprehension of a person requires of me that faculty of emotional resonance which Rodgers and his followers in America call "empathy"[3] and

[2] E. Minkowski, *Vers une cosmologie*, Editions Montaigne, Aubier, Paris, 1936.

[3] Carl Rodgers and Marian Kinget, *Psychothérapie et relations humaines*, Béatrice Nauwelaerts, Louvain, 1962.

which involves my own person. The one is a matter of analytical psychology, the other of phenomenological psychology: "Poets and painters are born phenomenologists," writes Prof. J. H. van den Berg,[4] one of the pioneers of that school.

In the context of this personal relationship my patient's dream touches me as much as it does him, speaks to me as well as to him. I ought to be listening to what his dream is saying to me, to my own soul; and because I listen I can help the dreamer to hear what it is saying to him. That is not all. God speaks to us through our dreams, as the Bible clearly shows. It is God who is speaking to this man through his dream. It makes no difference whether he is a believer or not. God speaks to everyone, to the wicked as well as to the righteous, as Christ reminds us (Matt. 5.45). But God is also speaking to me through my patient's dream, just as he speaks to me through the dreams I read about in the Bible. It is God whom I must listen to and understand.

So I am myself called in question before God by each of my patients and by each of their dreams. That is the occupational hazard of psychotherapy, as has been well shown by Dr. Paul Balvet, of Lyons.[5] One guesses that he is talking of himself when he describes the difficult crisis through which the beginner in psychiatry must pass. "He thought he was taking up what is termed an 'interesting' speciality," he writes, "only to realize now that it was his own neurosis that impelled him towards it, and that he was not taking it up because it was a speciality that had become popular over the last few years, but because he was looking for a solution to his own personal problems." It is true that in contact with the anxiety of others, I become daily more aware of my own anxiety, which I have been repressing just as everyone else does, in an attempt to look as if there were nothing the matter with me. The psychotherapist tries to help this patient to look at himself honestly, only to find that he is himself faced with the almost intolerable necessity of looking with equal lucidity at his own life.

So I feel myself really close to my patient, and am able to live and understand his dream. I too am in the race of life. It is a blind and compulsive race, in one direction only, with no going back, full

---

[4] J. H. van de Berg, *The Phenomenological Approach in Psychology*, Springfield, Ill., 1955.

[5] Paul Balvet, "Problèmes de vie du psychiatre", in *Présences*, No. 87, 2nd Term, 1964, published by the Prieuré de St.-Jean, Champrosay, Seine-et-Oise.

of surprises, obstacles, and disappointments, and considered by some to be pointless. The animals, probably, do not know any more than we do where they have come from and where they are going. But they do not ask themselves such questions. It is the questions my patient and I ask ourselves about the meaning of life that differentiate us from the animals and make us human beings. And if we try sometimes to avoid the questions and forget them, in order to attain an apparent peace of mind, our dreams will insist on raising them again for us.

Where, then, are all these dreamers going as they press stubbornly and painfully on in haste and anxiety, as if they had an appointment which must on no account be missed? Are they not all searching for a place, an obscure and unknown goal which beckons them irresistibly? Are we not all engaged in a quest for an unknown destination, "a place to live in", as Rousseau said?

A spinster says to me: "All my life I have felt as if I was on a station platform." Nevertheless she is in a useful job and is a great help to others spiritually. But she feels that only marriage can secure a definite place for her in society. This is an illusion, surely. Another woman, who has made a good marriage, tells me that she always sees herself as "a goldfish going round and round and finding nothing but itself". Clearly such feelings arise subjectively from within the persons who experience them, and not from the external circumstances of their lives. This inner malaise makes them constantly wait for something from outside, which never comes.

A man dreams that he is an official representative at the funeral of a former colleague. The obsequies are being conducted with great pomp and solemnity; but he cannot find the seat that has been reserved for him, and no one seems able to tell him where it is. He searches feverishly for it, but in vain. The theme of the seat that cannot be found recurs in dreams with great frequency, with all kinds of variations. Sometimes it is a meeting, or a drawing-room, or a banquet: all the seats are occupied by strangers who do not even bother to answer the dreamer as he inquires about his seat. What is this place that all men are looking for, consciously or unconsciously? I believe it is the place of perfection, which in fact does not exist in this world—a place that will give real security and protection from disappointment. Listening to the accounts of so many dreams, generally dramatic, often startling, sometimes idyllic, I can see that like me all men are searching for an unknown place where we hope to find the answer to all our problems, all our dissatisfactions and doubts.

People often say to our anxiety-ridden patients that they ask too much, that they see everything too much in terms of black and white, and that they must reconcile themselves to taking things as they find them, accept the fact that things are all in varying shades of grey, and adapt themselves accordingly. But those who profess this cut-price philosophy are probably doing so only in order to reassure themselves. It helps them to repress the longing for perfection which sleeps deep in their own souls, and which would arouse the same anxiety in them if it chanced to be reawakened. What is the meaning of this nostalgia for perfection which some admit and others hide, but which is inevitably there in every man and woman? It is our home-sickness for Paradise. The place we are all looking for is the Paradise we have lost. The whole of humanity suffers from what we might call the "Paradise Lost" complex.

3

Biblical Perspectives

AND SO we have come right round to the biblical view of man, to biblical anthropology, in the current phrase. In the beginning the Bible places man in the Garden of Eden. A place for him! A wonderful, peaceful place where he lives in harmonious familiarity with Nature and with God. It is not a place of inactivity and rest for man. God calls him to work: he is to till it and keep it (Gen. 2.15). But it is a place of perfection where no anxiety comes to make man want to leave it. We know what happened, how man opened his heart to evil, and lost his inner peace. Then God drove him out of the Garden of Eden, lest he should eat of the tree of life, and live for ever in that tragic condition. And so we see man committed to his life of endless wandering.

The tragedy, however, had already begun inside the Garden of Eden. After the Fall, the Lord called to Adam: "Where are you?" (Gen. 3.9). Adam hid himself. The place had already ceased to be paradise for him. His hiding-place among the trees was not his place, but an alibi. With his disobedience, fear had entered his heart, and with it distrust, disturbing his relationship with God, as well as that with his wife and with his place. He had already begun to flee from place to place, seeking in vain his lost happiness and security. He was disappointed in his wife, and disappointed in himself. Disappointment was to be his continual lot, driving him on relentlessly.

The march of history had begun. Evil was to reveal its full dimension in the murder of Abel by Cain (Gen. 4), and in the remorse that was to pursue the murderer. God said to him: "You shall be a fugitive and wanderer on the earth" (v. 12). Then we see Cain

founding a city (v. 17). The story shows the whole of civilization as
an attempt by man to make a place for himself, where he may
settle down and, freed from his nomadic life, regain his lost security.
Civilization develops in an immense process of evolution right up
to our own day, but still fails to rescue man from his anxiety. Civilizations come and go, all of them mortal, as Paul Valéry said.[1] Man
goes on across the centuries, always looking for a place.

Nor is it only for himself that man is looking for a place. He is
looking for a place for God as well—he wants to localize God.
Primitive religions and, later, mythologies, localized divinities in
streams and stars or on Olympus. The Israelites put monotheism in
place of this innumerable multitude of gods distributed in as many
different places. It was a tremendous spiritual revolution: Yahweh
revealing himself as the only God, eternal and universal.

This universal God proves, however, to be too big for them. They
need a place, at least a meeting-place, where they can find him and
worship him. While Moses is on the summit of Sinai, facing the
immensity of the heavens, and listening for the voice of God, they
make for themselves a god to their own scale, the golden calf. Here
at least was something accessible, visible, and localized. They could
sing and dance around it, crying: "These are your gods, O Israel,
who brought you up out of the land of Egypt!" (Ex. 32.4). Moses'
anger burns hot. He breaks the tables of the law which he has received from God. The golden calf is an idol, a false god; but it is
more—it is the proof that the people have understood nothing of his
preaching, that they have failed to comprehend the greatness of God
that he has revealed to them.

Nevertheless Yahweh does not condemn the people's need to
localize their God. On the mountain he has already given Moses
instructions for the making of the ark (Ex. 25.10–16). This is not an
idol, but it is a place, a sacred object, containing the testimony
which reminds the people of the covenant which the one universal
God has made with them. The ark is portable; the poles of acacia
wood overlaid with gold by which it is to be carried remain constantly in the four gold rings, ready for immediate departure. All
around there is to be a court, where all the Israelites may gather.
So God is in the midst of his people, and marches with them in the
desert. You see how carefully Yahweh gives his instructions. He
condemns any representation of his transcendent Person, which

[1] Paul Valéry, "La crise de l'esprit", first letter, *Variété 1*, Paris, 1924.

might become an object of worship. But he nevertheless understands that man needs a place in which he may worship.

When the Israelites settle in the promised land, and become, under David, a powerful nation, the king's great ambition is to build a temple in place of the nomadic ark of the desert, finally to localize God (II Sam. 7.1–17). Yahweh's reasons for refusing to allow David to carry out his project, and then allowing Solomon to do so, are not clear. I believe one may see here a further sign of the two-fold solicitude I have just pointed out: the fear that the localization of God will make men forget his universality, and the recognition of their legitimate need to worship the one universal God in a particular place.

Solomon in his wisdom realizes the difficulty of reconciling the two factors. In his prayer at the dedication of the temple, he says: "But will God dwell indeed with man on the earth? Behold, heaven and the highest heaven cannot contain thee; how much less this house which I have built?" (II Chron. 6.18). But he goes on: "Hearken thou to the supplications of thy servant and of thy people Israel, when they pray toward this place; yea, hear thou from heaven thy dwelling place; and when thou hearest, forgive" (II Chron. 6.21). Seven times in the course of this magnificent prayer for the people he makes reference, in various ways, to this possible correlation between the human place where the faithful pray and the divine and universal place where God hears them. Furthermore, Solomon, knowing that God could not be confined within a temple, had waited for God to localize himself, after a fashion, when he invaded the temple in the immaterial form of a cloud (II Chron. 5.11–14).

But this localization of God was to have its dangers for the faith. It was responsible for a narrowing of their idea of God which favoured a form of nationalism which proved to be Israel's undoing. Henceforward the temple was to become the object of the religious and patriotic fervour of the people. We are given a wealth of detail concerning its construction, dimensions and decoration. This is a way of underlining the importance of the event. There are innumerable passages celebrating the love of the believers for their temple, the pride they took in it, the joy they derived from spending rapturous days in it. But from there to making it the symbol of their national pride is only a short step—as if God were not the ruler over the whole earth.

As a result, when the temple was destroyed the people of Israel were thrown into complete disarray. Then arose the prophets, Isaiah, Jeremiah, and Ezekiel, to remind them of the universality of God. He rules over the whole of history, and even Nebuchadnezzar, the enemy of Israel, is an instrument in God's hand (Jer. 43.10). The Word of God can be heard in foreign lands, in Chaldea or Egypt, and it was revealed to the exiles rather than to those who had remained among the ruins of Jerusalem.

In the terminology of Martin Buber, to whom I have already referred, we can say that in Solomon's time the temple had been a Thou-Place. When the glory of Yahweh invaded it like a cloud, it was a meeting-place with Yahweh, whom Buber calls the eternal Thou. But in time the temple had become a That-Place, a thing to be described and admired. Yahweh himself had become a That, an object of theology and piety, too limited, too localized, a prisoner in his temple, and the prophets had to reaffirm the sovereign greatness of God, so that he should be a Thou once more. "I do not discover the man to whom I say Thou," writes Buber, "in any particular time or place." And so God breaks out of his prison, and calls Nebuchadnezzar to destroy the temple.

This is strikingly expressed in André Neher's fine book on Jeremiah.[2] He recalls first that Jeremiah came from Shiloh, which had been a holy place long before Jerusalem. Of Shiloh, Yahweh had already said: "It is my dwelling-place"—and yet he had trodden it under foot. Then, to explain Jeremiah, Neher refers to the Book of Job, which warns us, he says, "that the wildest and most sacrilegious illusion ... is to cut down God to the average human scale, to localize him in a particular point of space and time." So Jeremiah "reintroduces the unknown into the equation linking God and man". In rediscovering the eternal Thou and establishing a personal relationship with Yahweh, Jeremiah advances beyond the narrow, localized concepts of his contemporaries. He speaks of a God on a whole world scale who rules over the whole of history, transcending the limited picture of him given by the theologians. He rediscovers the living God, the God of Abraham, of Isaac, and of Jacob, the God of the nomadic patriarchs, the Most High God, whose priest is Melchisedek, a universal priest since he is "without father or mother or genealogy, and has neither beginning of days nor end of life", but resembles the Son of God (Heb. 7.3).

[2] André Neher, *Jérémie*, Plon, Paris, 1960.

And so throughout history the pendulum swings between localization and universalization. The faithful, in their fervour, need to
localize God to look for him in a certain place where he has revealed himself to them. Then their faith comes to identify him with
the place, in a spirit of geographical or religious particularism
which sets Constantinople, for example, or Geneva, against Rome.
But there also arise from time to time prophets whose message is:
God is greater than you think! Such a one was Pope John XXIII,
or among Protestants Karl Barth. Nevertheless this recall to uni-
versalism cannot at the same time deny the necessity of the mediation of particular places.

When Jesus is talking to the Samaritan woman beside Jacob's
well (John 4.5–26), she raises the question of places with him: "Our
fathers," she says, "worshipped on this mountain; and you say that
in Jerusalem is the place where men ought to worship." Jesus
answers: "The hour is coming, and now is, when the true worshippers will worship the Father in spirit and truth." He thus firmly proclaims the universality of God. He refrains, however, from denying
the importance of places. He had in fact already said to her: "You
worship what you do not know; we worship what we know, for
salvation is from the Jews." Here we have the same problem of the
need to reconcile localization and universality, and it is approached
with the same wisdom as it was in the case of the ark of the covenant and the building of the temple at Jerusalem.

Localization can lead to strife and argument, to intransigence and
schism. It lies at the root of theological controversies such as that
referred to by the Samaritan woman, since theologians must lay
down *where* the truth lies. This they must do because man needs a
place, if he is not to be rootless. Even his faith in a unique and
universal God must evolve on a particular terrain. He has to base
himself on a place, a firm jumping-off point, if he is to develop fully
and eventually take in a wider horizon. Those churchmen who are
working for a closer understanding between the different Christian
denominations are well aware of this. There is no question of disregarding the insight that each Church has and merging them all in
a vague syncretism. Localization could lead to a kind of cornering
of God, a hiding of him away. But it can also be a road towards the
universal, as Jesus suggests to the Samaritan woman.

There is, then, a necessary movement between localization and
universalization; but it is one which moves away from a particular

localization or conception of God so as to be able to challenge it. Bishop J. A. T. Robinson in his book *Honest to God*[3] attempts this kind of challenge. Traditionally, we locate God in the sky, he explains. We look upwards towards him. But in the space-age it is no longer possible to know which is up and which is down. We must be constantly revising our image of God. Pastor Bernard Martin undertakes a similar task in his book *Si Dieu ne meurt . . .*[4]. In the light of modern psychology he calls in question not only the concept he had of God, but his own person and his ministry. In some respects this is also true of C. G. Jung in his *Answer to Job*[5]. He suggests not only the idea of a progressive historical transformation of our conception of God, but also that of the psychological evolution of God himself. This is a bold concept, which runs counter to our traditional view of an immutable God. It must be recognized, however, that there are plenty of biblical texts which also contradict the idea of an immutable God—for example, all those which speak of God repenting. The God of the Bible is a God who acts; and he who acts is no longer immutable. Jung's view throws quite a new light upon the fact of the incarnation of God in Jesus Christ.

What makes it possible for these authors to set off in this way on a voyage of discovery towards new spiritual places, is the fact that they have all undergone a long and sound training in their traditional surroundings. The place they are leaving behind, and which they are calling in question and seem almost to be denying, has served as the firm base from which their innovating effort has been made.

Teilhard de Chardin[6] was constantly preoccupied with this problem of his place. What was his place? Was it in his vocation as a priest? Or as a scientist? He always tried to bring them together instead of separating them; but he realized that such a synthesis was not easy in a period such as ours, which keeps the two domains of the sacred and the secular so radically separate. God has been localized and relegated to the Churches, to their welfare and missionary activities, and to the realm of theological discussion. Mixing with scientists through his work as a geologist, Father Teilhard suffered, as a priest, from the fact that the exciting field of present-

[3] SCM Press, London, 1963.   [4] Buchet-Chastel, Paris, 1964.

[5] Translated by R. F. C. Hull, Routledge, London, 1954.

[6] Pierre Teilhard de Chardin, S. J., *The Making of a Mind: Letters from a Soldier-Priest, 1914-1919*, translated by René Hague, Collins, London, 1965.

day scientific research was looked upon as a secular domain, in which God had no place. His work, too, is like a prophetic cry: God is greater than you think! Is not the evolution of the world and of man the permanent creation of God?

Father Teilhard de Chardin then wrote his *Messe sur le monde*,[7] in which he assimilates the whole world to the Body of Christ consecrated by the priest on the altar. He realizes full well that such a view runs the risk of being called pantheistic. In his letters from the Front[8] during the 1914–1918 war, and subsequently in many others of his books, he defends himself against this accusation, which indeed has constantly been made against him. The problem is obvious: either God is too rigorously localized, he is turned into a local or national God, or an abstract God confined to the religious sphere and apparently shut out of the real secular world, separated from practical living as well as from scientific research; or else, as a reaction against this restrictive view, God is seen to be universal, filling the whole world—in which case there is a risk of losing sight of the true God, the God who is a person, and slipping into a vague pantheism. How are we to reconcile our need both for a universal and for a personal God?

It seems to me that the Bible gives a clear answer. The God of the Bible is indeed a universal God, but he is a God who nevertheless chooses places in which to reveal himself to men. He is a God without frontiers, omnipresent, never the prisoner of any particular place, but not an impersonal God floating everywhere and nowhere. He breaks into history and geography because he speaks to men and enters into dialogue with them; and a dialogue always takes place at a particular time and place. There is a *kairos*, a moment in time when God reveals himself. Similarly he chooses places in which to reveal himself. This was Jacob's experience: in exile, while he slept "in that place", he dreamt he saw a ladder set up between earth and heaven, and on it the angels ascending and descending. God said to him: "The land on which you lie I will give to you and to your descendants." And, when he awoke, Jacob exclaimed: "Surely the Lord is in this place and I did not know it" (Gen. 28.10–22).

He is, then, the universal God, but he localizes himself, or rather chooses particular meeting-places in order to make contact

[7] "The Mass on the World", in *Hymn of the Universe*, translated by Simon Bartholomew, Collins, London, 1965.   [8] *The Making of a Mind.*

with men. There are many instances in the Bible—God's dialogue
with Adam in the Garden of Eden, with Abraham at Haran, with
Moses in the burning bush on Mount Horeb, with Isaiah in the
temple at Jerusalem, with Jeremiah at Anathoth, and throughout
the New Testament, right up to the Revelation to St. John on
Patmos. St. Paul proclaims to the Athenians "the God who made the
world and everything in it," ... who "does not live in shrines made
by man." He is universal. He is, he says, "not far from each one
of us" (Acts 17.22–31). Nevertheless St. Paul makes constant reference throughout his ministry to his concrete, precise, localized experience on the road to Damascus, when Jesus spoke to him (Acts
9.1–9; 22.6–11; 26.12–18; Gal. 1.15–17; II Cor. 12.2–4).

Taken as a whole, however, the Bible brings to this problem of
the localization of God an answer that is at once vaster and more
precise. It reveals to us, in fact, that God's purpose is the salvation
of the world. It is not a matter of the salvation merely of the human
race, but of the whole of creation, which waits, as St. Paul says,
"to be set free from its bondage to decay" (Rom. 8.19–25). There
could be no clearer assertion of the universality of divine action.
Universal history, and the whole evolution of Nature, are the
realization of this plan by God. But he proceeds step by step,
through a series of mediations of localizations. He makes a covenant
with Noah (Gen. 9.17). He makes a covenant with Abraham (Gen.
15.18). He chooses a people for himself, the Israelites, and makes a
covenant with them (Ex. 24.8). Later on, Jesus chooses the Apostle
Peter as the foundation of his Church (Matt. 16.18). These are so
many places, that is to say particular events, which mark out the
divine itinerary towards a goal which is universal.

Seen in this light, all churches, all rites, and all theologies are provisional stages, instituted provisionally by God in order to bring the
human race to full fellowship with him. There is a text in the Book
of Revelation which lends support to this view. Remember the
building of the temple at Jerusalem, which demonstrated the
Israelites' need to localize God. Now, when St. John, on Patmos,
sees the New Jerusalem coming down from heaven, he observes:
"I saw no temple in the city, for its temple is the Lord God the
Almighty and the Lamb" (Rev. 21.22). No more temple; no more
need to localize God. The heavenly Jerusalem is the last place given
by God, the place of his final triumph, where man can at last know
the universal God without any particularized mediation.

This universal goal is announced right at the start by God to Abraham: "By you all the families of the earth will bless themselves" (Gen. 12.3). Later, he says to Moses: "All the earth is mine" (Ex. 19.5). Nevertheless, in God there is no contradiction between the particular and the general, between the local and the universal. He knows that men need provisional places if they are to be brought to him. He chooses holy places for himself—Anathoth, Shiloh (I Sam. 1.24), Jerusalem (II Sam. 6.12). After the Exile he brings the Israelites back into their holy city. The beautiful books of Ezra and Nehemiah movingly recount the heroic rebuilding of Jerusalem and the temple.

Every religion and every church has its holy places, its places of pilgrimage, Mecca or Benares, Tinos or Lourdes. They can be instrumental in provoking fanaticism or religious particularism; but they can also be places where men meet the one God, the Father of all believers and of all unbelievers. For many people the fervour of fanaticism is the first stage in a long spiritual journey which will lead gradually to charity and understanding towards others.

When the time was ripe in the plan of salvation, God sent his Son, Jesus Christ. As St. Paul writes: "Christ Jesus, who, though he was in the form of God," was "born in the likeness of men" (Phil. 2.5–7). To be in the likeness of men is to be bound to places. As we have seen throughout this discussion, having a place is the sign of being within the concrete reality of the world; it is the sign of our humanity. In Jesus Christ it becomes the sign of the incarnation of God. Jesus therefore needs a birth-place, because every human being must have a birth-place. God chooses the place: the stable in Bethlehem. The gospels tell the story of his earthly ministry. Christ's mission is universal, but it is accomplished in particular events, in personal encounters, in clearly-defined places, leading right up to the place called Golgotha (Matt. 27.33), and Joseph of Arimathea's tomb (Matt. 27.57–60), the Cross planted in the ground and the cave hewn out of the rock which symbolize Christ's solidarity with the earth. Finally, Jesus himself identified himself with the temple of Jerusalem (John 2.19–21), thus proclaiming himself to be the place of the New Covenant.

Bethlehem, Golgotha! Places which have become familiar and personal to us, and which belong to Christians throughout the world. Why those rather than others, unless it is because God chose them to be the scene of events unique in history? And because God chose them they have taken on a universal significance: they are the symbols of the universal divine mercy. Many other biblical places have this double significance, both particular and general. On the one hand they recall the historical events which took place there, and on the other they are symbols of the eternal verities.

The same is true, in the opening verses of the Bible, of the earth itself, which God gives to man so that he may live on its fruits. It is true of Nature, over which God gives man dominion (Gen. 1.28). And it is true of the Garden of Eden, which he entrusts to man's care and which he instructs him to cultivate. That is to say, that in giving man his place, God also gives him a mission and a responsibility. Noah's Ark is a perfect example of a place given by God—a place of refuge, the instrument of his providence (Gen. 6.14; Heb. 11.7). The story enchants us with its concreteness, and the naïve charm of the picture it suggests, of the elephant, the tiger, and the lamb embarking with Noah. It expresses also, however, a universal truth—that man's salvation is to be found in obeying God.

Egypt represents the servitude from which God wants to deliver man, the alienation from which he purposes to free him. Later on, at the time of the prophets, it represents the vain hope of military or political help from outside, which will bring nothing but disappointment if it is not within the purpose of God. Egypt also represents, as Dr. Aloys von Orelli has pointed out, the gnosis, the wealth of spiritual knowledge which may lure man into pride. Thus it is the opposite of the desert into which God led the Israelites after he had brought them out of Egypt. The desert is deprivation and poverty, the place where man can rely on no security whether material or spiritual, but only on God. The Israelites would have perished there if God himself had not given them food and drink (Ex. 16–17).

The whole story of the Exodus is full of symbolic meaning. It proclaims that God himself leads man where he wills, despite the delays occasioned by man's resistance and disobedience. God describes in advance to Moses the Promised Land which he destines for his people (Ex. 3.8). On the way he manifests himself to the Israelites "by day in a pillar of cloud to lead them along the way, and by night in a pillar of fire to give them light" (Ex. 13.21). He leads them into the desert, and makes them wander there for forty years (Num. 32.13), because they have not dared to cross over Jordan to enter the country he has given them. But he is tenacious of his purpose, and brings them into the land at last, and marks out the territory that each tribe is to occupy. Then he establishes cities of refuge, where a man who has killed another unintentionally may escape vengeance (Josh. 20). He himself chooses the places where his worship is to be conducted (Deut. 12.5).

The symbol of the wilderness recurs over and over again in the Bible. The scapegoat was driven into the wilderness after it had had laid upon it, in solemn ceremony, "all the iniquities of the people of Israel, and all their transgressions, all their sins" (Lev. 16.21). The desert here would seem to represent the unconscious mind into which we repress all our guilt. The Israelites must always have been afraid of seeing the scapegoat come back from the desert in which it wandered, just as we live in constant fear of our guilt-feelings coming back to the surface of our conscious minds. In any case, the well-known Parisian psychiatrist, Henri Baruk, has stressed the psychological importance of the scapegoat as pointing to man's need to get rid of his feelings of guilt.[9] He has even said that this was what prompted him to learn Hebrew, so as to read the Bible in the original and be better able to understand its psychological teaching.

Above all, however, the desert represents the place where all men can find the temporary retreat they need. When Elijah was discouraged to the point of wishing to die, because all his striking successes had come to nothing, he betook himself to the desert (I Kings 19.4). There he sought and found personal contact with God. God revived his spirit and invested him with a fresh mission. So, the desert is the prayerful meditation to which God invites us at decisive moments so that we may rediscover his inspiration. It is a time of fruitful solicitude between two periods of social activity.

It was in the desert that John the Baptist called on his contemporaries to come and recognize and confess their faults, and repent in preparation for the coming of the Kingdom of Heaven (Matt. 3.1–2). It was into the desert that the Apostle Paul went after his conversion. He stayed there for three years in order to meditate upon the tremendous task that awaited him. The desert is the dramatic place where man finds God, but where he must also measure himself against the Devil—for Satan follows God about everywhere, like a shadow.

[9] H. Baruk, *Psychiatrie morale expérimentale*, Presses Universitaires de France, Paris, 1960.

The desert is not the only place in the Bible that takes a symbolic significance in this way. There are many other places which awaken all sorts of echoes in our minds. I remember a remarkable essay by Pastor Roland de Pury on Jerusalem and Babylon,[10] which represent, throughout the Bible from the Tower of Babel (Gen. 11.1–9) to the fall of Babylon (Rev. 18.2), the antithesis between the City of God and the forces of evil. Similarly rivers, seas, mountains—Sinai, Horeb, the hill of the Sermon on the Mount, the Mount of the Transfiguration—all places can take on symbolic meaning which arouses in all believers the memory of their own personal spiritual experiences.

This is what makes the Bible so movingly poetic. It is as poetic as a legend, an epic, or a fairy-tale. This, too, is why it has on occasions been interpreted as a work of the imagination. That may be true of some of its books, such as that of Job, which are exceptional in character. In recognizing the symbolic meaning of places we must not forget that they are, above all, places—that is to say, a material reality which is the context of human life. The Bible is not a fairy story. Stories begin with the traditional: "Once upon a time there was . . ." You will not find that in the Bible, which tells true stories, about things that actually happened, and in order to make this fact clear, it always indicates the place where the event occurred.

One of the first things that strike us about the Bible is the abundance of place-names, many of them particularly difficult to pronounce! Why this insistence on giving us so many names? I think we ought to see in this a sign of the realism of the Bible. It affirms that it is concerned with real historical events by giving precise details of the names of the people involved, of the places where the events took place, and their date.

I have referred elsewhere to the frequency of proper names of persons in the Bible, sometimes whole chapters full of them. I see this as a demonstration of the personalism of the Bible, because the proper name is the expression of the person, of his individuality, his unity and his totality. The Bible contains no theoretical teaching about man, and this makes the formulation of a biblical "doctrine of man" particularly difficult. It tells real-life stories, things that happened to this man or that, to men of flesh and blood, and it furnishes their names in order to emphasize that reality. The same applies to those other proper names, the names of places, which

10 In *Dieu Vivant*, No. 12, 1948, published by Editions du Seuil, Paris.

provide the precise historical and geographical context of each
biblical story.

The same is true of dates. Note, for example, the care taken by
the prophets to state the year, month, day, and even sometimes the
hour, together with the place in which God spoke to them and entrusted them with his message. Similarly, when you make an
agreement you must sign it with your name, but you must also
indicate the place and date.

God does not preside only over the general destiny of the human
race. He often gives individual orders, sending a certain man to a
specific place: Joseph, Jacob's son, to Egypt (Gen. 45.8); Elijah to
Zarephath (I Kings 17.9); Jeremiah to the potter's house (Jer. 18.2);
St. Joseph to Egypt, to save the infant Jesus from Herod's mas-
sacre (Matt. 2.13); Jesus himself to the desert to be tempted there
(Matt. 4.1); or to Jerusalem, to suffer martyrdom (Matt. 16.21);
Philip the Apostle, at noon, to the deserted road from Jerusalem
to Gaza, to baptize the first African there (Acts 8.26); St. Peter to
Joppa, to the Roman centurion's house (Acts 10.20); St. Paul to
Europe (Acts 16.9), or to Jerusalem, to be arrested (Acts 20.22), and
to Rome, to preach the Gospel there (Acts 19.21).

What I want to emphasize in giving these examples is that divine
inspiration does not consist only of moral exhortations or religious
revelations, but also of precise and concrete instructions. It often
happens that the recipients of these instructions do not understand
them at the time, but only after they have obeyed them. The thing
that shows up the realistic nature of God's guidance is that it often
involves for the believer not merely an idea but an act, not merely a
message to deliver but a place to which he must go. It sometimes
happens that God leads us by an obscure intuition which makes us
go to a particular place without our knowing what awaits us there.
It sometimes happens, too, that he leads us by means of events that
seem to have no religious significance. There is no such thing as
chance.

Thus, place-names are the mark of realism, and those in the Bible
bear witness to the concrete nature of the life of faith. God is everywhere, it is true, but he reveals himself in particular places. The
history of our faith is necessarily tied to places. Even when the
Bible speaks eschatologically, it uses the language of incarnation.
St. Paul speaks of the resurrection of the body (I Cor. 15.35–44).
And when St. John, on Patmos, sees the heavenly Jerusalem coming

down from heaven at the end of time, "prepared as a bride adorned for her husband" (Rev. 21.2), it is still a place that he is describing. It has walls whose dimensions the angel measures with the help of a reed; there are trees of Life, planted in the middle of the city (Rev. 22.2). It is the place where "death shall be no more, neither shall there be mourning nor crying nor pain any more" (Rev. 21.4).

4

Our Places Change

THESE FEW indications that we have just drawn from the Bible unreservedly confirm what we observe as doctors; namely, that man
is an incarnate being, who needs a place and who needs to be
attached to it and to be rooted in it. In the opening chapters of this
book I have described the pathology of deprivation of place. I
described abnormal situations such as family conflicts and deportation, which involve a brutal separation from one's place.

Man can also suffer, however, from the disruption of the place
he occupies in quite normal circumstances, if the disruption goes
beyond his capacity for adaptation. A man becomes attached to his
place, he becomes one with it. It becomes a part of his person, of
his inner self, so that anything that happens to his place also affects
his person. It is true that he has a remarkable capacity for adaptation, much superior to that of the animal, governed as it is entirely
by its instincts. Nevertheless his capacity to adapt himself has its
limits, and if the evolution in his environment becomes too rapid, it
may demand a rate of transformation in man which is beyond his
capabilities. This is what happened, for example, during the two
centuries that separate Vasco da Gama from Pascal.

For thousands of years the known world had been strictly limited.
Look at a map of the ancient world: the whole of the Mediterranean
basin is carefully drawn. There are a few prolongations towards
Great Britain, Germany, and the East, but they soon become uncertain in outline. Alexander's armies had indeed pushed on as far
as China, but this extension had never really been assimilated. And
then, suddenly, in the space of a few generations, the face of the
world had changed. The voyages of the great navigators, followed

by the discovery of America, immeasurably extended the boundaries of the world. Man's mental picture of the place in which he lived was called in question. Instead of locating himself on a map, he had to use a planisphere, and there is no centre on the surface of a planisphere. The earth was no longer built on the human scale.

At the same time the Copernican revolution in astronomy enlarged the heavens even more than the earth. Here again, as with the conquests of Alexander and his lieutenants, the ancients, with Pythagoras, had already glimpsed the truth, but it had never become integrated into the human imagination. For centuries men had gone on thinking of the earth as a fixture, a solid base, immobile and unshakeable, at the centre of the universe. They could, of course, imagine a space above and a space below, a heavenly vault and a shadowy Hades, but that was still in relation to a fixed point. The sun, the planets, and the stars moved round him, but man was at rest in the centre, attached to the earth.

Then suddenly, with Copernicus, the earth is seen to be no longer the motionless centre of the universe. It is just one more planet in the solar system, which is itself a tiny part of the universe, which in turn is discovered to be unimaginably immense. This last is a discovery so disconcerting that it is appreciated only by a few scientists. Another century had to pass by before Galileo's work provided striking confirmation of the Copernican system and of the rotation of the earth. At once Galileo was subjected to persecution. He was compelled to retract, on his knees. There is a legend that as he got to his feet he said: "But it *does* move!" However that may be, one can measure, in that persecution, the strength of man's resistance to anything that upsets his traditional place.

At that moment this resistance was expressed by the Roman Church, which had meanwhile had to defend itself against an equally agonizing upheaval. At the same time as Copernicus was putting forward his views, Luther and Calvin had made their appeal to the sources of the Christian religion, and had called in question the authority of tradition. Now, the universal acceptance of ideas consecrated by tradition constitutes a form of security, a religious environment, and it was this security which was threatened by the critical thought of the Reformers. In the face of this danger the Catholic Church hardened its position at the Council of Trent. The trial of Galileo expresses the same stiffening against the crumbling of the traditional system of thought. Descartes exercised great prudence in the way he put forward his equally revolutionary ideas, for fear of suffering the same fate as Galileo.

It is necessary, however, to understand the psychological causes of the persecution of Galileo. To admit that the earth rotated was to reject an age-old security which seemed indispensable. This was a real crisis for man: his whole conception of the world was being upset; he must have felt as if the ground were suddenly slipping away from under his feet. Even today sensitive people can feel that same sense of vertigo. Quite recently, one of my patients told me that she experienced a certain anxiety at feeling the earth turning under her feet. It was about the time of Galileo's death that Pascal wrote of his anxiety when faced with the immensity of the heavens: "The eternal silence of those infinite spaces strikes me with terror."[1] The world had suddenly become too big. Man felt lost in it. He no longer even recognized himself in his place, so vast had it become.

We ourselves are living in a period analogous to that of Pascal. Once again a change has taken place in our conception of the scale of the world. The infinite space which frightened Pascal is no longer a picture in our mind's eye, but a reality in which sputniks and cosmonauts travel in increasing numbers. This is such an important transformation that it is going to demand an effort of psychological adaptation which man is not going to find easy. As I write these lines, the Americans have just achieved the first rendezvous in space, and the Russians have succeeded in the delicate operation of placing on the moon a television camera which is sending back pictures to us. Everyone feels that these are but the first steps in a grand adventure whose future development no one can foresee.

I fully share the enthusiasm aroused by these well-nigh incredible exploits, and I see in them one further stage in the dominion over Nature to which God has called man (Gen. 1.26). But I also think that they are going to have incalculable psychological repercussions, not only among the cosmonauts as they undergo this scientific training, but also among the rest of us who continue to crawl modestly about on the earth, or fly at an altitude which seems quite insignificant.

The reason is that we all carry about with us a picture of the world that is a part of ourselves. When I read, for instance, that a space machine has missed the moon, and has gone on to lose itself

---

[1] Pascal, *The Pensées*, translated by J. M. Cohen, Penguin Books, 1961, No. 91, p. 47.

in space, it makes me shudder. Suddenly nothingness is no longer just "nothing at all", but a tremendous reality. Nothingness, which had already been obsessing modern thought, has been brought close to us, or at least a striking mental picture of nothingness. We had already the concept of death—but that at least left a tomb. And, after all, we had got used to it.

Well before the cosmonauts had begun taking off on their flights, Teilhard de Chardin was remarking that the anxiety and anguish which characterize the modern mind derive, at least in part, from the revolution wrought in our conception of the world by discoveries in the field of geology and astronomy. "For our mind to adjust itself to lines and horizons enlarged beyond measure, it must renounce the comfort of familiar narrowness ... Conscious or not, suppressed anguish—a fundamental anguish of being—despite our smiles, strikes in the depths of all our hearts and is the undertone of all our conversations. This does not mean that its cause is clearly recognized—far from it."

"In the first and most widespread degree," he continues, "the 'malady of space-time' manifests itself as a rule by a feeling of futility, of being crushed by the enormities of the cosmos.

"The enormity of space is the most tangible and thus the most frightening aspect ... Enormity of duration ... Corresponding enormity of number—the bewildering number of all that has been, is, and will be necessary to fill time and space."[2]

I feel that Teilhard de Chardin is right on this point: that psychoanalytical factors (which I fully recognize) are doubtless not the only causes of the wave of anxiety which is breaking over the human race at the present time. The reason why one of the signs of our time is the alarming increase in neuroses, is that it is one of the outcomes of the social and spiritual evolution of our age. It is disturbing to live in a space that is curved—the very idea defies our powers of pictorial imagination. Such a space is a purely mathematical entity, inconceivable, foreign to our minds, like the dimensions of geological and astronomical time which are equally beyond our mental grasp. What about when our grandchildren go off for a weekend on the moon? Doctors, psychotherapists, and clergymen, be prepared!

But the transformation of our social environment is taking place

[2] Pierre Teilhard de Chardin, *The Phenomenon of Man*, translated by Bernard Wall, Collins, London, 1959, pp. 227–8.

quite as rapidly as that of our astronomical ideas, and it is an equally important factor in our distress. In the ancient city man lived within a solid framework. The importance of the family, ancestor-worship, an authoritarian political organization, a rigid system of customs, and a certain religious unity compassed him narrowly about. For centuries society evolved only very slowly. In the Middle Ages the individual was even more of a prisoner within his surroundings, his guild, his social caste, and a whole host of taboos. When the Crusaders set off for the Holy Land they took with them their rigid feudal hierarchy. In the time of Pascal, of which we were speaking, the navigators who rounded the Cape of Good Hope, or passed through the Straits of Magellan, were still scarcely more numerous than the cosmonauts of our own day. Man was still closely bound to his place.

Since the Renaissance, since the French Revolution, and above all since the industrial revolution and the period of technical progress which have caused a prodigious development in the means of communication and transport, man's place has suddenly expanded to include the whole world. A century ago my father used to go for his holidays to St. Cergue des Voirons, about ten kilometres from Geneva. It was quite a business, a real expedition. Nowadays, a Finn will spend his holiday in Florida, and an American in Greece.

There is a general mixing of men and of ideas. A third of the population of the United States moves house every year. Followers of the most diverse ideas are constantly mixing and meeting—pious Christians and fanatical atheists, impenitent conservatives and militant communists, idealists and existentialists. We are constantly being submerged in quite contradictory philosophical doctrines, political propaganda, and social and artistic ideas. Time was when each man lived shut up in his own little garden. Now the world is swept by one tidal wave after another. How can you ask young people to hammer out a personal spiritual place for themselves in the midst of such a maelstrom?

Morals are changing as rapidly as ideas. For centuries they evolved extremely slowly. Each generation was almost the same as the preceding one. Every man's behaviour was governed by a powerful force of convention. Each country had its own customs and inviolable local traditions. Now, in one of the young African countries, one whole section of the population is beginning to adopt the American way of life, and these new customs exist alongside the most primitive traditionalism. One can eat strawberries in autumn, brought from the antipodes. Sex, from being taboo, has become commonplace; the rare visit to the theatre has given way to the craze for the cinema; and the peaceful habit of reading aloud in the family of an evening has been succeeded by the kaleidoscope of television.

I have already spoken of the marital conflicts which are increasing in number, but which for us are still pathological cases. Meanwhile the structure of even the most normal family is changing profoundly. The solid hierarchical framework of authority is disappearing. I have treated many women, whose nervous anxiety was at bottom due to the fact that their husbands had opted out of their position as head of the family. One often finds parents who lean on their children more than their children lean on them; and children, even in excellent families, who are as good as abandoned. I am not one of those who sigh for the good old days, which were not good at all, and which would be intolerable today. But we are still looking for a new structure of society which will both permit the full development of the individual and assure the sort of cohesion in the family that will make it a "place" in the full sense of the word.

In my view this is above all the task of the woman, who feels more strongly than the man the importance of places. It has been said that, without women, men live only in monasteries, barracks, or slums. But while it is true that the married woman knows well how to create a place for her husband and children to live in, there are many spinsters who are much less good at making a place for themselves. They used to remain tied to their parents' home, or to that of a brother. Nowadays they are emancipated, at least in our western countries. It is a tremendous change that has taken place. The reason why more women than men are to be found in the psychotherapist's consulting-room is that the social status of women has evolved to a greater extent than that of men.

True, they would not want to go back to the time when a woman was not a person, but a thing, at the mercy of men. Nevertheless, liberty has brought them a whole sheaf of problems, and, especially in the case of spinsters, the problem of loneliness. They need not only a career, but also a place of their own. I have sometimes had to advise them to rent a flat instead of living here and there in furnished rooms. Having a home of her own is particularly important for a woman. To put a name-plate on her door, to be in the telephone directory, is a sort of promotion for her, it means she has become a person. Many have hesitated a long time before following my advice, and have told me later what a difference it made to their lives. They could have visitors, they had a place of their own.

Technical progress has completely changed the scenery of our lives, the appearance of our towns, of our countryside, of our buildings and houses, and this change has exercised an influence over the evolution of our customs. It has been said that with all our powerful modern techniques we have not yet managed to build a town worth living in. We need not be surprised at this. Architecture and town-planning are not concerned only with technical problems. In many respects the growth of industry has seriously disfigured places in which compact masses of human beings live. Think of the frightful state of our big mining towns, and the industrial sectors of our large cities.

This is no doubt only a transitory situation. Louis Armand has shown[3] that what he calls the first industrial revolution, that of coal in the last century, required the concentration of factories around the mines and railway stations, whereas the present revolution, that of electricity, of electronics and of automation, allows wide decentralization. But who has not noticed the tremendous resistance shown by the workers against leaving the surroundings they are accustomed to, ugly as they are! It is not possible to close a mine without arousing protests which are due not only to fear of unemployment, but also to people's attachment.

In a most interesting book[4] Henri van Lier has likewise shown that the products of technology were horrible in the age of the "dynamic" machine, of the steam-engine type. Today, however, in the age of the "dialectic" machine, they are, he says, beautiful, moving, and even susceptible of bringing about a renascence of art, morality, and humanism. But what old engine-driver will willingly leave his unaesthetic machine to go and press multicoloured buttons on an electronic control-panel?

The siting of a factory or a new town in open country arouses a strange sense of unease, even if public transport or good roads make it easy for the workers to travel to and from their work. This is a problem which is exercising the minds of architects today. In order

[3] L. Armand and M. Drancourt, *Plaidoyer pour l'avenir*, Calman-Lévy, Paris, 1961.
[4] Henri van Lier, *Le nouvel âge*, Casterman, Tournai, 1962.

to be welcoming and acceptable, a place must have a past. Whether or not one is aware of it, a real place is not only a geographical location. It must also be located in history. Think, for example, of the attractiveness to tourists of cities such as Rome, Athens, or Florence. People do not go there only to visit museums and palaces. They have an atmosphere which is the result of a long past, and which is sensed intuitively by the visitor, even if he is not very cultured. This is why they are called the High Places of culture.

What a privilege it is, too, for my wife and me to visit different countries in the way we are able to do. We are welcomed everywhere by friends who take us into their homes, introduce us into their own lives, incorporating us into their personal environment. There are some people who have little interest in getting to know the places in which others live. They prefer to stay at home, in their own familiar places, and they criticize me for being so fond of travelling. There are others who travel a great deal, but always stay in international hotels, where they find the same breakfast, the same cuisine, and the same service as they are used to in their own country.

My colleagues who practise in mushroom satellite towns have told me how their inhabitants remain strangers to each other, isolated, how difficult it is to arouse any community feeling. The fact is that they are all newcomers, come from no one knows where. There is no kernel of old local traditions. So now attempts are being made to graft a new town on to an old village, as has been done, for example, in France, in the case of the atomic city of Pierrelatte.

This is only one example of the complexity of the problems which face the architect, and of the passionately interesting nature of his vocation. It is he who creates man's place, his public places as well as his private one. All that we have thought about so far on this subject underlines the extreme importance of the architect's mission in the world, and shows that the architect is transforming man himself when he builds him new places to live in. He must move forward in accordance with modern methods and modern needs, but without introducing so much in the way of innovation that men can no longer adapt themselves to the places provided for them. There has recently been built in Geneva a house for infirm old men, a building in the modern style, all glass. Those poor old men no longer find it easy to adapt themselves to a place that is so foreign to them.

It is through places, also, that communities are formed. Technology, however, has given us a world that is extremely impersonal. How, then, can we arrange our environment so as to give back to a depersonalized humanity the sense of community? Consider, for example, how the advent of the motor-car has transformed both our habits and the physiognomy of our towns. But it is only on foot that man really meets man. In his car a man has only just time to make a quick friendly gesture or to shout an insult as he passes. It is far from the case, however, that technology has brought only ugliness. Engineers, with their barrages, have created everywhere in our Alpine valleys lakes of movingly poetic beauty.

For centuries the peasants have been the surest supporters of the *status quo*. Their conservatism derived from the very fact of their attachment to the land, to the little place that was always there, handed down from generation to generation, and cultivated by each in the same manner, with the oxen and plough their distant ancestors used. Today they are centres of revolt, setting up barricades on the roads with their tractors as a sign of protest, and raising insoluble problems for the governments of their countries. The government is annoyed with them, and accuses them of being themselves the authors of their misfortunes because they insist on sticking to their old customs, to their old ancestral methods, to their little patches of land, and because they will not change in keeping with the rest of the world.

Then many of them go off to the town in search of a more propitious place for themselves, only to experience, for the most part, the worst results of rootlessness. It is in fact in the vast urban conglomerations of our time that one finds the most misfits and vagabonds. I am reminded of the Abbé Pierre, who has brought to the notice of our generation the distress of those who have no place to call their own. And of the splendid work done by that great-hearted woman, Mlle. Suzanne Nouvion,[5] who devotes herself to the welfare of the outcasts of Paris. Both can tell us how many of them there are in a big modern city, and its surroundings—men and women "always looking for a place", and always in vain.

Until quite recently the churches have shown themselves even more conservative than the peasants—Christian churches at that, despite the revolutionary ferment of their Gospel. Marxism knew what it was about in undertaking a desperate struggle against them.

[5] Suzanne Nouvion, *Le célibat laïc féminin*, Editions Ouvrières, Paris, 1962.

But now we see the churches changing before our eyes. It is precisely the criticism of Marx, Nietzsche, and Freud, as well as that
of the existentialist philosophers and of their own theologians that
is forcing them to forsake their old routines of thought. With the
ecumenical movement, however, the social physiognomy of the
Church is changing as well.

The *rapprochement* between the churches under the impulsion of
Bishop Söderblom, Dr. John Mott, and their spiritual heirs in the
Ecumenical Council of Geneva, had already made considerable in-
roads upon an age-old tradition of separatism. It is not to be wondered at that they encountered powerful opposition, particularly
from the most fervent communities, those that were surest of their
own rightness. Christian people had lived for so long between four
walls, oblivious of practically everything that was going on in the
chapel next door. Then suddenly the walls were thrown down. What
a change of place! One that might well bewilder the most
devout of believers. The process had been speeded up since the third
Assembly of the World Council of Churches at New Delhi in 1961,
when the Eastern Church joined the World Council. The incomparable spiritual riches of the Orthodox tradition are being discovered
anew. But it will take a long time for them to be assimilated.

In many respects the Roman Catholic Church was better known,
but it seemed to be an immovable colossus, imprisoned by its truths
and its glories as well as by its past errors. Then suddenly with
Pope John XXIII, with the Second Vatican Council, and with Pope
Paul VI, it is being transformed almost more rapidly than the six-
teenth-century Reformers could have hoped. It is not difficult to
imagine the bewilderment of pious Catholics in face of the abandonment of the traditional use of Latin or the schema on religious
liberty. At the end of the second session Pope Paul VI found it
prudent to put a slight brake on the zeal of the innovators so as to
allow the rest to catch up.

As we have already clearly seen in the course of this study, our
environment is bound to change—our spiritual environment even
more than our material environment. But the changes must not be
too precipitate, or else they will outrun man's power to adapt to
them. I speak here as a doctor: the doctor must always pay attention to proper dosage. People want to know what is good and what
is bad. Those who think along doctrinaire lines give answers in
terms of absolute and contradictory theories. But experienced

doctors point out that it is all a matter of dosage. In the same way people want to know whether tradition or innovation is good or bad. Here again the study of man teaches us that it is all a matter of dosage: that to stand still may be fatal, but also that one cannot tear a man brutally from his place without risk of mortal injury.

As we have seen, we all have within us our picture of the world. We also have our own picture of man, and this picture has become as blurred as the other. This is due largely to the advent of psychoanalysis which characterizes our century. On the one hand, psychoanalysis heals people suffering from anxiety, but on the other it sows the seeds of an anxiety of its own in all men's hearts. The Rev. Fr. Oraison, who is both priest and psychoanalyst, has described[6] this modern insecurity which derives from the fact that psychoanalysis has put an end to the "myth of man as a reasonable being and master of himself".

Where Copernicus revealed the external infinity of space, Freud has revealed within us an infinity that makes us feel just as dizzy. The dimensions of the mind have increased so far beyond measure that we are no longer able to grasp them.

The mind is also a place. It is the emotional environment of the person. Think of the description of the mind that was still in vogue less than half a century ago. We calmly enumerated the "faculties of the mind"—the will, the imagination, and so on. They were absolutely reliable. Now we have been shown that we live on a volcano, on an abyss of inner conflicts and explosions which send up only a few tiny bubbles to the surface. And then, it used to be possible to classify the virtues and vices. We knew the difference between right and wrong, between good folk and bad. Now it is all inextricably mixed up. We are no longer certain of what are the true motives of our own behaviour.

The whole of psychology has been turned upside down by the discovery of the unconscious factors, almost always the inverse, as Jung has pointed out,[7] of our sincerest aspirations. Psychology now sees our minds as torn by the constant interplay of contrary impulses. Psychology is said to have become dynamic, where formerly it was static. We might well say that it has become pathetic. For psychology is ourselves, the inner place in which we live our lives.

[6] Marc Oraison, *Une morale pour notre temps*, Arthème Fayard, Paris, 1964.
[7] C. G. Jung, *Psychology of the Unconscious*, translated by B. M. Hinkle, New York, 1916, reprinted, Routledge, London, 1951.

See, then, how our place has changed, how quickly it has changed, and is still changing, throwing us into uncertainty as to what our place will be tomorrow. I have certainly not described this transformation in our picture of the world and of ourselves in order to deplore it. Man must explore his environment, interplanetary space and the depths of his own mind. But in the course of this exploration he goes from one surprise to another. What seemed simple appears more and more complex; what seemed fixed is seen to be moving; what seemed sure is thrown into doubt. Man is too interested in truth to refuse to revise his conception of the world and of himself. Man is a remarkably adaptable creature, more even in his mind than in his body. But he must pay the price of his perpetual and laborious adaptation.

I have described the mind, the psyche, as the place of the person. But the body is no less so. And so the word "place" takes on once again its concrete, material, physical meaning, the primacy of which I have already insisted upon. The whole of the work done in the fields of physiognomy and typology illustrates the fact that the body reveals the person. The body finds it harder to tell a lie than does the mind. A young man is telling me his reactions to a friend's suicide. He felt a sort of dissociation of his being: his body wept, whereas inertia descended upon his mind, and it became numb as it watched his body weep. No doubt his body was expressing the truth about his person.

Generally speaking, we are readier to believe our minds than our bodies. At least we seek the agreement of our minds in order to preserve the harmony of our internal environment. H. F. Amiel remarks in his *Journal* for 29 August, 1876: "Thirty years ago, I felt for two weeks that my body was outside my real self; I regarded it with curiosity, as an alien thing, and the sound of my steps on the floor made me turn and look. There is therefore no vigorous adhesion between my appearance and my reality."[8] Such adhesion is nevertheless necessary for the authentic manifestation of the person.

To rebel against one's body is to enter into conflict with one's natural environment. Such conflicts are harassing, exhausting, and destructive of the person. How many people there are—and this is particularly true of women—who cannot accept some bodily misfortune, often a defect which no one notices, whereas they feel that

[8] *The Private Journal of H. F. Amiel*, translated by V. W. and C. V. W. Brooks, Macmillan, New York, 1935, p. 477.

nobody sees anything in them but that. Sometimes the defect is purely imaginary! They think they are too tall or too short, too fat or too thin, that their hair is too greasy or too dry, or their breasts too big or too small. All that is required is an unkind remark, or some chance comment overheard, for the whole thing to turn into an obsession even in the case of the most attractive women, who can be quite overcome by really surprising doubts about their ability ever to look nice or be loved.

And then there is the slow decay of the body which old age brings, and all the complicated and costly artifices which women—and sometimes men too—employ in order to hide it, and of which they become the prisoners. This often brings about an ever-increasing divorce between the person and the body, a sort of lie told not only to others, but also to oneself. True elegance requires integrity in one's attitude to oneself and to self-expression in one's toilet. Often, for example, a woman has told me that as a little girl or in adolescence she suffered from never having been given a new dress, having instead always to wear clothes passed on by an elder sister or by charitable neighbours. She felt vaguely that this constituted a sort of devaluation of her as a person. A dressmaker once told me of the joy it gave her to help a customer to find the dress that suited her body best, and so to acquire greater self-confidence. This reminds me of Bacon's remark to the effect that one commands Nature only by obeying her.

By all means let us influence Nature, but without contradicting or betraying her. Unfortunately not all beauty specialists, dress designers, milliners, and hair stylists have this conception of their vocation. "I always do my own hair," a pretty woman says to me, "in a natural style, for fear of its being out of keeping with my appearance. Only once I had it done by a famous Parisian hair-dresser. He made a grand job of it, in accordance with his own ideas. All my friends complimented me on it. But by the next day I couldn't stand it any longer. It was pretty enough, but it wasn't *me*, so I undid it all." "How had he done it, then?" I asked. "Just imagine! He'd given me a halo!"

5

The Healing of Persons

TALKING OF HALOES, of course, reminds me of Pascal's remark:
"Man is neither angel nor brute, but unfortunately when he wants
to be like an angel he behaves like a brute."[1] This is often quoted
in connection with the disdain of the body which is so common
among religious people of all shades of belief. They contrast the
ideal life of the soul with the sordid necessities of that of the body. I
have already written elsewhere about this negative attitude, and
pointed out how far removed it is from the biblical view of man. It
is generally the result of a puritan upbringing, full of moralistic
prejudices. Here are two further examples: a pretty woman confides
in me that her first act when she goes into a hotel bedroom is to
turn all the mirrors with their faces to the wall. Another tells me
that she has never been able to look at herself naked without a feeling of shame. "This body of mine," she adds, "is my enemy."

This rejection of the body is merely a symptom of a more general
rejection of life as it is and as God has given it to us. "I am discovering now," a woman patient says to me, "that I had taken
refuge in the 'spiritual'. It was my little cabin." What takes place is
in fact that the person's real place is rejected in favour of an imaginary place. Accepting life means accepting that one has a body and
identifying oneself with it, as well as accepting the limitations it imposes on our ambitions, especially when it is ill, infirm, or old.

The word "accept" may lead to misunderstanding. It might give
the impression that the subject gives unwilling consent, that he re-
signs himself with a bad grace to an inevitable servitude. On the
contrary, genuine acceptance brings liberation, and a much fuller

[1] op. cit., No. 329, p. 114.

fulfilment than all our airy dreams. Dr. Jacques Sarano has demonstrated this clearly in his book *Essai sur la signification du corps.*[2] We must get beyond the dualism of mind-body, which has been made familiar to us since Descartes. For we do not live in two places, our mind and our body, or in three—mind, body, and spirit —but in one only. Harmonious living, like a classical drama, demands unity of place.

So it is that many organic affections are the bodily manifestations of emotional disturbance, as we have been taught by the psychosomatic school of medicine which has come to us from America. So it is, conversely, that bodily exercises can effectively contribute to the healing of psychic disturbances. This is the case, for example, with Schultz's system of autogenic training,[3] which is so popular in Germany, and with yoga, which is of oriental origin. The principle is also used in the method evolved by my fellow-countryman Dr. Vittoz,[4] and introduced into France by his pupils, Dr. d'Espinay,[5] Mlle. Henriette Lefebre, Dr. Ledoux, and others. It seems to me to have the great merit of de-intellectualizing the treatment of neurosis, and of showing the patient that what his body feels is more important than what his mind imagines.

This also explains why gymnastics, especially the dance, singing, and all the arts of bodily self-expression, have great therapeutic value. It is not a matter of merely of accepting willy-nilly that one has a body, but of rediscovering its value, of using it as a genuine manifestation of one's person, and of becoming aware once more, as Dr. Sarano says, of its spiritual significance. The body is the place of love. The sex act is not merely the expression of one's feelings, but the sublime gift of oneself, a true spiritual testament.

The medicine of the person, as it has come to be known, lays great stress on this demand for profound accord with the body. This is expressed, for example, by Professor Karlfried von Dürckheim in his book on the *Hara*, or vital centre of man.[6] The Hara, as he has learned from the Japanese, is the abdomen, the centre of gravity of

[2] Published by Delachaux and Niestlé, Neuchâtel and Paris, 1963.
[3] J. H. Schultz and W. Luthe, *Autogenic training: a Psychophysiologic Approach to Psychotherapy*, Heinemann, London, 1959.
[4] Chauchard, Ledoux, *et al.*, *Le Dr. Roger Vittoz et l'angoisse moderne*, Editions du Levain, Paris, 1965.
[5] P. d'Espinay, *La psychothérapie du Dr. Vittoz. Comment combattre l'anxiété par le contrôle de soi*, Tequi, Paris, 1965.
[6] Karlfried von Dürckheim, *Hara, The Vital Centre of Man*, translated by S. M. von Kospath and E. R. Healey, Allen and Unwin, London, 1962.

the body—the place of the place, one might say. To place this centre of gravity in the right place, neither too high nor too low is to put one's whole person on a firm base. That implies a proper attitude of the body, and at the same time signifies a proper attitude of the person in his life.

The medicine of the person considers man *in situ*, in his relationship with his environment. Thus it takes its place in the line already traced by Hippocrates when he wrote his treatise *On airs, places, and waters*. Man, then, is to be seen in relation and interaction with himself and others, with the world and with God. Society, the world, and God are his external place; his body, mind, and spirit are his internal place. God has created us in our totality; he has given us our place; he rules over our physical as well as our spiritual lives. Thus, the acceptance of one's body is much more a spiritual problem than a psychological one. That is why among the followers of the medicine of the person there are not only psychiatrists and psychotherapists of every school of psychological medicine, but also a great number of surgeons and other specialists in physical medicine —ear, nose and throat specialists, ophthalmic surgeons, gastroenterologists, and radiologists.

It was a surgeon from Strasbourg, Dr. Ernest Irrmann, who produced an excellent treatise on the practice of the medicine of the person and on the theoretical principles that may be deduced from it.[7] Surgeons sometimes say that they have little understanding of the jargon of the psychoanalysts. But they understand very clearly the importance of the body for the person, and they have a lot to teach us on the subject. The psychoanalyst, following Freud's instructions, refrains from undressing his patients, whereas the patient willingly shows himself naked to the surgeon, which is a quite concrete and effective way of entrusting himself to him. We are always talking about personal contact—and the hand of the doctor palpating the abdomen is contact *par excellence*. We talk about confidence—what greater demonstration of confidence can there be then the exposure of the body to the scalpel in the hand of the surgeon?

Last year in New York we had a teach-in on the person, with several doctors who were specialists in various branches. A surgeon referred to the problem of those who have had a limb amputated.

[7] E. Irrmann, "Introduction à la médecine de la personne", in *Présences*, No. 89, p. 63, (Prieuré de St. Jean, Champrosay, Seine-et-Oise).

Even when we have a tooth out we do not feel the same as before and we cannot keep our tongue away from the fascinating void. The man who has lost a limb has lost his place. He must adapt himself to a new place in the form of his mutilated body. The job of the surgeon is not only to carry out the operation with impeccable skill, but also to understand the disturbance caused in his patient, and to help him towards reconciliation with his body.

The vague, almost unconscious awareness we have of the clearance required by our body in order to avoid bumping into things when it moves, is termed a schema by the psychologists. I have a patient who is exceptionally tall. He automatically bends his head when he passes beneath the pendant light in the waiting-room when I go to fetch him. The paraplegic, condemned to spend the rest of his life going about in a wheelchair, must incorporate it into the schema of his body in order to go through doorways without difficulty. And that is no small matter. More generally, the problem arises for all those who are infirm: they have to learn to accept the limitations of their disabled bodies. Mlle. Suzanne Fouché has done much to help us to understand this problem, showing us that as doctors our task is to help all our patients to accept their bodies as they are. And the only way to help them is to achieve the same harmony within ourselves.

It is not a matter only of their health and ours. It is a matter of our development, of that plentitude of human life which requires that we should be integrated within ourselves. All that I have said elsewhere about accepting our age, our sex, our parents, our environment, accepting even disease and sin, is concerned with this problem of place. All those things make up our real existence. They are the place in which we are called to live, instead of in some other dream-place. The problem, then, is an existential one. For centuries idealist philosophers have been pleased to argue about the essence of things and the nature of man. Those were mere abstractions, against which the existentialists have struck a decisive blow.

The latter have rightly reminded us that we are incarnate. To designate existence, the Germans use the word *Dasein*, literally "to be there". "There" is a place. There is no true existence that is not dependent upon a place: *hic et nunc*, here and now. Similarly, Paul Ricoeur of the Sorbonne says in his book *Finitude et culpabilité*[8]

[8] Paul Ricoeur, *Finitude et culpabilité*, Editions Montaigne, Aubier, Paris, 1960.

that it is "the *here* of my body" which always makes my perception of any object finite, in that it depends on the viewpoint at which I stand. One can indeed say that a guilt complex always involves a certain rebellion against the fact that the human condition is finite, and not infinite.

It is also because of this finiteness that one cannot be at the same time both well and ill, that the points of view of the healthy and of the sick cannot ever exactly coincide, and that the experience of sickness is a strictly personal matter which one cannot fully understand without being sick oneself. There is a gap between health and sickness, over which one passes from one place to another. Past health is the place to which the subject has been accustomed, and which he must leave. Sickness is a new place which he must of necessity accept. All our patients have reached this state of crisis as regards their place, and the manner in which they resolve it will have a great influence on the course of their cure. To fall ill is not only to suffer, to show lesions and symptoms, to fear the threat, more or less remote, of death. It is also to be wrenched violently out of the habitual framework of one's life. It is to lose one's place.

There is a place one must leave, a deprivation of place. Family, job, meeting friends, shopping, pastimes, opening one's mail, a hundred and one little habits, hunting or fishing—in short, action, liberty, particularly liberty of action, this is the place in which one has lived one's life. Even if one was sometimes discontented with it, one discovers how attached to it one is when the time comes to leave it. Sickness inevitably brings its own kind of alienation with it. We find ourselves completely dependent upon others, even for those trivial things which are sometimes far more troublesome to ask for than important medical attention. One woman patient does her utmost to hide her illness. She knows full well, she tells me, that if she admitted to being ill, she would become a mere "thing", delivered defenceless into the hands of her family.

As soon as you fall ill, everyone gives you advice, sometimes excellent, sometimes absurd, and everyone is hurt if you do not follow the advice that has been offered. The authority of the doctor alone makes it possible for you to escape all this domineering kindness. Everyone blames your past behaviour: "Didn't I tell you that you were overtiring yourself?" When you are ill you are in a state of inferiority to all who are well, however kind they are. A sick person never feels himself to be properly understood, and he also often misunderstands the real meaning of things said to him or measures taken on his behalf. Mme. Pastorelli gives an excellent description[9] of the ditch that is inevitably dug between the sick and the healthy despite the best of intentions, a ditch which grows deeper if the illness is a prolonged one. "He who goes down to Sheol," says Job, "does not come up; he returns no more to his house, nor does his place know him any more" (Job 7.9–10).

But the sick person has also a new place to accept, to make his. This new, unknown place is the state of sickness. His place henceforth is his bed, which takes on an unsuspected dimension, as does everything that is within reach, notably the drawer in his bedside table. Professor J. van den Berg gives[10] a percipient description of the little world of the sick person confined to bed. There is a new timetable, governed by medicines and sickroom routine. There is the time of waiting for the doctor's visit, and all one would like to say to him and then cannot. Visits by friends and relations have a changed tonality. People make jokes in order to hide their emotions. And then there is silence, the long silence that is so difficult to fill when one is unused to it. And in fact nowadays, so many people caught in the inexorable machine of active life have lost the habit of silence. In the silence unaccustomed thoughts come into the sick person's mind, so that he wonders if they are not abnormal.

The change of place is most complete when the patient has to go into hospital. I have often had great difficulty in securing a patient's consent to his transfer to hospital. That must surely have happened to my colleagues as well. Or else one has to put an end to useless argument by an act of authority. And then there it is, the alienation of sickness, the patient powerless to escape when the ambulance comes for him. The causes of this resistance are of course extremely complex, the true ones often being unadmitted, and even unconscious. But among them, no doubt, is the patient's fear of losing the little independence he has left. Once in the hospital one is at the mercy of any and every doctor or nurse, and one cannot leave when one likes. It is even worse when it is a case of going into a psychiatric hospital, and Professor Baruk has made a vigorous denunciation[11]

---

[9] France Pastorelli, *The Glorious Bondage of Illness*, English translation, Allen and Unwin, London, 1936.

[10] " 'Garder le lit', Essai d'une psychologie de malade", *Situation* 1, Utrecht and Antwerp, 1954.

[11] *Psychiatrie morale expérimentale.*

of the dishonest stratagems which are sometimes used, and in which he sees a violation of the person.

Quite recently I was seriously ill, and had to spend six weeks in hospital. For the doctor, being ill himself is an important experience. The doctor is always thinking of other people's illnesses. I recall an evening discussion on the medicine of the person, in which some of our colleagues had been asked to talk about their own experiences of being ill. It was profoundly moving. How well they understood, when it concerned themselves, that disease does not only have an objective and scientific aspect, but has also a quite personal meaning—that it involved the purpose of their lives.

I in my turn went suddenly over from the place of health and action to that of sickness and inaction, and I did so without great difficulty. That is due, I think, to the fact that I do not suffer from that vagabond complex which I described in the first chapter of this book. On the contrary, I am at home anywhere. This confirms the law to which I referred, that just as a person who has been deprived of his place may go on looking for a place without taking root anywhere, so one who has known a real place is able to change from one place to another and establish himself in each. So I was able to find myself in sickness, and subsequently in hospital, not, of course, free of problems, but without injury or anxiety. On the contrary, I was grateful for the solid and unshakeable support of my wife and children, and for the numerous tokens of affection of which I was the recipient.

I am shy, of course, very shy. I have always found it hard to leave my solitude and enter into company. I am also very independent. I like to manage for myself, and hate to ask for anyone else's help. But I have not the vagabond complex. At least, not in the psychological sense of the expression, for there is a spiritual sense described by the author of the Epistle to the Hebrews when he recalls all the faithful who "acknowledged that they were strangers and exiles on the earth . . . seeking a homeland" (Heb. 11.13–14). That I have always felt; perhaps because I have known since childhood that my parents were in heaven, and that death alone would reunite me with them.

It is less by inclination than by vocation that I interest myself in the world and in people. It is because God has called me to try to understand and help them. But I am fully aware of the limitations of our knowledge and our capacity to help in this world. It is in the

Beyond that we shall find the answer to all the problems that remain insoluble for us. Thus the threat of death which hung over me was a trial for my wife, for my sons and my family, for my friends, for my patients who suddenly had my support taken from them, but for me scarcely at all. I did not know whether I preferred to live or to die. So I never prayed God to preserve me from death, trusting in his sovereign will. Others prayed for me, with wonderful fidelity. Priests said Mass with special intention for me. To all of them I am most grateful. Their prayers were answered. And now I can take advantage of my convalescence to write this book.

However, the patient's capacity to adapt to his new place, either sickness or hospital, does not depend only on his own personal state of mind. It depends quite as much on the person of his doctor and the atmosphere of the hospital. I had the good fortune to be in the care of Professor Eric Martin, Dean of the Faculty of Medicine at Geneva University, and one of the pioneers in the practice of the medicine of the person.

When you are ill you are of course principally concerned that your doctor should be professionally expert. You expect him to make a correct diagnosis and prescribe the most effective treatment. You do not expect him to hide medical incompetence under a display of amiable sentiments. But how much better when, along with the technical skill, he has also those human qualities which make the doctor a healer of persons! How much better to have personal contact with him, to feel that he understands and even guesses your problems—the problems which are raised by the illness itself. For that will also contribute to the success of the treatment he gives you. Medicine is full of surprises. Even the most carefully thought-out courses of treatment may fail to bring about the desired result. And sometimes failure is due not so much to objective factors as to an imponderable, the morale of the patient. In order to sustain morale, it is not always necessary to call in an expert psychiatrist. The important thing is to talk to the patient, and really to listen to him. Professor Martin would come on a Sunday afternoon, without his white coat and without any assistant, to sit by my bedside and have long and intimate talks with me.

I was also able to see that when a hospital is run by a doctor of the person, the whole atmosphere of the institution becomes personal, and that this is extremely important for the patients. The head nurse becomes a head nurse of the person, as was Mlle.

Rossier in that hospital. Along with her professional skill she has a personal care for each patient, as also have all those who work under her direction. For the morale of the patient, his capacity to adapt himself to the new place in which he has to live, depends on the harmonious and personal collaboration of all the doctors, all the nurses, and the whole staff. We spoke of that in 1964, on the occasion of the inauguration of the Clinique Marie-Louise, which Dr. Giacomo Rizzi had built at Monticelli, near Parma, as a psychiatric "hospital of the person". It is not enough in a hospital that the medical superintendent should himself be a doctor of the person. He must awaken all those around him to the meaning of persons, from his deputy to the kitchen-maid, in order to foster a community spirit throughout the establishment.

This is why the new superintendent of the university psychiatric clinic in Geneva, Professor Julian de Ajuriaguerra, told me that he devoted half his time to his staff, doubtless not only to instruct them in the psychological and social factors attendant upon disease, but also to help each member in his own personal difficulties. For doctors, nurses, the porter, almoners, and cleaners all have their problems too. They are accustomed to attending to others, devoting themselves to others, but keeping their own worries secret. And the fact is that where morale is concerned no one can bring to others more than he has himself.

I was speaking recently with a psychiatrist who acts as consultant in a general hospital. I was talking of all the conflicts, the jealousies, and injustices that can arise in a hospital among the doctors, among the nurses, between the medical staff and the domestic staff, and of all psychological troubles that can result. I asked him if he did not think that medical efficiency would be improved if an attempt were made to resolve them. "Indeed it would," he said, "but first you would have to convince those in charge of the different services. It is easier to convince the manager of a factory, who is quick to see that the services of a psychologist improve the financial return made by the enterprise. In a hospital the profit motive plays no part as it does in a factory."

Dr. Heinrich Huebschmann, of Heidelberg, has told[12] the story of one of his tuberculosis patients who was on the way to being cured when the administrative authorities, who have their own

---

[12] H. Huebschmann, "Le malade et son monde vu par un praticien hospitalier", in *Au service de la personne*, Nouvelles Editions Latines, Paris, 1959.

reasons for what they do, had him transferred to another hospital. There he fell into a rapid decline despite excellent treatment. All hope of a cure was abandoned, and he was sent home to die. "At the last minute," wrote Dr. Huebschmann, "he insisted on being taken back to the first hospital. Once again there was an astounding improvement. He gained twenty pounds in six weeks. His fever disappeared and expectoration ceased—and all with a minimum of antibiotics. Today that patient is cured." That story seems to me to have the precision of a laboratory experiment. Dr. Huebschmann stresses the equal value of the two hospitals, "both equally well equipped; each tried to use modern remedies and therapeutic techniques; they were both excellently run, and the respective superintendents were both good Christians." The only difference was that one was a hospital which practised the healing of persons. In it there reigned a community spirit such that the patient felt himself to be understood and accepted as one of the community. In the other, he was only a number, a case.

The first hospital was the Ludorf Krehl-Spital, which was for a long time under the direction of the late Professor Richard Siebeck. I once heard him pay an eloquent tribute to his head nurse: "She was herself so fully a person that everyone who came into contact with her became a person." Yes, there is a contagious personal quality that can transform the atmosphere of a hospital, impersonal as it so often is, and affect all who work in it, and the patients as well.

On this subject, here is an interesting detail connected with places. Dr. Scherding runs a sanatorium for tuberculous women on the Plateau d'Assy, in France. He told us that when he is informed of the arrival of a new patient, he finds out whether there is in the house another patient from the same place, so that he can put them together in the same room. They can talk together about their home district, and this helps the new arrival to adapt herself to life in the sanatorium.

In this way their stay in hospital can be a real revelation for some patients, their first experience of a model society. This is especially true of patients whose condition is aggravated by a vagabond complex; patients who have possibly gone from one doctor to another, from one medical service to another, without ever finding any personal contact, without every experiencing the social climate in which one feels one is being made welcome, in which one becomes a person, in which one discovers what real team-work is, and in which one feels one belongs. The medicine of the person in a hospital is the result of the efforts of all, the fruit of mutual confidence among all who work and live there. Fellow-doctors and nurses, if you want your patients to be really open with you, be honest and open with each other.

And you will discover, in yourselves and in your patients, the often surprising effect of such openness. It is well worth the time spent upon it, and it may contribute to healing. Of course, medicine was simpler in Virchow's time. It was thought that disease was always the effect of an organic lesion, and nothing else. So, with his eye to his microscope, the doctor looked for the lesion. He was glad when he found it—with the pleasure that comes of being able to "localize" the trouble. But when he found none, he simply declared: "It's nothing—just nerves."

Of course we still need the pathologist with his microscope. But we have learnt that disease is a far more complicated affair; that "nervous", even existential, factors are at work in every disease, whether organic or not; that these factors cannot be tracked down under a microscope, but only by spending time listening to our patients.

What we must do, therefore, is to establish personal contact with the sick, so as to integrate them into the community, whereas the tendency of the healthy has always been to keep away from the sick, especially the mentally sick. You will remember the story of the schizophrenic whom Jesus healed in the country of the Gerasenes. The evangelist records that he "lived among the tombs" (Mark 5.3). The tombs: the symbolic place of those who are excluded from human society. For centuries still the mentally ill were made to feel rejected in this way by the human community, deprived of a place. Their liberation from their chains by Pinel marked a step forward in their restoration as persons. Nowadays efforts are made to make the psychiatric hospital a real *place*, with flowers on the tables, communal activities, parties, and a coffee-bar.

Consider, too, the lepers, who in primitive countries must leave their places, their huts and families, and take to the bush to live alone, as soon as their disease is recognized. But to a certain extent all our patients are also people who have lost their place, people in search of a place. They need medicines, it is true, but they also need to be welcomed back and reintegrated into society. I spoke recently on this topic at the French Congress of Rural Medicine.

The country doctor often feels inferior to his colleagues in the town. He has less opportunity to supplement his technical medical knowledge. As soon as he comes upon a serious case he must pass it on to the hospital in the city, which has at its disposal equipment that is not available in a village. But the country doctor, though he may not be sufficiently aware of it, holds a trump card which the hospital specialist lacks. It is his familiarity with the environment of his patients; he knows their homes, and the gossip and conflicts of the village. He can talk to them about their cows, and the ill effects of the drought or the hailstorms. This is the privilege too, to a lesser extent, of the family doctor in the town, and it is what gives his vocation its interest.

All the sick have this double need, for first-class technical skill, and for personal contact. Ideally they should go together, and that is what the medicine of the person is. It is not sufficient, for instance, for a surgeon to be assisted in his work by a psychologist who can give him information on the mental state of his patients, as is often done nowadays. It is very important that the surgeon himself should take an interest in those on whom he is to operate; that he should go, for example, to the patient's bedside on the evening before the operation, as Dr. Jean de Rougemont has described, and sit down for a friendly chat with him. His moral influence may perhaps be greater than that of the psychologist.

The same applies to a course of psychoanalysis, which is also a surgical operation. Just as, during the operation, the surgeon is only a technician, pure and simple, so the psychoanalyst must maintain the cold Freudian silence. This reserve can be an indispensable instrument, during the treatment, for forcing the patient to go to the limit in self-exploration, instead of escaping into interesting discussions, or into deceptive emotional outbursts. The close and unwearying attention of the doctor gives the patient the feeling of existing, of being accepted and understood.

When a patient says to us: "You understand me," that means, "You accept me, you accept me just as I am." And finally: "I feel that you are loving me." My friend Dr. Susumu Akahoshi has recently published a book called *The Psychology and Psychopathology of the AMAE*. The Japanese word AMAE means the need to be loved. The author is a true healer of persons, a complete doctor, since after having been a surgeon for a long time he turned to psychiatry. He thus made in his own vocation the synthesis of body and mind, and to this he adds the spirit, as he brings to that vocation all the fervour of his Christian faith. I am unable to read his book, since it is written in Japanese, but I am very impressed by the fact that in that language there is a word for the immense, primordial, and universal need of man to be loved.

This need is particularly intense in all cases of neurosis, perhaps in part, I think, because neurosis is often a secret malady. It attacks eminent men and women, people who are much in the public eye, whom everyone admires, on whom everyone relies without any suspicion of the awful anxieties and obsessions they hide in their hearts and which come to the surface the moment they are alone. They are usually careful not to let it be known that they are coming to consult us, knowing that their friends and relations would not understand: "But why do you need to see a doctor, you who seem so strong?" The homage they receive from society does not cure them. One of them said to me in a letter: "Everyone esteems me, but no one loves me."

So they feel they are living double lives, that they show a brilliant façade to the world, behind which they hide extreme distress. They often feel guilty about it. Sometimes they despise themselves. They need to find a place in which they can at last be honest, and that place is our consulting-room. Much has been written on the subject of "transfer". Freud saw in it only an emotional phenomenon in which the patient relives in the presence of the doctor the feelings of a child towards his father. Dr. Maeder has shown[13] that there is in this something more than an emotional phenomenon. It is the experience of the spiritual phenomenon of personal contact. Through this particular interpersonal relationship, he says, the patient is reconciled with society, and is enabled to return into the human community in general.

In an analogous fashion, we may say that the patient, having found one real place, will become capable of establishing himself in any other place. In so far as I become something of a father for my patient, my place becomes in part his place, and this frees him from his vagabond complex. The transfer stage is only a transitory one, but it is indispensable to reintegration into life and into the world. Through us and our place, the patient is attached once more to society, and often also to God and the Church, which then become

[13] Alphonse Maeder, "Le rôle du contact affectif en psychothérapie", in *Revue suisse de psychologie pure et appliquée*, Vol. X, Ch. 4, 1951.

for him the best possible place. Nevertheless I ought to say that it is often very difficult for a patient who has been cured, or at least undergone an improvement in his condition, to feel at home in the Church, even if he wants to. He finds it so impersonal, so cold and conventional, after the stirring experiences he has had in the psychotherapist's consulting-room.

The giving of a place to those who have none seems to me to be one way of defining our vocation as healers of persons. As we have seen, one becomes a person only if one really has a place. So in helping our patients to find their places we are helping them to become persons. And that place is no abstraction. It is our consulting-room, the fireside, the photographs on the mantelpiece, the clock they detest, the books on the shelves, all the little details with which they have become familiar during those hours that have been so important in their lives. When I moved house, one patient whom I had been treating for a number of years took more than three months to feel at ease in my new consulting room. And how many patients find it hard to leave when the consultation is over, to leave this place!

Giving a place to those who have none!

PART TWO

The Two Movements

6

Two Gospels

GIVING A PLACE to those who have none! This maxim brings us back to my student friend of whom I spoke at the beginning of this book, and who said he was always looking for a place. He happened to come back to see me recently, and I asked him how he was getting on. You can imagine how glad I was to hear his reply: "Very well." Had I anything to do with it? I really do not know. I am not even sure that I was not an obstacle in the way of his cure, despite all my goodwill and the friendship which unites us. Perhaps my fireside was a place of refuge and security amid the storms. But for a place to be really beneficial, one must be quite free and at ease in it. That is not as easy to bring about as you think.

One day he said to me: "You are influencing me too much." I protested: I am so careful to respect the liberty of others, I take so little pleasure in dominating others, influencing others—surely not! But after all, it might be true. We can exert influence without knowing it, even when we are being careful not to give advice. The influence we exert depends not so much on what we say as on what we are—or rather, on what the other person believes we are, and what he thinks we are thinking.

Our dialogue suffered from one serious handicap. The reader will remember that this student had had a strict religious upbringing. I too am a Christian, and he knew this. He could not have ignored the fact, even if I had carefully avoided any mention of my own beliefs. Therefore he could not help identifying me with the religious world of his childhood, attributing to me the concepts which his parents had tried to inculcate in him, both good and bad. So the influence we exert does not depend on what we are really thinking, but upon what people think we are thinking.

I have said that that student always felt torn between two worlds —an ideal world of faith, symbolized for him by St. Francis of Assisi and Pascal, and the "everyday" world, that is to say the practical reality of life, where one has to fight to avoid being crushed, to defend oneself, to be hard when necessary, because life is hard. Now he certainly classed me as belonging to the world of religion and high moral standards, even if I spoke against moralism and took special care to help him to accept the hard reality of life. He must have seen me as a representative of religion, a symbol of the idealist, religious attitude, which floats in a cloud of fine sentiments above the reality of life. When he said: "You are influencing me too much," was it not because he was afraid my influence might make worse the thing that was tearing him apart, by making him even more sensitive to the call of faith, contrary to the inevitable realities of life? So he had also to defend himself against me, and against the influence he felt me exerting over him. It is not possible to be truly at ease when one has to be on the defensive.

He said of my last book: "The beginning is all right, but it suddenly turns into a sermon, and that's a pity!" That was another remark that touched me to the quick. I know very well what that word "sermon" means to those who have been disappointed or hurt by the Church: fine phrases, easy bromides, far removed from the realities of life; high-sounding uplift which is not only irrelevant, but not even put into practice by the person who preaches it. But it is also no doubt true that though I have often denounced it, I fall into the same fault myself. It is a fact that those whom the Church has disappointed or hurt, like my student friend, have a quick ear for the sermonizing tone the moment it appears.

And how could I be free from it? Like everyone else I am stamped with the mark of my upbringing. I am the product of the Church and of the religious experiences which have bound me to the Church. I am a churchman, and all churchmen are given to preaching sermons (there are of course many others who do it without being in any sense churchmen). It is better for me to recognize it frankly than to try and defend myself against the charge. The psychotherapist's consulting-room is a place for truth. It requires of me the same attitude of truth as it demands of the patient. If I want to help him to become himself, to show himself as he really is, surely it is necessary for me to be myself and to show myself as I am. Even if I hid my private thoughts he would feel them.

Psychoanalysts sometimes reproach me for not maintaining the moral neutrality which they consider to be the basic principle of the exercise of their vocation, because I do not hide my convictions. I am in full agreement with them when they say that psychotherapy ought to be non-directive. I think I take as much care as they to avoid the "sermon", moral exhortation and advice. But who can claim to be really morally neutral? No one, in my opinion—neither they nor I. We can indeed watch that we say nothing openly that might betray our secret reflections and judgements, but they are none the less there, and do not escape our patient's intuition.

He will imagine them even when they are not there, as you will see. A certain patient lives too far from Geneva for me to be able to see her as often as is necessary. So I refer her to a psychoanalyst in her own district, one with whom I have a relationship of mutual respect. But with his agreement she continues to see me from time to time. It is a dangerous situation: how will she avoid making harmful comparisons between him and me, even if we both try to be non-directive? And this is how it is that she tells me that he has advised her to give herself to a man who is courting her—an estimable man, but married.

This young woman has high moral principles, and so she has some scruples about throwing herself into an adventure of this kind, and she brings me her scruples. She certainly does not wish, she says, to deny herself his love out of mere moralistic prejudice more or less tinctured with a false shame of sex, or with hypocrisy. After all, she thinks, the moral problem is not hers but the man's, since she is quite free to do as she pleases. But one of the Ten Commandments comes into her mind: "Thou shalt not steal." Is she not going to steal from the wife the husband who belongs to her? Shortly afterwards, however, she gives way to her love, and invokes the "influence" of her psychoanalyst to justify herself.

Nevertheless, if I mentioned it to my colleague, he would doubtless protest, as I did myself when the student said to me: "You are influencing me too much." "I never gave her any such advice," the psychoanalyst would probably say. It is the girl herself who must have thought that she would scarcely be acting more virtuously in rejecting her lover than in giving way to him. Everyone remembers the words of Jesus in the Sermon on the Mount: "I say to you that every one who looks at a woman lustfully has already committed adultery with her in his heart" (Matt. 5.28). I do not suspect my colleague, therefore, of having given advice, any more than I have done myself. I too took the greatest care not to make any pronouncement about the struggle of conscience which was going on in our patient, for one does not know by what roads a soul must travel in order to achieve its full stature. This does not stop that young woman thinking and believing that my colleague approved of her amorous adventure, and that I for my part disapproved of it. She attributed to each of us a judgement that neither of us had pronounced. It was not long, however, before she broke off the affair, since it did not answer her deepest aspirations.

As you see, in such a case it is not so much a matter of doctrines explicitly professed by a psychoanalyst or a believer. It is much more a matter of the contradictory convictions that are attributed to them. Many people, both unbelievers and Christians, make this mental distinction between psychology and faith. This is the problem I am going to deal with in this Second Part. I put it in the middle in order to make the point that it is the axis, the pivot of my book, and, I may say, its justification. For this is a problem which has been on my mind for a long time, and my reason for writing about it now is to show where my thoughts on the subject have taken me.

I am conviced that the opposition between psychology and Christian faith is not as great as many psychoanalysts, theologians, and educated people at present believe. Freud was a man of exemplary moral conduct, who most scrupulously confessed the slightest dishonesty to himself of which he could possibly be aware. In this connection, see his book on the psychopathology of everyday life.[1] It would be impossible to praise too highly the moral and spiritual merits of C. G. Jung. As for Alfred Adler, as Dr. Reissner has shown,[2] of the "Big Three" he is the nearest to Christian doctrine.

From the first there have been psychoanalysts who professed the Christian faith. One of the earliest was Professor Pfister,[3] of Zürich, who carried on an extremely interesting correspondence with Freud on this subject. I cannot name all the others, such as Dr. Nodet, of Bourg-en-Bresse, or Dr. Baudouin, of Geneva. Others have found faith after having already practised psychoanalysis for

[1] S. Freud, *The Psychopathology of Everyday Life*, translated by J. Strachey, The Hogarth Press, London, 1960.

[2] Albert Reissner, "Three Great Schools of Psychotherapy and their Attitude towards Religion", in *Ministerium Medici*, No. 2, Amsterdam.

[3] Oscar Pfister, *Au vieil Evangile par un chemin nouveau*, Fischboucher, Paris, 1920.

a long time, such as Dr. Alphonse Maeder and Dr. Théo Bovet, of Zürich. These two last were pioneers of the medicine of the person, along with other psychiatrists and psychoanalysts of every school of psychology.[4]

I do not include myself in the list, because I am not a psychoanalyst. It was on the advice of psychoanalyst friends of mine that I gave up the idea of specializing. To some extent the reason was so that I could remain in my own place, a little garden open to all the winds, without any enclosing wall. So I belong to no particular school of thought, and all the seeds that blow from any direction into my garden may germinate there. Moreover I can cultivate an interest in the whole of medicine, and not in psychiatry alone. Because of my independence of mind I feel called to reflect upon this confrontation of the truths revealed by psychoanalysis with those of the Bible. Are they really in opposition to each other, as is so often thought, and as the patient I quoted just now believed? Why is it that so many people set them in opposition to each other?

Many men—authoritative in their fields—have made for themselves a synthesis of the data of psychoanalysis and those of religion. To the list of doctors I have just given should be added all those pastors and priests who, without abandoning the Christian ministry, have become psychoanalysts. They are numerous, and include Weatherhead,[5] in England, Fr. Godin,[6] in Belgium, Fr.

---

[4] Notably Paul Plattner, in Berne; Aloys von Orelli, in Basle; Bernard Harnick, in Zürich; W. Scheidegger, in Hilterfingen; Madeleine Rambert, in Lausanne; Helen Roesli, in Zürich; W. Bitter and his partner, in Stuttgart; Frau Sommer, in Berlin; Klaus Thomas, also in Berlin; Rudolf Jentzsch and his wife, in Brunswick; Gretel Glunkler, in the Hohe Mark; Karlfried von Dürckheim, in Todtmoos; Urban, in Leipzig; Szalay, in Budapest; Fr. Racanelli, in Florence; R. Assagioli, the leader of the Psychosynthesis movement, also in Florence, and his collaborator in Los Angeles, Robert Gerard; G. Rizzi and Tina Rabaglia, in Parma; Declich, in Sondrio; Ramón Rey Ardid, in Saragossa, and Soto Yarritu, in Pamplona; Gordon Johnsen, in Norway, and R. Eeg-Olofsson, in Stockholm; Van den Speck and L. van Loon, in the Hague; Paul Linck and Louis Kling, in Strasbourg; Charles Brisset, in Ville d'Avray, and Claude Veil in St. Mandé; Dominique Bonnet in Paris; Hélène Brunel, in Montpellier; Henri Martel, in Lyons; André Sarradon, in Marseilles; R. Pierloot and his young pupil Elisabeth Houben, in Louvain; A. Aspiotis, in Athens; Akahoshi, in Tokyo; Reissner, in New York; Loomis, in Hemet, California; Knapp, in Charlottesville, Va.; and Vitols, in Goldsboro, N.C.

[5] L. D. Weatherhead, *Psychology, Religion and Healing*, Hodder and Stoughton, London, 1951.

[6] André Godin, S. J., *The Pastor as Counsellor*, translated by Bernard Phillips, Gill, Dublin, 1966.

Oraison[7] and the late Fr. Lepp,[8] in France. There is therefore a
great diversity in individual attitudes: among the Christians there
are fervent believers in depth psychology, and others who are
opposed to it, sometimes violently; and among the foremost of the
psychologists some are believers, others agnostics, and yet others
atheists. But although their individual personal convictions are so
varied, this does not stop people from attributing to the two groups
in general—the Christians on the one hand and the psychoanalysts
on the other—two apparently incompatible bodies of doctrine. We
must therefore take things as they are, admit that it is difficult to
bring psychology and religion together, and try to find a way of
overcoming the difficulty.

Let us then come back to the problem of places, and to the
student who told me that my book began well, with an objective
psychological analysis, but that I then spoilt it by sermonizing. I
hope, at any rate, that he has not retained a similar impression of
the discussions he had with me. I have no desire to address moral
exhortation to a man suffering as he did from an inner blockage
which was quite beyond the power of his will to shift. And yet, if
I had wanted to preach him a sermon, I could easily have found a
theme for one: I could have said to him: "You are looking for a place
to tie yourself to. But the Bible, on the contrary, calls on us to remain unattached! Blessed are the poor, blessed are they who are
free of all attachment, who have cast away all their riches!" It is in
such terms as these that some conceive of a so-called Christian
psychotherapy which is really only preaching at the patient. Like
my specialist colleagues, I have always stood out against such a
concept of the doctor's function.

This is not to say that there is not some truth in the preaching.
Abraham is called "the father of all who believe" because he
obeyed God's command: "Go from your country and your kindred
and your father's house to the land that I will show you" (Gen.
12.1). Go from your place! He had to leave Ur of the Chaldeans for
the uncertain life of the nomad, for a country in which he was soon
to know famine (Gen. 12.10). God leaves him no illusions: "Know
of a surety that your descendants will be sojourners in a land that
is not theirs, and will be slaves there, and they will be oppressed for

---

[7] Marc Oraison, *Une morale pour notre temps*, Arthème Fayard, Paris,
1964.
[8] Ignace Lepp, *La morale nouvelle*, Grasset, Paris, 1963.

four hundred years" (Gen. 15.13). Now Ur, the land of his fathers, was a highly civilized place. It has been described as a sort of socialist paradise, since the excavations that have been made there have revealed that all the fruits of men's labour went to the State, which in return guaranteed an egalitarian distribution to the whole populace, thanks to a perfected system of ration coupons.

And here we have Abraham obeying, leaving his place, going out into the unknown, in perfect submission and confidence towards God alone, breaking every natural bond, and disregarding every prudent consideration that might have held him back. St. Paul quotes the Scriptures: "Abraham believed God, and it was reckoned to him as righteousness" (Rom. 4.3). Abraham's self-abandonment to God was total. Think of the sacrifice of Isaac (Gen. 22.1–18), which the Moslems commemorate with great fervour, because this rigorous dependence on God is the dominant trait of their religion. But these are views common to all the biblical religions. Isaac, Abraham's cherished only son, was the child of a miracle. Sarah gave birth to him when she was already in advanced years. He was Abraham's treasure. And God put him to the test by asking him if he was ready to sacrifice him. Detachment! Renunciation!

God also takes Moses out of his place, away from the comfortable rural life he was leading in Midian, keeping the flock of his father-in-law Jethro (Ex. 3.1), and thrusts him into one of the most dramatic adventures in history. He must face the power of Pharaoh, the enemy; he must face his fellow Israelites, from whom he had fled because they had seen him kill an Egyptian; he was to wander for forty years in the desert, and would not ever be able to enter the promised land (Deut. 31.2). Separation! Similarly God took Amos, the little shepherd, "from following the flock" (Amos 7.15) and from dressing the sycamore trees, to send him to the court of King Jeroboam. Gideon, with incredible labour and zeal, had gathered an army of 32,000 men. God made him demobilize 31,700 of them, for fear that if he won he would attribute the merit for it to himself instead of to God! (Judg. 7.1–8). And Jeremiah, who ended up lamentably in exile to Egypt, announcing that "none of the remnant of Judah who have come to live in the land of Egypt shall escape or survive or return to the land of Judah, to which they desire to return to dwell there" (Jer. 44.14).

I do not want to go on quoting examples, but I must quote Jesus himself: "Foxes have holes, and birds of the air have nests; but the Son of man has nowhere to lay his head" (Luke 9.58). Here he gives himself as an example of one who has broken every bond that trummelled him—the perfectly free man. On the eve of his Passion he announces that he is "leaving the world" (John 16.28), and giving his life: "No one takes it from me," he says, "but I lay it down of my own accord. I have power to lay it down, and I have power to take it again; this charge I have received from my Father" (John 10.18).

And so much of what he said echoes these texts. He invites his first disciples, Simon, and Andrew his brother, to leave their nets. "I will make you become fishers of men," he says (Mark 1.17). Leaving their nets meant leaving their place—the beautiful shore of Galilee—and leaving their occupation. He takes them with him into his wandering life. He promises eternal life to "every one who has left houses or brothers or sisters or father or mother or children or lands, for my name's sake" (Matt. 19.29). At times he expresses the point with a harshness that shocks us: "If any one comes to me and does not hate his own father and mother and wife and children and brothers and sisters, yes, and even his own life, he cannot be my disciple" (Luke 14.26). The learned Dominicans who translated the Jerusalem Bible are careful to comment in a note on the use of the word 'hate': "Hebraism expressing complete and immediate detachment." Separation! Detachment!

To the rich young man, who longed to "inherit eternal life", Jesus replied: "Sell all that you have and distribute to the poor, and you will have treasure in heaven; and come, follow me" (Luke 18.22). Everyone knows the first of the Beatitudes: "Blessed are the poor in spirit, for theirs is the kingdom of heaven" (Matt. 5.3). In the parable of the Great Feast, Jesus speaks of those who will not enter the Kingdom of Heaven because they are too attached to their earthly preoccupations; one has "bought a field" (a place!), another "five yoke of oxen", and a third has just got married (Luke 14.15–24). What a difference from the Mosaic law, which excused newly-married men from military service for a year! (Deut. 24.5).

Detachment from one's place, from material goods, from affections—who could deny that this is one of the major themes of Christian preaching? "Blessed are they who have no place, for they are better prepared to answer God's call." But if that part of me which is the believer might have said it, the psychologist in me would have objected, as any psychologist would. We have all seen so many of those men and women who have never grown up because they have been repressed by a religious upbringing, and have been trained since infancy in systematic renunciation.

Moreover, it is not only psychologists who would object, but also socialists. Karl Marx was not entirely wrong when he said that religion was the opium of the people. To how many generations of miserable exploited people has the Church preached resignation, acceptance of one's lot, surrender, and submission? The privileged classes, for their part, have found themselves quite at ease in the Church, where they are told that the immense wealth of Solomon was a sign of God's blessing.

So, while the psychologist attempts the difficult task of giving a place to those who have none, of reactivating the atrophied affectivity of those who are alone, of giving back to the neurotic the capacity of enjoying earthly pleasures, the Church teaches them disdain of such things, and detachment from them. This contrast is carried over into a much more general context to which I must refer.

"Be yourself," says the psychologist, "instead of imitating fine examples or reciting a lesson you have learnt! Assert yourself, dare to show yourself as you are, be true to yourself!" And his patient thinks of what he has always been taught as divine truth: "If any man would come after me, let him deny himself and take up his cross and follow me" (Matt. 16.24).

"Become a man," says the psychologist, "get rid of that childish timidity which stops you from growing up! You have retained a naïvety that doesn't suit your age any more." And the patient remembers that Jesus said: "Let the children come to me, and do not hinder them; for to such belongs the kingdom of heaven" (Matt. 19.14).

"Learn to defend yourself," says the psychologist. "Life is a struggle. The man who does not defend himself is pushed under without pity. Learn to say no. The man who cannot say no is had for a sucker by everybody." And the patient thinks of the words of Jesus: "But I say to you, Do not resist one who is evil. But if any one strikes you on the right cheek, turn to him the other also; and if any one would sue you and take your coat, let him have your cloak as well; and if anyone forces you to go one mile, go with him two miles" (Matt. 5.39–41).

"Do not be afraid of showing your feelings," says the psychologist, "instead of hiding them. Your heart is full of hate against your father, yet you pretend to love him and obey him. Your mind is full of rancour and secret rebellion poisoning it. Express it frankly!" And the patient thinks of Jesus: "Love your enemies and pray for those who persecute you" (Matt. 5.44). "Blessed are the meek, for they shall inherit the earth" (Matt. 5.5). "Forgive, if you have anything against any one; so that your Father also who is in heaven may forgive you your trespasses" (Mark 11.25).

Of course, as I have already indicated, the psychologist does not say these things explicitly, or at least only rarely. And if he does, he is being untrue to his doctrine of moral neutrality. These are views which the patient attributes to him, and the patient does so because he is intuitively aware of the tragic clash of the two gospels. He feels it in much more delicate questions put to him by the psychologist: "Have you talked to your father about these complaints you have against him?"

There are indeed two gospels in the eyes of the public, and even in the eyes of many doctors and theologians: a gospel of psychology, and a biblical gospel; a gospel of self-fulfilment, and a gospel of self-denial; a gospel of self-assertion, and a gospel of renunciation; a gospel of sincerity, and a gospel of charity. I hope there will be no misunderstanding as regards this—I am using the word gospel in a loose, secular meaning, as when one speaks of the communist gospel. The true meaning of the biblical Gospel is the revelation of the redemption of the world by Jesus Christ, but that is not what is meant here, and I doubt if any psychologist would venture to argue about that kind of revelation, which pertains exclusively to the realm of faith, and is not accessible to psychology.

What I am talking about is the advice that might be given by a psychologist compared with that of a theologian—or the advice that people *think* the psychologist and the theologian are giving, apparently in contradiction of each other. All our patients feel this contradiction, even if they have not been brought up as Christians, though of course it is the latter who feel it most acutely. One such remains silent in my study for a long time. What is he thinking about, I ask myself. Suddenly he puts a direct question to me: "In your opinion, what is the meaning of self-denial?" This, then, is the argument that is going on in his mind: must one be oneself, at the risk of denying what one has been taught is right, love of one's neighbour, and humility? Or ought one to deny oneself, at the risk

of insincerity, and of failing to achieve the self-fulfilment which
psychology talks about?

The conflict, I repeat, seems to me to be more apparent than real,
theoretical rather than practical. If I am setting it out here in an
acute form, in terms of black and white, that is because I think it
is useful to say straight out what many people think to themselves
without daring to say it openly. The conflict exists in people's
minds, if not between psychology and religion, at any rate between
their understanding of psychology and of the Christian faith. There
are many facts, observable by anybody, which lend support to this
view of psychology and religion as being in opposition to each
other. How many mediocre personalities are there in our churches—
people who have not the courage to live full lives, to assert themselves and make the most of themselves, and who look upon this
stifling of themselves as a Christian virtue, whereas faith ought to
create powerful personalities?

I recall the case of a man of exemplary character and conduct.
He adored his mother, and she him. She used to say that he was the
best of sons, most considerate towards her, and that he had never
caused her a moment's anxiety. Her dearest wish was that he should
get married, but he seemed scarcely to have any wish to do so. She
herself advised him to see a psychoanalyst who would be able to
persuade him, perhaps. Then suddenly the once submissive son began bitterly to accuse her of having always been a domineering
tyrant over him. As a result, he claimed, he had suffered terribly.
He could not even buy himself a tie of the colour he preferred, because his mother would at once declare that it was ugly. She could
not bear being contradicted, and he had had to knuckle under. But
it had always been against his will, and now, he said, he had had
enough.

The poor woman was nonplussed. Surely she had made sufficient
sacrifices for him! She lived only for him, and tried only to please
him. And she was so sure of his love. Someone had led him astray!
It must be the influence of that unfortunate psychoanalyst. She had
brought him up so carefully, reminding him always of St. Paul's
exhortation: "Children, obey your parents" (Eph. 6.1). He was so
good, he would not hurt a fly—and now he had suddenly turned so
aggressive. It was unbelievable! He could not really believe the
things he said. Someone must have put it into his head. She was in
despair—her son had been quite altered.

He used never to miss going to mass, and now he had stopped going, and said that he only went to avoid her unbearable nagging, and that anyway he had never had any real religious feeling or personal faith. That psychoanalyst must certainly be an atheist, and doing the work of the devil. He was turning a good boy away from religion, and sowing disharmony in a united and happy family. Unless it was the influence of that girl that her son had started seeing. He was making a secret of it, the naughty boy—he who always used to tell her everything—but she had spotted it all right! The girl was not the right sort, but a brazen hussy who showed no respect for her whatsoever. She was the daughter of divorced parents, badly brought up, and she did not dress in a suitable manner. She had no sense of duty, and was only interested in having a good time. The "young idea"! Her son would never be able to be happy with her.

Whatever that unhappy mother thought, her son's psychoanalyst was not an atheist. He even had religious convictions that were much more mature than hers. And, on his side, he reflected on the situation. What a lot of cases of maternal possessiveness he had seen like this one! And what a tragedy it was! It had nothing to do with religion. Jesus himself had to defend himself, and vigorously, too, against his mother's attempts to control him. But what a pity it was that there was so often a sort of conspiracy between religion and maternal domination. The mother sincerely invoked the authority of religion and the respect of children for their parents which it demanded, in order to justify her behaviour, which was really only the satisfying of her maternal instinct. Unfortunately that distorted the meaning of religion.

The psychoanalyst had to try and save the boy without arguing with a mother who would be incapable of understanding what he was doing. It could only be like two deaf people talking to each other.

Unfortunately it sometimes happens that pastors or priests naïvely throw their weight on the side of a domineering mother whose great piety they admire. Take, for example, the case of a young woman whose mother was an invalid. She had devoted herself without reserve to taking her mother's place, running the house, and bringing up her younger brothers and sisters. They had left home, and she remained her mother's favourite daughter. Her mother could not do without her. The daughter happened to get a chance of going abroad. A wise country doctor urged her to take the opportunity: it was her last chance of making something of her life. But she went to see the parish priest.

"Going away! You can't think of such a thing! Your mother is ill, and all your brothers and sisters have left home—it is your duty to stay and look after your mother." And so she stayed. Why her, rather than her brothers and sisters? I saw her twenty years after that, after her mother's death, with all the psychological complications that had made their appearance in the meantime. She was obsessed with the feeling that she had spoilt her life. The family was quite astonished that I should support her in her plan to take up her studies once more. Everybody had become quite accustomed to looking upon her as the unselfish daughter, devoted to others, and asking nothing for herself. Ought she not to be still looking after her old father?

But it was very late now to be taking up studies again and training for a job. When the right moment has been allowed to slip by, it is terribly hard to begin afresh. It is like running after a train one has missed. She felt useless, incapable of succeeding. In the course of her talks with me she necessarily became aware of her real situation, of the truth of which she had had a vague presentiment— enough to cause her such anxiety that she had been incapable of facing up to it on her own. Fortunately I had the support of her spiritual director at that time, a remarkably understanding and intelligent man. He came to see me, and we prayed together for healing for her.

He must nevertheless have been somewhat disturbed when she exclaimed to him: "Don't talk to me about God or Jesus any more! I have been deceived! I have been deceived in their name! People have preached self-denial at me in their name, and I thought I was obeying them."—"You are not rebelling against God," the venerable priest assured her; "you are protesting against the false picture of God that you have been given."—"What do you mean, a false picture? I've been to lots of retreats, run by famous priests, and they all talked about self-renunciation. Isn't that what the Church teaches?"

I was myself somewhat handicapped in my task with her, as I was with the student. For her, too, I represented the religious world in which she had been brought up. I could see that she had an ambivalent attitude towards me, as she had towards the Church. She said to me as well: "Don't talk to me about God, or Jesus—I have been deceived in their name!" Fortunately there remained the third person of the Trinity, and she confided in me that she prayed to the Holy Spirit. Clearly, serious psychological errors had become subtly mixed with orthodox Christian teaching. How was the truth to be disentangled from error? That is no small task. The dialogue must be thoroughly frank and honest. Are there not some who finally reject religion simply because they have not been able to put self-assertion and self-denial in their proper perspective?

There are indeed two gospels: a gospel of abnegation and meekness, and a gospel of self-assertion and self-fulfilment. When I give a lecture in a medical college, when I tell the story of a case I have dealt with, when I demonstrate the importance of the religious life in the psychological destiny of men, and the liberation that can be wrought through faith, there are Freudian professors there, especially in America, listening politely to what I have to say. But their thoughts, I have no doubt, are meanwhile going over the many cases they have dealt with, in which religion has been an enslaving power rather than a liberating one. It is not surprising that they have argued with me, sometimes calmly, sometimes passionately.

Objective, academic arguments of that kind, however, scarcely ever go to the root of the matter. For the deep sources of our intellectual beliefs remain hidden. They lie in each person's emotional history, which is not brought out in such discussions. Is this not precisely what the psychoanalysts tell us? A certain Freudian psychologist, for example, has become a psychoanalyst after having been ill himself, and having been cured by psychoanalysis. He cannot, therefore, look upon psychoanalysis simply as a therapeutic technique. For him it has been a message of salvation. He has adopted it as if it were a gospel, a doctrine of truth about human life capable of liberating men and women. He has undergone a real conversion which, like all conversions, has made him a proselyte who wants everyone else to find the truth he has found.

Moreover, anyone can observe that his conversion has made him a man full of charity, showing inexhaustible solicitude towards his fellow-men, an example to all those true believers who judge their neighbours harshly. Did not Christ say that the tree is known by its fruits (Matt. 7.20)? That psychoanalyst bears good fruit. He is a living and eloquent example for his patients. They will spontaneously aspire to be like him, and they will adopt his outlook on life, even if he never discusses it with them.

7

Two Movements

LOOKING FOR a place—leaving one's place. Giving to those who
have none a place to which they can attach themselves; or urging
the need for detachment. This is how the theme of man's place made
it possible for me to grasp and express the dilemma I had to deal
with, various aspects of which we have been looking at. I tried to
give a place, or rather to be a place for that student who was looking for one, so as to liberate him from his vagabond complex. I
was careful not to talk to him about Abraham, whom God called to
leave his place to become a vagabond of the faith.

One thing, however, struck me: there was in fact a radical difference between Abraham and the student, namely that Abraham
had a place, whereas the student had none. Abraham, as we saw,
had an excellent place—the high civilization of Chaldea. The
student was looking everywhere for a place because he had been
denied one.

Similarly, Jesus had had an excellent place in his childhood.
Later he characterized his apostolic ministry by saying of himself:
"The Son of man has nowhere to lay his head" (Matt. 8.20); but
before that, up to the age of thirty, he had had a place. He had had
a united family, and what a family! The love of the Virgin Mary,
his mother, full of grace (Luke 1.28), blessed among women (Luke
1.42), chosen by God with all those exceptional precautions which
C. G. Jung refers to in his *Answer to Job*. And the wisdom of his
father, St. Joseph, a true head of the family, attentive to God's
warnings (Matt. 2.13). Joseph himself initiated him into the ritual
duties which formed such a solid framework for the life of the Jews
of his day, and which Robert Aron has described in detail in his

book on the obscure years of Jesus' life.[1] It was indeed an exemplary family and social environment, a place.

The detachment of a child from his parents' home is never as easy as that of the ripe fruit falling from the tree. Witness the fact that even the Virgin Mary did not accept it without difficulty. But if the family is healthy and the parents united, the detachment takes place as well as possible, and, in particular, it becomes an occasion of growth for the parents as much as for the child. But when the home has not acted as a real place, detachment becomes impossible, and the situation turns into tragedy. Neither the parents nor the child can grow any more, because they have become bogged down in an endless argument which only exacerbates their mutual complaints and prevents them from liberating themselves from each other.

It is a striking thing to see a young person thus blocked in his proper development. One feels he ought to be getting away from the parents whom he criticizes so severely, that he ought to be eagerly seeking new horizons, forsaking his unhappy past, integrating himself into a new environment and making a future for himself there. But no—he only apparently turns his back on his parents, despite his violent outbursts against them. In reality he retains them within himself. He is full of the painful memories of his childhood, unable to detach himself from them and face the world freely.

It is one of the laws of life that one stage successfully completed prepares the way for the next, while failure in one stage lays in advance a heavy handicap on the next. The resentment that the child harbours from the past fills his mind and falsifies his outlook. Because he has been the victim of injustice he can see nothing in the world but injustices done to him. Because he has not been loved, or not loved well, he can neither love nor believe in and accept love. He is still the prisoner of the past even when he tries to leave it behind. If I may be permitted a paradox, he remains fixed in the place he has not had.

It is true that one must first have a place in order to be able to leave it afterwards. "For everything there is a season, and a time for every matter under heaven," says the Preacher (Eccles. 3.1). It is not always the same time. There is a time to cling to one's parents, and time to detach oneself from them. In all things there is a time

[1] R. Aron, *Jesus of Nazareth: The Hidden Years*, translated by Frances Frenaye, Hamish Hamilton, London, 1962.

for attachment and a time for detachment. He who does not attach himself properly at the time for attachment cannot detach himself properly either at the time for detachment.

"Why should what was true yesterday no longer be so today?" I was asked by a patient of a dogmatic turn of mind. The doctor has a different mental outlook, because he is always attending the school of Nature. He sees that in Nature everything has its rhythm, its complementary alternations. It is a fact that during the phase of dilatation of the heart, for example, the nervous centre which controls its contraction cannot be excited. There is a time when the buds burst into leaf, and a time when the leaves fall. But only those that have grown in spring can fall in the autumn.

One must first have a place before leaving it. One can abandon only what one has got. One can give up only what one has received. There is a radical opposition between "being denied" a thing, and "leaving" it. Being denied a thing means being prevented from having it before one has known what it is to have it, and so one has a longing for it which is all the greater for one's not having had it. More than anything else it is a piece of bad luck which one cannot do anything about. On the other hand, leaving a thing is a free act.

It would be absurd and unjust to urge detachment upon a man who had never received the thing in question. Unfortunately it is often done. What occurs even more often, is that a man who is the victim of this denial hears renunciation being preached as if it were meant for him, when he cannot renounce because he has not received. Abraham, however, is called upon by God to leave his place, the exemplary place which he has really had. Similarly, the brothers Simon and Andrew whom Jesus calls upon to leave everything have first of all had a place and an occupation. In the case of Nathanael, Jesus says to him: "When you were under the fig tree, I saw you" (John 1.48). Under the fig tree was his place.

The rich young man was told by Jesus to sell his goods (Mark 10.21). The young man had first received his goods, had enjoyed them and become attached to them, and Jesus does not blame him for that. But now the time for detachment has come, so that he may be able to attach himself to the person of Jesus ("and come, follow me", Jesus says). Thus there is a rhythm between attachment and detachment. One must first receive, in order to be able to give. One must first possess, in order to be able to give up.

One of my patients had suffered severely in childhood from the

denial of affection. The result was an inferiority complex, utter
self-doubt, and withdrawal into solitude. I sent her to a foreign
colleague who reminded her that "It is more blessed to give than
to receive" (Acts 20.35). He encouraged her to come out of herself
and of her resentful attitude, to give herself generously to the welfare of others, and to her profession which she did not like. Then
she would find happiness, he said. Of course it was true, and she
knew it. But it was the very thing she could not do. She felt she had
nothing to give. When we give of ourselves we do it spontaneously,
without wanting or trying to. Because we have received, we need to
give what we have received. And the more my patient told herself
she must give, the less able was she to do so. She was quite surprised when I talked to her about receiving first, of opening herself
first to the joy of receiving. The giving of herself would come
later. It would come on its own when she had received what she
lacked. "A man who has not got happiness," wrote Amiel, "cannot
impart it."[2]

Father Teilhard de Chardin gives an admirable description of
this necessary alternation between receiving and giving in his
Milieu divin.[3] He recalls the ancient proverb: *Nemo dat quod non
habet*—No one gives what he does not possess. "How would man
give himself to God if he did not exist?" he writes. "What possession could he transfigure through his detachment if his hands were
empty?" The author speaks of the priest who is often asked:
"Which is better for the Christian, activity or passivity? Life or
death? Growth or diminishment? Development or curtailment?
Possession or renunciation?" And as a priest he replies: "Why
separate and contrast the two natural phases of a single effort? . . .
Develop yourself and take possession of the world *in order to be*.
Once this has been accomplished, then is the time to think about
renunciation; then is the time to accept diminishment for the sake
of *being in another*. . . . First, develop yourself."

He recognizes that books about the spiritual life "do not generally throw this first phase of Christian perfection into clear enough
relief". From this come all the conflicts we were considering in the
previous chapter. The key of the problem is indeed in the assertion
that there is a necessary alternation. Teilhard de Chardin concludes:

---

[2] *Amiel's Journal* (8 Dec. 1869), translated by Mrs. Humphrey Ward,
Macmillan, London, 1904, p. 163.
[3] *Le milieu divin: An Essay on the Interior Life*, pp. 77f.

"Thus, in the general rhythm of the Christian life, development and renunciation, attachment and detachment are not mutually exclusive. On the contrary, they harmonize, like breathing in and out in the movement of our lungs." Similarly Amiel writes, on 16 August, 1875: "Life is but a daily oscillation between revolt and submission, between the instinct of the *ego*, which is to expand, to take delight in its own sense of inviolability, if not to triumph in its own sovereignty, and the instinct of the soul, which is to obey the universal order, to accept the will of God."[4]

There are, then, in fact, two movements—movements which are successive and complementary. We shall see that they correspond to the gospels of which I have spoken, that of self-fulfilment and that of renunciation, that of psychology and that of religion. They correspond, in general terms, to the respective tasks of the doctor and the psychologist on the one hand, and those of the priest and the pastor on the other. The doctor seeks to give to the deprived the thing they lack—health, strength, a place, integration in a social environment. The minister of religion sounds God's call to detachment from all earthly possessions, a call which he addresses to those who have them in abundance.

Amiel, with his puritan upbringing, has a bad conscience when his "instinct of the *ego*" makes him "expand". He places the Christian life only in the second movement. Teilhard de Chardin, on the other hand, rightly joins the two movements in the same Christian life, for it is the same God who calls both the doctor and the minister of religion to the service of men: the former particularly to give to the poor the wealth they lack, and the latter particularly to detach the rich from the slavery of their possessions. But I have said that these two functions only approximately differentiate our respective vocations. In fact, they overlap. The minister also brings to the deprived possessions which they have been denied. "You give them something to eat" (Luke 9.13), Jesus said to his disciples in front of the hungry crowd. And the doctor and the psychologist also, when the right moment comes, lead men beyond the pure satisfaction of their needs towards a more complete development, which is to be found in self-giving. Teilhard de Chardin gives elsewhere[5] this fine maxim: "The secret of balance and happiness

---

[4] *Amiel's Journal*, translated by Mrs. Humphrey Ward, p. 222.
[5] *Le milieu divin*.

consists in centering on oneself, de-centering on one's neighbour, and super-centering on one greater than oneself."

My chief task here as a doctor, however, is to enter into concrete detail, in order to show how these two movements work together in practice, and to demonstrate the importance of the order in which they occur. Here, then, are some examples.

I treat a person suffering from anxiety-neurosis. His symptoms derive from heavy and deep-seated emotional pressures. It is no small task to relieve them. Astonishing and dramatic sessions with him go on for several months. Gradually he is becoming aware once more of all the things that caused such grave injury to him in his childhood, and it is a real torture to him to go over them again in telling me about them.

He says something of this to his pastor, who naturally knows nothing of all this, knowing him only as a most faithful parishioner, with a certain prejudice against psychologists. The pastor, with the best of intentions, says to him: "It isn't good to dwell on one's past. Forget all that!" Yes, indeed, if only he could forget! But that is the very thing he cannot do. Or to be more exact, he had forgotten it too well, since the terrible memories have been repressed into his unconscious. That is why he is ill. Neither he nor I derive any pleasure from bringing out into the light of day all his hidden sufferings. He must first reawaken the memory of them and look them in the face by speaking of them. Then after that he will be able to forget them—that is to say that they will lose their power to fascinate and paralyse. The story of the past must first be told before we can close the book.

A certain woman patient behaves like a child, not only in her life, but especially in my consulting-room. She says herself that she would like to be a baby again, so that her mother could take her into her arms and comfort her. I could say to her: "Be your age; you aren't an infant any longer, so act like an adult!" One doctor has already said that to her, and it did her no good. You cannot become adult to order, by an effort of will. When children grow up it happens on its own. Suddenly they want to act like grown-ups. All at once a child pushes his mother away: "Don't keep kissing me all the time like that; I've had enough; I'm not a baby any more!"

He is able to do this, however, precisely because he has been surfeited with kisses in his early years, whereas my patient has not. A friend once wrote to me: "Can a person be really adult if he has never been a real child?" It is necessary first to be a child, to know to the full that protected and pampered place which is childhood, before being able to leave "childish things". I must allow this patient to express her childish needs which have not been satisfied. Then she will feel accepted, just as she is, and will be able to develop from then on.

Another child exclaims: "Leave me alone! I want to do it myself!" because you want to help him to make his new mechanical toy work. Let him do it by himself, then, and be glad of the ambition for autonomy which is awakening in him. Perhaps he will not manage to do it, and that will be a useful and not at all humiliating experience for him. If, however, you said, before he tried on his own, "Let me show you, because you won't manage on your own," you would be putting a harmful doubt into his mind. He does not yet understand the difficulty of what he has set out to do, and so he will think that you lack confidence in his ability to surmount it.

There are several ways of saying to a child who has hurt himself, "Don't cry!" There is a way of doing it that is full of tenderness, so that the child will feel the maternal love reaching out to console him. But there is also a harsh way of saying it, which really means: "You ought to be ashamed of yourself for crying over such a trifle." There must be many who as a result retain throughout their lives a false shame about weeping. There are some who have admitted that they hesitated a long time before coming to see me for fear of weeping in my consulting-room.

There are families where weeping is inconceivable, even at the time of a bereavement. In such families joy is not manifested either, because all the emotions are buried beneath a stoic hardness. This hardness was taught by Dr. Dubois,[6] of Berne (I always wonder if he met Freud at the Salpêtrière[7]). In fact he showed great love towards his patients, and great understanding, since before Freud he was maintaining that psychological conflicts could bring on illness, even without there being any organic lesion, an idea which was quite new at that time.

But Dr. Dubois was a stoic by temperament, and he still believed in the primacy of reason and the will over the emotions. He actually

[6] Paul Dubois, *The Psychic Treatment of Nervous Disorders*, translated by S. E. Jelliffe and W. A. White, Funk and Wagnalls, New York and London, 1908.

[7] *Translator's note:* A geriatric and psychiatric hospital in Paris.

refers admiringly to what he calls "Christian stoicism", which allows one to bear everything without betraying any emotion. This is stoicism, all right, but it is not Christianity. Jesus wept over Jerusalem (Luke 19.41), and he wept over the death of his friend Lazarus (John 11.35). One must first be able to express one's feelings, to cry or laugh spontaneously, before attaining that self-mastery which is so often the very thing that the nerve sufferer lacks, and which Dr. Dubois called Christian stoicism.

Professor Loomis,[8] of Union Theological Seminary, New York, is also speaking of a two-stage rhythm when he says of the development of the child: "In order to form friendships with others, one must first be separate." Yes, to be separate, to be an individual, is to become a person, to become conscious of one's own existence, and it is a necessary preliminary stage if any genuine community bond is to be established with others. This word existence brings us back to the burning question raised by the quotation I made from Teilhard de Chardin. "How could man give himself to God if he did not exist?"

Perhaps the ordinary man in the street does not realize the gravity of this problem. The feeling that we exist seems so simple and natural to those of us who have been able to develop normally. Recently three of my patients told me, one after another, that they doubted their own existence. That means that they had the impression, almost impossible to express, of being automata or ghosts. They seemed to live, they acted, spoke, laughed, and cried, but always with the feeling that it was not really they who were doing so, but a being that was a stranger to themselves, or rather the appearance of a being. In such cases the psychologists talk of a failure in the formation of the ego, and consider it as an aggravating factor. Sometimes I have had psychologists refuse to accept such patients whom I have wanted to entrust to them, on the grounds that psychoanalytical treatment would be incapable of doing any good.

How can one reassure a person who doubts his own existence? Clearly it does not suffice to assure him that he does exist. The feeling he has of not existing is obviously impervious to any attempt at logical refutation. And how is he to be cured if he does not re-

[8] Earl A. Loomis, "Le rôle de l'inconscient dans la haine du différent, du nouveau et de l'inconnu", in *Les conférences du Cénacle libanais*, Beyrouth, No. 7, 1964.

discover the certainty of his own existence? I ought to say "discover", rather than rediscover, since these are people who have never yet been conscious of their own personal existence. It is not, therefore, a psychological problem, in the proper sense of the term, but a problem of the healing of the person.

There are some who say to such people: "Give yourself to the service of others. It is in giving oneself that one finds oneself." This is a quite useless exhortation, and generally harmful. In order to give oneself, one must first possess oneself. A person who does not feel that he exists cannot give himself either—he feels he is pretending to give himself. Alexandre Vinet said: "I want man to be master of himself so that he can better be at the service of all." To be master of oneself involves first of all consciousness that one exists. One must first become a person in order to be free to give one's person. Sometimes another exhortation is added to the first—a religious one, but equally ineffective. "Seek contact with God. It is in listening to him, by entering into a personal relationship with the personal God that one becomes a person." But it is equally true that for contact with God one must feel one exists.

And yet such patients often themselves feel intuitively that their problem is really a religious rather than a psychological one. I remember a young woman who was having at the same time psychotherapeutical dialogues with me and impassioned theological dialogues with a pastor—echoes of which she naturally brought to me. This particular pastor and I held each other in the highest esteem, and we did not mind each other's efforts to help the same person. I even think that our complete collaboration, each in his own sphere, was a factor in our success. The pastor has great psychological experience, and I am quite sure that he did not fall into sermonizing.

It was, however, following upon a religious experience that that patient was liberated from her doubts about her own existence. After dramatic interviews and exchanges of letters with the pastor she suddenly made a sort of "Pascal's wager"—"If God exists and I exist, I am willing to do whatever he asks!" An idea came into her mind, really rather an odd idea, but she obeyed it without hesitation. This reminds me of Christ's remark: "If any man's will is to do his will, he shall know whether the teaching is from God or whether I am speaking on my own authority" (John 7.17). One piquant detail: At the height of her argument with the pastor, the patient had telephoned me to ask me for "a drug that stops you thinking", and I had prescribed a tranquillizer which had perhaps made her decisive interview with him easier.

Afterwards she wrote me a magnificent letter. She realized that her illness and her religious anxiety, her dialogues with me and her stubborn debate with the pastor were a sort of substitute for living. She needed them in order to feel that she existed, for if one is fighting, one has the feeling that one exists. It is almost Descartes' *Cogito ergo sum*—I think, therefore I am—I churn out thoughts, I argue, I fight for ideas, therefore I am. But it is tragic. She wanted to be healed, and she was afraid of being healed, afraid that healing would deprive her of the arguments without which she feared she would no longer feel that she was alive. I need hardly add that she has had, since then, plenty more important problems to bring to me, and plenty of interviews with her pastor, but they have been free of the terrible handicap of doubting whether she existed.

This doubt whether one exists may have its distant cause in an emotional injury in childhood. A young woman retains the awful memory of a certain event—she had at the time a conflict with her father, over a quite trivial matter. But she held out against him because she was certain she was in the right. The father, in order to break her resistance, had "sent her to Coventry", pretending not to hear her when she spoke to him, depriving her of her good-night kiss, and for three days forbidding anyone to speak to her—in short, treating her as if she did not exist. What he did, in fact, was to destroy her consciousness that she existed. We feel we exist in so far as others accept, respect, and welcome our existence, in so far as they prove it by listening to us, answering us, and entering into dialogue with us.

The essence of psychotherapy is the open-hearted talk, the expression of one's thoughts in the confidence of being really listened to and understood, entry into personal communication and receiving a response—in short, the living experience of dialogue. The whole remarkable work of Victor E. Frankl[9] demonstrates this, and Professor D. F. Tweedie, of the Fuller Theological Seminary, Pasadena, California, has made a study[10] of the similarities and

9 V. E. Frankl, *Die Psychotherapie in der Praxis*, Deuticke, Vienna, 1947.

10 D. F. Tweedie, Jr., *Logotherapy and the Christian Faith; an Evaluation of Frankl's Existential Approach to Psychotherapy*, Baker Book House, Grand Rapids, Michigan, 1961.

dissimilarities between this "logotherapy" and Christian faith. When I have to talk about myself, I tell of how as a child I was uncommunicative, unsociable, and odd, due no doubt to the fact that I was an orphan. Of all my teachers there was only one, my Greek teacher at school, who understood what I needed. He invited me to his house, and into his study. Imagine the effect on me of that intellectual High Place, with a man whom I revered listening attentively and kindly to what I had to say. I found a real "place" there, and my Greek teacher was my first psychotherapist. The personal contact which he generously offered me there, and which others offered me later on, had such an influence on me that it determined my vocation. Many people have been able as a result to come to me to have the same experience in their turn. I had, therefore, to receive the treasure of personal contact myself before being able to bestow it on others.

I once asked the zoologist, Professor Portmann of Basle, if it ever happened that his fellow workers were injured by an aggressive animal. "Never," he answered, "because the first bit of advice that I give to anyone who comes to work in my Institute is to keep talking to the animals." "But I don't know what to say to them, those animals of yours!" exclaimed a young girl assistant. "That doesn't matter. Say 'Blah-blah-blah' to them; the important thing is that they should feel you are talking to *them*."

Of course one has to say something other than blah-blah-blah to a child. There are some parents who never talk seriously to their children, as if the latter were not really persons, and their ideas of no importance. "In our family," one such writes to me, "the children were not allowed to be real people, to be persons with desires, tastes, and opinions." It is by daring to express his desires, tastes, and opinions, and through feeling that they are respected, that the child becomes aware that he exists, of being a person distinct from other persons. It is a violation of the person of the child to try to direct him in everything according to what his parents think best, without heeding his own preferences. He comes to the point where he no longer knows what his desires, tastes, and opinions are, and an individual without any personal desire, taste, or opinion does not feel that he exists, either. This can be observed in families with high moral or religious pretensions. The parents are so sure they have a monopoly of absolute truth that any other view than their own can only be a grievous error in their eyes. They are so sure of their judgement in all matters, that they impose it on their children—for their own good, they think.

This often goes along with the teaching of self-abnegation. While still quite young the child must learn to forget himself, to disregard his personal desires, to behave in accordance with the requirements of others, seeking always to please them rather than himself. Of course the parents head the list of the "others" who must be pleased and have constant service rendered to them, whereas they themselves scarcely ever bother to gratify any of the child's pleasures, which they look upon as mere selfish whims. And they accuse him of selfishness if he manifests any personal aspiration. So one meets honourable (and honoured) parents, who even look upon themselves as excellent parents, and who without realizing it at all, are exploiting the willingness of one or other of their children to an unbelievable extent. The child soon becomes the Cinderella of the family. It is true that there is usually only one of the children treated in this way. The rest accept the principles of self-abnegation only in so far as they wish to, and they know quite well how to derive their own share of profit from the little victim who cannot refuse them anything.

Of course it is possible to think that the unhappy child was already predisposed towards neurosis because he was more sensitive than his brothers and sisters; and also more credulous, since he believed all he was told, including all those fine theories about self-denial, without seeing that his parents preached them but did not practise them. But that comes from a still deeper cause—he is a child who has received less love than his brothers and sisters, and he is unconsciously trying to win more love by means of his endless devotion. It is in vain, of course, because the parents have a slight unconscious feeling of guilt over exploiting him in the way they do, and this feeling prevents them from really loving him. But their behaviour only makes the child's neurosis worse. Thus everyone —the victim, his parents, brothers and sisters—are the prisoners of the attitude they have adopted; all play their roles, whether of exploited or exploiters, and none of them realizes it.

Before giving up one's selfishness, one has to express it in living. One has to express it, at any rate, to the legitimate extent to which all living beings need to assert their personal lives. This is their right, and even their duty. Moreover, contrary to what those who have been brought up in this doctrine of self-abnegation think, a certain more or less conscious egoism always lurks behind the pleasure one derives from devoting oneself to others. I am only too well aware of it in my profession of service to others! It gives me pleasure, a pleasure no different from that sought by people who are accused of being selfish because they are interested only in themselves. My devotion is no more disinterested. And now that my health is going to oblige me to cut down on my activities, I shall be a little frustrated, and I shall have to accept it.

But the stifling of the child and of his will can also come about spontaneously, without his being subjected to the preaching of self-abnegation. Take, for instance, the case of a woman whose parents were always quarrelling. The conflict created unspeakable anxiety in her mind, and so, instead of trying to satisfy her personal desires, she began while still quite small to calculate her behaviour so that she avoided as far as she could anything that would start her parents quarrelling. As she was her father's favourite, and since he never scolded her, she would take the blame for her brothers' and sisters' misdeeds, and so spared them a scolding, while at the same time sparing herself the pain of seeing them punished, which always hurt her as much as if she were being punished herself.

There is, of course, great virtue in this, but it is quite premature in a child. Really she has had no childhood; she has not known the legitimate carefreeness of the child; she has forgotten herself before becoming properly aware of herself. She effaced herself, and behaved in accordance with the requirements of others at an age when a child ought to be discovering himself. She took refuge in solitude because she was not like other little girls any more. Her fragile shoulders were weighed down by a care that was too heavy for them. This separated her from the real life in which—despite all the fine idealist doctrines—everyone must fight for himself.

So here we are on the threshold of another problem, the question of non-resistance or self-defence. I have already touched on it in my book *The Strong and the Weak* and in the shorter work *To Resist or to Surrender?*. To give way may sometimes be a victory, and sometimes a defeat. It is a victory if the one who gives way is strong and courageous, and above all free within himself to defend himself. He is then well aware of his desire to defend himself, and still restrains his fists. His generosity of heart enables him to overcome his natural reaction which prompts him to fight. On the other hand it is a defeat in the case of a man paralysed by a psychological complex so that he is incapable of resisting and defending himself. We doctors, of course, generally see people who give way, not so much from virtue as because of a psychological blockage.

How happy we are when a sick person who has never been able to defend himself begins to do so! "No, no, and no! I do not accept this world the way it is," a young woman exclaims; and I think to myself: "Good! That's the dynamism of life asserting itself!" Another patient arrives in a state of great excitement: "Blows, blows," she says, "we came to blows! For the first time in my life I defended myself!" She had always put the second movement—self-denial—before the first, namely self-defence. The serious thing is that she sincerely took this reversal for a Christian virtue. In the religious and moral teaching she had received, Christianity was identified exclusively with non-resistance.

That is naturally very pleasant for the parents, brothers, and sisters in a family, or for colleagues in an office, who soon get used to leaving out of account the demands of the weak person who always gives way. So, when he begins to defend himself, the equilibrium of the community is upset, and he draws bitter reproaches upon himself. Everybody is against him, because everybody is put out at not being able any longer to exploit his convenient passivity: "Aren't you ashamed," they say, "you who call yourself a Christian, to behave in such a selfish and wicked manner?" Thus religion is appealed to in order to justify the injustice. Religious blackmail of that kind is very common. The strong invoke Christian principles in order to obtain the submission of others, when really it is they who are in the wrong, and ought to give way.

It is dishonest to identify Christian morality with systematic non-resistance. "Argue your case with your neighbour himself" (Prov. 25.9), says one of the Proverbs. Jesus himself took a whip (John 2.15). And at the very moment of his arrest he took good care to say to the disciple who had used a sword that he could easily defend himself victoriously if he wanted to: "Do you think that I cannot appeal to my Father, and he will at once send me more than twelve legions of angels? But how then should the scriptures be fulfilled, that it must be so?" (Matt. 26.53–4). The last sentence touches upon the problem of "motivation", dear to the psychoanalysts: as they have shown, it is not so much the way a person behaves, as the underlying motives that dictate the behaviour, that have moral importance. If his motives are unconscious and automatic, due to the repression of his capacity for self-defence, their moral value is nil. In the case of Jesus in the Garden of Gethsemane, the moral value is total, since he shows himself to be free, and motivated solely by his desire to obey God. A little while before, he had said: "For this reason the Father loves me, because I lay down my life, that I may take it again. No one takes it from me, but I lay it down of my own accord" (John 10.17–18). It is therefore inner liberty, which confers authenticity on an attitude. The strength of Gandhi in his non-violent but victorious campaign against the British Empire lay in his undoubted liberty of mind. And the same is true for every man in his daily life.

But for the common run of mortals, what is a freedom that they have never dared to use? A myth, is it not? Therefore, if the second movement, that of non-resistance, is to have any value, it must at least sometimes be preceded by the first movement, of self-defence. If we have never yet defended ourselves, if we have never let our instinct of self-preservation have its way, we cannot know whether our non-resistance is courageous or cowardly. We must first exist, defend ourselves, succeed, assert ourselves, before showing ourselves generous. If we do not, we merely allow ourselves to be pitilessly devoured by all and sundry. "Whatever allows itself to be devoured, is devoured, and nobody thanks one for it," writes the gentle Amiel (28 April, 1861).[11]

[11] *Amiel's Journal*, translated by V. W. and C. V. W. Brooks, p. 148.

8

Premature Renunciation

WE MUST ASSERT ourselves, then, before we deny ourselves. We must know what we want, and struggle to achieve it. A young person in particular must have ambition. Soon enough life will compel him to cut back on it. But before that he must fight, or else his renunciation is nothing but capitulation, a betrayal of himself. Ambition! It so happens that my student friend is talking to me about it now. He had repressed it. He tells me that he used once to despise all those who looked for success in life. He criticized them severely, and called them plotters and climbers. He thought of them as rats in the rat-race. And he called himself a rat when he allowed himself to indulge in some selfish manœuvre to gain his own ends.

Now he says to me: "When all's said and done, it is legitimate to fight to achieve your aims if you have some talent you ought to be using." What helped to cure him, I believe, was a time that he spent in a professional job away from student life. He just had to learn to defend himself. He was quite surprised himself at his own success, though it was at the cost of a change in his outlook. His fine idealism gave way, and he was forced to be tough. He gained in authority, to his own surprise. He was respected. He said to me: "Ambition is the very force of life, the expression of a natural need to fulfil oneself in life, and to bear fruit."

Yes, a force of Nature. I am writing these lines in Malaga, watching the sun rising in kingly majesty from the sea. What beauty! What grandeur! It puts me in mind of an adolescent starting out on life, with the immensity of life before him, as Apollo has the immensity of the sky in which to drive his chariot. He can adopt the well-known motto: *Quo non ascendam?* Whither can I not ascend? He has the ambition to make something of his life, something as perfect as the regular track traced out by the sun in the sky. For him this is the time for the ascent, for self-assertion and self-manifestation. In the bright sun of Malaga my wife and I are watching day by day the miraculous explosion of spring during these early March days. The leaves are appearing on the trees, and the roses opening —Nature is not neurotic! She lives each moment as it comes, which is the advice that Dr. Georges Liengme, one of the first psychotherapists, used to give to those who suffered from neurosis. And Nature, more easily than men, will accept being stripped bare in autumn.

It is understandable that the ancients should have made Apollo the god of harmonious balance, the god of expansion, and also the god of the arts, which are for artists self-assertion and self-expression. For that is indeed the meaning of art, of all the arts, from the inspired daubings of infants to the art of constructing cyclotrons, those new race-courses in which the physicist organizes races and collisions for atomic particles.

It is understandable that the ancients should have also made Apollo the god of medicine, for medicine is the art of awakening and directing the forces of nature. More exactly, Apollo was the chief god of medicine, for there were three gods of medicine, as Paul Diel shows us in his book *Le symbolisme dans la mythologie grecque*.[1] The other two, Asclepius and Chiron, presided over medical, physical, and psychological technique. But it was still necessary for Apollo to rule over them to keep them in their right places as technicians, and to ensure that the harmoniously balanced doctor is not too exclusively the slave of his technique. How wise the ancients were!

Let us come back to the adolescent on the threshold of life. Perhaps his parents teach him the importance of humility, like the parents of whom I was speaking just now, who taught their children self-denial lest they became egoists. But in their heart of hearts are not these parents quite as vainglorious as their son? Is not their attitude to him determined by their wounded pride, because they have reached the second movement, when many long-cherished ambitions must be renounced.

They are probably a little jealous of their son, who is only setting out on life, and they allow themselves to indulge in what the Germans express by an untranslatable word *Schadenfreude*, the joy

[1] Payot, Paris, 1952.

of destroying the joy of others. He is proud and happy at having obtained a good mark for a philosophy essay or at having constructed a scale model aeroplane, and he is dreaming already of becoming a philosopher or an engineer. Then his parents say to him: "You'll see, it won't last! You don't do what you like in this life." Really they are as proud and happy as he is of his successes, but they hide it for fear of making him conceited. They sincerely believe that they are teaching him the wisdom of living. But is it not because they themselves do not really accept that at their age they must learn to give up, that they preach giving-up to their son, who is at the stage of the first movement, the age of expansion?

The young must live their youth, the simple, confident, and careless ambitions of adolescence. They must not assume adult responsibilities too soon. This, too, is why some people may regret having married too young. A woman, for instance, received a proposal of marriage long before she had any real desire to marry. Having been very strictly brought up, she had hoped to enjoy the liberty proper to her age, and it was of this period between childhood and marriage that she was deprived. She passed straight from the tutelage of her parents to that of her fiancé, soon her husband, generous though he was towards her. He was, in fact, a worthy man whose suit she had no reason whatever to refuse. But it was a premature marriage. She loves him, and yet her husband's love for her weighs upon her and constrains her, because she received it before she desired it. The constraint takes the form of a doubt as to whether she really loves her husband. She is afraid to tell him of her doubt, and this separates her from him.

One sometimes sees also a girl so happy to have got engaged very young, so dazzled by her unexpected good fortune and by the prestige of her fiancé that she no longer wants to go on with the work she has undertaken. She abandons her studies, gives up her music lessons and her social activities before having made anything of them. From then on her engagement fills her life. She wants to see her fiancé every day, and does not know what to do with herself if he is too busy to be with her. She thinks she is growing up, but in reality she is prematurely restricting the horizons of her life.

If the engagement is broken off, she is left alone in a desert. She sees that she has no personal life. If she marries, then perhaps only much later, after her own children are married, she will realize that she had given up too much of her personal life. By then she will feel that she is too old to take up her studies again or start a career. She may blame her husband, claiming that it was he who made her give up her interesting activities. It may be true, perhaps because he was jealous and she gave way to his jealousy. But, equally, that may not be the case, and the husband will feel hurt and protest against the injustice of her complaints.

Marriage, one's job, and life itself necessarily involve renunciation. But that ought in fact to be a second movement after the first movement of the free expansion of youth. Parents who put the brakes on their adolescent children confuse these two movements together. Self-assertion must come before self-denial. And one is the better able to deny oneself for having first asserted oneself. "In my family," a woman says to me, "we were not allowed to show any ambition whatsoever." But surely her parents, in that case, *had* an ambition, without realizing it, namely that of being an exemplary family, a family without ambitions? Other parents restrain the development of one child for fear of his overshadowing the others. And they restrain each of the others for the same reason! They succeed in this way in making them all jealous of each other, and implant in their minds the false notion that no one can assert himself without detriment to others.

A negative education of this kind destroys a child's self-confidence and pushes him into neurosis, because it blocks the spontaneous force of life within him. This vital impulse may perhaps make a child indulge in some rash expense, the attraction of which the parents cannot understand. They consider it to be foolish, and take the child severely to task over it. It is even worse when the parents say nothing, but their attitude is such that it could never enter the child's head to indulge any of his whims. Years later he will confess to me that he still has a strong feeling that he ought not to be spending money on himself, though he is generous towards others. A spinster has remained with her aged parents. She has a good income. Not having a home of her own, she ought at least to be able to furnish her room in accordance with her personal taste. "Just imagine," she writes to me, "I'm thinking of spending eighty pounds on a wardrobe for my room. Don't you think I'm mad?" I am very glad. Life is just beginning to burst into bloom again in her.

Many people do not like life. Their upbringing has left them with a prohibition inside of them, which says: "Living prohibited." "Don't talk to me about eternal life!" cries one of my patients. "I hate life as it is—how do you expect me to want it to be eternal?" God created life, and Nature, and the forces of Nature. He gave their motions to the sun, the stars, and the earth. He brings the trees into leaf, and gives the young their desire to grow and develop. To put a brake on this vital impulse on the excuse of teaching the child wisdom or Christian humility, is to fail to understand the rhythms of Nature implanted by God. If the child rebels, his parents take this to be the very explosion of pride they were afraid of. And if the child submits, he will turn into a model of virtue and abnegation of whom everyone will take advantage, and whom no one will respect.

A young woman is much appreciated in the office where she works, because she willingly takes on all the unpleasant jobs which her comrades and her chiefs push on to her. She is eager to do favours for everyone, and never asks the tiniest favour for herself. She likes to think of herself as setting a shining example in the office, where she sees clearly that the law of the jungle prevails. But despite her undoubted nobility of soul, she has a total lack of authority and influence over the others.

They even behave as if they were jealous of her; and so they are, because they have probably got a bad conscience over abusing her willingness, and they hide their sense of guilt behind criticisms and unpleasant teasing. She makes them feel awkward about their selfish tricks, even though she assists them in their manœuvres. She is a silent but living accusation among them, and they defend themselves vigorously against it. At the same time as they exploit her they look upon her as abnormal, ill—and they are not altogether mistaken. They never suspect what secret storms rage beneath her inexhaustible smile.

I have seen many of these apparent sheep who can suddenly turn into wolves if the dyke that has been holding back their aggressiveness gives way. They often feel uneasy themselves. Between their placid exterior and the violence in their hearts there is too great a contrast. They are vaguely and painfully aware of this. One of them tells me that he has had enough of his "counterfeit goodness". Another comes back from a visit to another country, where a charming girl has said to him: "I like you a lot, you are so nice." Her words had wounded him deeply. They seemed to put his whole problem in a nutshell: that girl saw him as a delectable companion, but not as a man—she could like him as a friend, but not love him.

"I had formed an ideal picture of myself," a woman says to me, "I thought I was a model of virtue, of morality, of sweetness and love." And another: "I hate this lie that has taken on the colours and the mask—almost the radiance of love." Yet another suffers acutely, though always in silence, from the spitefulness of a sister-in-law. I make her say aloud in front of me: "My sister-in-law can go to blazes!" We were both surprised at the liberating effect of that little ceremony!

A self-effacing man, sensitive and humble, and full of self-doubt, but full of gentleness too, tells me that none of his predecessors in the job he now has could stick it. The man in charge is a very able man, but a martinet. Conflicts had constantly arisen, and had always ended in the only possible way—with the departure of the subordinate. But his practice is never to answer back. He carefully avoids any quarrel, and is quite proud of his success. He does not defend himself, and everything is all right. But in the course of our conversations he begins to wonder if this self-denial is really genuine. And then, suddenly, one day he tells his chief exactly what he thinks. The chief cannot get over it—such a docile employee! He always seemed to agree with everything, and here he is complaining like the others! Then, shortly after that, my patient arrives with beaming countenance, and says: "Just imagine, I touched eighty on the motorway!"—"Ah!" I said to myself, "He's on the way to being cured!" And in fact he begins to gain confidence in himself, to take on bigger responsibilities, and soon he announces to me that the terrible headaches from which he has suffered since childhood have disappeared.

The men of the Bible all asserted themselves firmly. Consider Jeremiah, who stands up to his contemporaries, and even to the prophet Hananiah (Jer. 28). Nevertheless it is the timid Jeremiah who says to the Lord: "I do not know how to speak, for I am only a youth" (Jer. 1.6). But when faced with the errors of his people he speaks out: "My heart is beating wildly; I cannot keep silent" (Jer. 4.19). Moses also is timid, and says: "Who am I that I should go to Pharaoh, and bring the sons of Israel out of Egypt?" (Ex. 3.11). Yet he learned how to assert himself! Think of Isaiah, boldly answering God's call: "Here I am! Send me" (Isa. 6.8). Read the Bible again, and see! Men everywhere facing the worst difficulties and opposition. The apostle Peter, on the day of Pentecost, speaks to the crowd and founds the Christian Church through his confident preaching (Acts 2). For him this was the time of affirmation, before the time of renunciation and martyrdom which his Lord had foretold for him (John 21.18).

Nevertheless to assert oneself does not necessarily imply being a missionary, singing the praises of God's love and urging men to answer it with their faith, their love, and their obedience. Often it means daring to air one's grievances, resentment, and rebellion. In this respect, too, the Bible is no less in accord with psychology. One may even say that it is here that the Bible most clearly confirms the law of the two movements. Job cries out in revolt against the unjust suffering that has befallen him, and he cries against God, as C. G. Jung has emphasized. Jung,[2] like Job, can neither understand nor accept a God who is cruel and deaf. Job appeals to God's goodness, justice, and pity; and God answers him only with a brutal manifestation of his sovereign power. This overwhelms Jung, as it had outraged Job. That is why Jung's book, which had a cool reception among theologians, does not seem to me to be so far removed from the biblical view as they think.

Job proclaims his rebellion with indomitable tenacity in the face of the pious attempts of his friends to keep him quiet and make him submit. "Let me have silence, and I will speak," he says to them (Job. 13.13). Nothing could be worse than to listen to a rebel impatiently or wearily, as if trying to show him that he can express his revolt provided he gets it over quickly, and that it is only the first step towards abdication. How long does it take a rebel to unload all the complaints that have piled up in his heart? Ask the psychologists. Nevertheless the Book of Job ends with a religious experience which Jung does not seem properly to have understood. It seems to me to consist not so much in the triumph over Job of a cruel and powerful God as in the fact of the personal contact that Job finds with him, and this is precisely because Job has been bold enough to assert himself before him: "I had heard of thee by the hearing of the/ear, but now my eye sees thee" (Job. 42.5).

Jonah also rebels, but in this case it is against God's mercy. God has forgiven the Ninevites, to whom he had told Jonah to announce his anger. Jonah sulks in the shade of a castor oil plant. He cannot accept that God should change his mind! In the castor oil plant which God has caused to grow, and which provides a beneficent shade, but which is attacked by worm, so that the next day it

---

[2] *Answer to Job.*

withers, Jonah sees an image of those divine contradictions which outrage him, for from God come blessings at one moment and misfortunes the next. So Jonah bursts out, without mincing his words: "I do well to be angry, angry enough to die" (Jonah 4.9). As regards rebellion, I ought to be quoting also numerous passages in the Psalms, in which the psalmist voices his indignation at the shameless prosperity of the wicked. Jesus Christ himself utters on the Cross a great cry of reproach: "My God, my God, why hast thou forsaken me?" (Matt. 27.46). God understands revolt, and allows it. He loves those who express it better than those who tepidly hide it (Rev. 3.15). For in respect of our heavenly Father, as with an earthly father, the way to adulthood lies necessarily through revolt.

I tended a girl who was the victim of a neurotic father. Actually the father, shortly before his death, had written me a fine letter telling me of his own difficulties, and confessing the wrongs he had committed towards his daughter, and saying how much he regretted them. That gave me a chance of replying and bringing him the assurance of God's forgiveness. The daughter's life was paralysed and empty. She had had to interrupt her intellectual and artistic studies, which she enjoyed, and for which she had a great gift. The reason was that study now reminded her of the way her father used to nag at her, and so to study would have been to obey him symbolically, to give him satisfaction, and a powerful unconscious force prevented her from doing so. Naturally she was also, and especially, suffering from a psychological blockage in regard to love and marriage.

As she was good at drawing, I asked her to do some portraits of her father. What portraits they were! She showed me several hundred, each more hideous than the last, and I examined them all with care. They were reminiscent of mediaeval pictures of the Devil, with their horrible grimacing faces. My patient was passing through her first movement, expressing all the wild hate that had piled up in her mind and poisoned it. I confess that I began to wonder whether it would ever stop. Yet when she talked one day about burning all the drawings, I begged her to think carefully before doing so.

My intuition told me that the first movement was not yet complete, and that the idea of burning the drawings might be the expression of a desire to put an end to this torrent of hostility by repressing it because it was becoming almost unbearable for her.

Then she decided to choose the drawings she wanted to burn—and they were not the worst. Later she went abroad, and a colleague took over my task. She is now married, active and happy.

"He who dare not hate cannot love," writes Dr. Nodet.[3] Psychoanalysis has revealed to us the tragic and indestructible link between hate and love. He who dare not say no, cannot really say yes either. All those who preach love and self-denial ought to learn that fact. To the child, his parents seem godlike. He cannot tell them of his hate and refusal, and the repression which results becomes for the rest of his life an insurmountable obstacle to self-giving, even in marriage or in religion. Here are the words of a woman who was very conscious of this: "I should like so much to be able to give myself completely, but I feel incapable of doing so!" So one must live through the first movement if one is to be able thereafter to take up the second successfully. The great risk if one tries to urge someone to be loving and forgiving is that he will pretend to love and to forgive.

The Bible tells of the conflicts between Jacob and Laban, and between Jacob and Esau. These narratives are most instructive. Jacob pours out his complaints to Laban, his father-in-law (Gen. 31.36–42). It is only after that that they are able to make a sincere pact together. Laban, indeed, had dealt very badly with his son-in-law. He thoroughly exploited him! He made him work for seven years, promising to give him his youngest daughter, Rachel, "and they seemed to him but a few days because of the love he had for her" (Gen. 29.20). But after this delay Laban deceived Jacob, and put his elder daughter Leah in his bed. And then he insisted on another seven years' work before he would grant him Rachel. I pass over the dramas of jealousy that resulted between the two sisters, made worse by the fact that Leah was fertile and Rachel sterile. I have already dealt with them elsewhere.

Jacob's character, however, was not a straightforward one, either. Instead of having a frank explanation with his father-in-law he went off without telling him, taking his wives and his flocks with him. Laban went after him, and demanded: "What have you done, that you have cheated me, and carried away my daughters like captives of the sword?" The affair is complicated by the fact that Rachel has secretly carried off her father's "household gods", and

[3] C. H. Nodet, "Psychanalyse et culpabilité", Chap. IV of *Pastorale du Péché*, Desclée de Brouwer, Paris, 1962.

she hides them so adroitly that Laban can search the whole camp without finding them. This allows Jacob to pose as the victim of un-founded suspicions. He forgets then how short the years seemed when he was working to win Rachel. He forgets too that he has en-riched himself considerably during his stay with Laban, and he bursts into reproaches and claims for more pay.

Thus, as in all human conflicts, there are wrongs on each side. Each sees only those of the other, or unconsciously covers up his own bad conscience beneath outraged protests. But this clearing-out of complaints brings a reconciliation which trickery, revenge, and flight did not procure—quite to the contrary. After the stormy explanation Laban and Jacob are able to make a covenant. They set up a monument as a sign of their agreement and of their will to respect each other's rights. On occasions the same sort of thing hap-pens to us, and we realize then that a first movement of frank ex-planation may be the precondition of a second movement of love, respect, and forgiveness.

What Jacob also forgot in his quarrel with Laban was that he had voluntarily stayed with the latter in order to get away from his own brother, Esau, whom he had already basely deceived in his youth (Gen. 27). And leaving Laban to go back to his own country meant going back to Esau, of whose vengeance he was mortally afraid. This was the context of his famous night at Peniel, during which he wrestled with God, and compelled him to give him a blessing (Gen. 32.22–32). This personal encounter with God introduces a new dimension into the whole problem of the conflicts of interest and character which occur among men. Simple frankness can bring about unexpected reconciliations, though they may be precarious. For lurking in the background of these conflicts there are always unconscious factors, and in particular repressed feelings of guilt which only the grace of God can wipe away.

We may well think that the peace which Jacob had just con-cluded with Laban prepared his mind for that deeper self-discovery which the story describes in the form of the struggle with God, from which he comes both wounded and victorious. I am careful, there-fore, not to look upon the psychological factors as being opposed to the spiritual ones. Rather do I see them converging and giving sup-port to each other. I believe it is utopian to believe in a secular morality, a morality of mere frankness, as if telling people what we think of them were sufficient to resolve all conflicts, without the help of divine grace. But I also think it is utopian to ask God to flood our hearts with fine feelings of forgiveness and love if we still have all our demands locked up deep inside our minds. For frankness facilitates the encounter with God, and dissimulation obstructs it. And so God rules over both movements, over the first as over the second. Both have their part to play in the divine plan.

An American religious magazine asked me for an article on forgiveness and mental health.[4] Perhaps the editor expected me to stress the salutary effect of forgiveness on mental health. Of course, if it is true forgiveness. But my experience is that true forgiveness is rare. It is particularly so, perhaps, among religious people who wish to witness to their faith by their conduct. A committed Christian finds it more difficult than an unbeliever to express resentment and dislike. What will people think of him, professing as he does the religion of love?

Then he makes an effort to forgive, and the need for an effort is the sign that he has not truly forgiven. I by no means deny the conscious sincerity of the effort, nor its moral merit, since he is making it in obedience to his faith, in order to put love where there has been hate, as the prayer of St. Francis says. But in St. Francis it was indeed a prayer, an appeal for decisive action by God, and not an effort to seem full of love when the hate is still there, though hidden. Premature forgiveness has a good chance of being false forgiveness.

This is a great problem for all churches, and for the mental health of their militant members. There are as many conflicts in the human society of the Church as there are in secular society. It is often even more difficult to forgive others their transgressions if those others are brothers in the faith who are themselves eloquent about justice and charity. The effort required for forgiveness is then greater still. One is silent instead of answering back, and one tries to smile and look benevolent. But then the psychological atmosphere becomes unhealthy. A strange anxiety often grips the hearts of those who are coming away from a Church Council meeting in which one has sensed the latent aggressiveness which has not been honestly brought out into the open.

True forgiveness is something quite different. It is a grace, and not the result of an effort. It is a liberation, not a burden. It restores harmonious unity to the mind instead of tearing it between

<hr>

[4] Paul Tournier, "Forgiveness and Mental Health", in *This Day*, St. Louis, May 1965.

two contrary forces. I always remember a certain French lady. She had a good presence, a firm, serious voice, and finely-chiselled features. The day after her conversion she exclaimed to me: "I was full of hatred." One felt how true that must have been from the way she said the word "hatred". And she told me how her hate had disappeared like a cloak falling from her shoulders.

The relationship which is established between the psycho-therapist and his patient is not without analogy with the situation of the Church. So long as the patient expresses resentment only against other people there is scarcely any problem, unless the doctor happens to think the patient is being unjust and does not dare to tell him so. But sooner or later the patient will be disillusioned or hurt by his doctor. Can he go on being completely honest, as his treatment demands? Will he for his part have the courage to tell the doctor the complaints he has against him, or is his attachment such that he will be tempted to bottle them up?

The exemplary relationship he has with his doctor is a vital treasure to him. And as soon as one has a treasure, one is afraid of losing it. How will the doctor react if he says something that will hurt him? Will he not lose interest in him? So perhaps the fear of losing the affection of his doctor will compromise his treatment. Last year I spent two months in the United States, on a lecture tour. On my return one of my patients admitted that she realized that during the last few months before my departure she had "humoured" me, carefully avoiding anything that might have cast a shadow over our good understanding, because she would not have been able to bear my long absence if we had not had time before I went to resolve by frankness any conflict that might arise between us.

Those conflicts can be violent. An old stock of aggressiveness, accumulated long ago against parents or other persons, may suddenly pour out upon the doctor the moment there is the slightest tension in the relationship. How is the doctor going to bear it? He knows well that this phenomenon is called negative transfer. But it is no use being learned; he is also a man, and he would not be a psychotherapist if he were not sensitive. So long as the patient is very infantile he accepts it easily, as one accepts a child's outbursts of temper. But when the patient is improving, when he is unwilling to be treated as a child any longer and so considers he has the right to take up a provocative attitude, the doctor in his turn may compromise the treatment by "humouring" his patient without really realizing it.

The doctor, too, may want to do honour, if not to his faith, like the people in the Church, at least to psychology, and to show that it sets us free and able to bear being attacked without answering back. Then, as in the case of Church people, repression of complaints may be mistaken by the doctor for true generosity. I believe these are more frequently than we think the causes of failure in psychotherapy. Whether it is the patient humouring the doctor, or *vice versa*, it is clear that in either case the first movement is avoided, and this will make access to the second movement difficult.

Faced with the enormous demands that neurotics make, I have sometimes been afraid of being swamped by them. I once slapped one of my patients. Oh, I am not boasting about it! I was fearfully abashed and humiliated. I confessed it as a sin. But if I hid my movements of anger so as to appear sinless, would that not be still more blameworthy? Perhaps, too, it did me good to be humiliated in front of a patient who admired me too much. Then she forgave me, and our relationship now is excellent. Another patient one day dashed out of the house slamming the door behind her. I very much wanted to run after her, but I knew that would be false. She must be allowed to live her first movement through to the end.

Yet another patient tended to be aggressive during our conversations. One day she arrived all smiles, relaxed, and friendly. I told her how surprised I was: "Well," she said, "in the train I suddenly felt such a wave of anger against you, and I was already afraid that my unco-operative attitude was spoiling our interviews!" There are, in fact, patients who are thoroughly well disposed towards us at a distance, but who become aggressive as the time for the consultation approaches. "So what do you think I did?" she went on, "I lowered the carriage window and shouted my hate for you out of it!" A psychotherapeutic train! In it she went through her first movement. But it would have been even better for her to have done it in my consulting-room.

9

Premature Abdication

I MUST TOUCH now upon an even more delicate subject. A very intelligent man comes to see me. He is not ill, he is an eminent man in his profession; only he is rather shy in company. He was brought up by admirable parents whom he still addresses only with grateful respect. It is perhaps a disadvantage to have parents that are too perfect, because it deprives you in adolescence of an opportunity of rebellion which can help you to learn to stand on your own feet. So far from rebelling, this man has never stopped trying to be like them and follow their good example.

I think I have already mentioned him. There is nothing tragic about his case, and I return to it only because it provides a good illustration of the complexity of the problem of renunciation. In fact his parents were pioneers in the fight against alcoholism. They never drank anything fermented or distilled, and devoted themselves single-mindedly to the rescue of alcoholics, whom they made to sign a pledge of total abstinence, which they themselves signed along with them in order to encourage them. Throughout his childhood the boy had been passionately interested in his parents' difficult and disinterested struggle against the scourge of alcoholism. When he reached the age of sixteen he wished to join in the battle, and he had signed a pledge of total abstinence for life. His parents were too wise to try and compel him; he signed of his own accord, but with all the solemnity which the act had in his eyes.

But what does it mean, to renounce something one has never possessed? He had never tasted the delights of alcohol—on the contrary, he had a horror of it. It was only much later that he realized that his renunciation was no such thing. He still had no desire whatever to partake of any alcoholic drink, but he was irked by the thought that his abstention was governed by a resolve made when he was so very young. I therefore decided, not without some hesitation, to absolve him from his vow at his request, so that he should be able to feel that he was his own master once more.

A pious young woman goes and spends a few days in retreat at a place of pilgrimage in the mountains. The setting is magnificent, the atmosphere one of fervent devotion. Since her childhood her religious ardour has attracted her towards an ideal of holy and consecrated life, in which she has been encouraged by the religious background of her family life. At youth meetings she has often heard estimable priests speaking about the value of renunciation, about the temptations of the flesh, and the excellence of virginity. She spends wonderful hours alone on her knees, in front of a statue of the Virgin Mary. And there and then she makes a mental vow of perpetual celibacy. She too, apparently, has made her vow freely, though clearly it has no canonical validity for the Church, which would require further precautions to be taken.

She, too, is renouncing something of which she has no knowledge or experience whatever. Her sincerity is complete, but there is a misunderstanding. She is renouncing marriage at a moment when she has not the slightest desire to get married. In actual fact she is at this very juncture postponing, without really knowing why, her answer to a proposal of marriage which has frightened her. When, shortly afterwards, she falls ill, we must not conclude that it is her oath which has made her ill. She was already ill before that. A Freudian colleague has attempted to explain to her the mechanisms of repression, without succeeding in making her understand, and certainly without liberating her from them. The treatment was turning into an argument which is not at all in accordance with Freudian principles.

It is only many years later that she and I can talk about all this without emotion bringing the dialogue to a full stop and inhibiting the process of recall. She sees quite clearly that her renunciation was unreal. The order of the two movements was reversed: her abdication, to be genuine, ought to have been a second movement, whereas there had been no first movement beforehand. The first movement in this case, it must be made clear, would not have been the exercise of the sex life, but full consciousness of sexual desire. True renunciation is not so much renunciation of a thing as of the

desire for that thing, an absolute refusal to give way to a desire—to
a quite lucid desire.

It is only now, with the easing of tension that the first months of
treatment have already brought about, that desire is awakening in
her—and it is not without some risk that it is awakening so late. She
is terribly shaken. She experiences a frantic desire to get married, is
furious at having missed her opportunity. It is perhaps too late.
Especially too late for an acceptable marriage. She finds it hard to
resist the advances of men she despises, and she is well aware of her
desire to give way to them. Now, her refusal is a real renunciation,
a real sacrifice!

Similar dramas can be observed in Protestantism, especially in
puritan circles. The problem of puritanism I naturally find intensely
interesting, since it can, on the one hand, produce remarkable
religious personalities, and on the other, sometimes lead to psychological disasters. Looking for a psychological interpretation of
puritanism, it seems to me to answer a human need to localize evil,
which to some degree goes along with the need to localize God
which I was dealing with in Chapter 3. Men in all ages have given
way to the desire to localize evil and the devil. In the physical sense,
think how doctors are glad to be able to localize their enemy in
order to be able to fight it: "The trouble is in the liver, in the
thyroid gland . . ." But in the moral sense the satisfaction is as great.
Take witch-hunting in the Middle Ages, for example, with the
magical practices which were meant to track down the witches responsible for misfortunes. What a relief it was for men who were
tormented by their bad consciences to be able to localize evil outside themselves!

Puritanism seems to me to derive from a similar tendency. It has
a Genevan origin which I cannot omit to mention. On 21 May,
1535, the people of Geneva, moved by the preaching of Guillaume
Farel, decided by a political vote to "live hereafter in accordance
with the Gospel". In the following year Clavin came to Geneva. He
stayed there at the request of Farel, and undertook to teach the
Genevans the full implications of the decision they had made. He
was soon instituting ecclesiastical discipline and a whole corpus of
strict moral and social legislation.

The first intention, therefore, was much more positive than negative, namely to ensure the continuance of genuine Christian living
rather than to give a casuistic and exhaustive definition of sin. But

as time went on it was this negative aspect which prevailed in Genevan puritanism and in its extensions in Scotland and the United States. From then on puritanism has taken on the appearance of an attempt to localize evil. By a kind of social convention, there is a list of forbidden things. The list may vary, of course, at different times and in different communities. Some, for instance, forbid smoking, the drinking of alcoholic beverages, dancing, and going to the theatre. But the psychological object is obviously that of ensuring a clear conscience for anyone who rigorously abstains from the forbidden things, and this is attainable, since the list, however severe, is restricted.

Thus the puritan industrialist of the last century could maintain a clear conscience if he lived in an exemplary manner, being extremely strict with himself where the forbidden things were concerned, but not noticing that he was exploiting the poverty of his work-people, even if he was generous in a paternalist sort of way. It is obvious that this is a negation of the universality of sin and grace which Calvin preached. Modern literature—Camus, Sartre, Simone Weil, and others like them, have awakened a boundless unease in us, and made us feel responsible for all the injustices in the world. We cannot get rid of our bad consciences on the cheap by living austerely—there is no other answer than the infinite grace of God.

Some religious sects, moved by the sincerest of desires to obey God's will, take this casuistry of moral defence to extremes. One of my patients had been admonished by her church council for having had a conversation in the street with a friend who was wearing a red jumper, which was looked upon as a sign of reprehensible frivolity and coquetry. This explains the paradox I have referred to, that such tendencies can forge outstanding characters who impose a high moral discipline upon themselves, and can at the same time be the cause of neurosis in their children.

A child brought up in an environment like that, in which all worldly pleasures are frowned upon, will forswear dancing, flirtation, theatre-going, alcohol, tobacco, nice clothes, and any interest in good food. He will retain perhaps for the rest of his life the idea that everything pleasurable is forbidden, and a sin. One day I shall have to tell him that enjoyment is permitted! But I am unlikely to have any success. All enjoyment, even before the idea of it rises to the surface of his conscious mind, awakens in him the distress that is characteristic of the violation of a taboo, and his pleasure is spoilt.

Do not blame his parents for having put constraints upon him. He has followed their example freely. He wants to be able sincerely to repeat with them the words of St. Paul: "For his sake I have suffered the loss of all things, and count them as refuse, in order that I may gain Christ" (Phil. 3.8). His parents had found the "pearl of great value" (Matt. 13.46), and in exchange for it they had joyfully sacrificed all this world's pleasures. And so for them it was a true renunciation, the sign of a liberating experience. The child, for his part, was giving up nothing, since he had known none of the things he was giving up. He had heard about Jesus Christ from the cradle, so that he could not be a new discovery for him. And so the Christian life appears to be for him an impoverishment, a dispossession, instead of a blossoming and a fulfilment.

He marries a girl who has inherited the same outlook as he has, and he feels that their vigorous moral code and their common religious background ought to augur well for durable happiness in their married life. But now the years have gone by. The husband has a good job, and he has met a less austere woman who has revealed to him the existence of unsuspected pleasures. He is ill-prepared to counter their attraction, because his childhood renunciation cost him no effort, no real struggle or sacrifice. And his wife, too, is unprepared for the strains involved. She sees nothing, so sure is she of her husband's fidelity. Then she goes down with tuberculosis. It is one of those cases where we can say with Dr. Huebschmann that "when the mind is silent, the body cries out".

St. Francis led the life of a rich young man before espousing Dame Poverty; St. Augustine a life of frivolity before giving it up. They could really talk about renunciation, because they had tasted deeply of the joys they subsequently renounced. You, reader, know how delicate a point this is. You may be wondering if I am not going to get round to urging people to sin, so that they will be in a position to renounce their sin afterwards. Formulated in this way, the law of the two movements would be an absurdity, since everyone sins. "None is righteous, no, not one" (Rom. 3.10). What is wrong with a moralistic education is precisely that it suggests to the child that he can be safe from sin, provided he abstains from a certain number of duly listed things.

He believes in the universality of sin and the universality of

God's forgiveness as a biblical truth which he has been taught since childhood; but he has not experienced them. He has heard the proclamation of God's grace before having wept over the reality of his own sin. That is what the first movement is—not the fact of sinning, since that is common to all, but the intense, humiliating, overwhelming emotion that accompanies the conviction of sin. Then, and only then, the message of grace takes on its full value. The conviction of sin is the place where we encounter God's grace. That is what the theologians mean by the phrase *felix culpa*, the happy fault, which gives us the opportunity of experiencing the divine forgiveness. This is also the lesson of the parable of the Prodigal Son.

Does this mean that it is useless, or even dangerous, to teach children religious truths, moral laws, and pious practices? I certainly do not think so. To allow them to grow up in complete liberty and in ignorance of the moral and spiritual exigencies of life would in fact be to deprive them of the opportunity of the rebellion, or at least the crisis of adolescence, through which they must pass before finding a more personal faith. But when that crisis comes, it is important to respect and accept it as the first movement that is the necessary preliminary to a return to the faith and a more thoughtful adherence to the ineluctable exigencies of life. The child will surmount his crisis only if he is free to express his doubts and his rebellion, to reject what has been inculcated in him. But then it will be seen that not all the seed sown in his mind has been sown in vain.

A young woman was in despair as a result of the demands made upon her by a strict religious sect. She worked for a charity under the direction of a perspicacious woman who said to her one day: "Now you must stop those religious arguments, shut your Bible, hide it at the back of your wardrobe, and go and see a psychologist!" You will understand that with her I did not open my Bible. She had had enough of people urging renunciation upon her in the name of religion. She was at the stage of the first movement, and needed to be free to discover herself. But when I see her now, and see all the good she does both in her family and beyond it, I know that she is the heir of a great spiritual tradition which had marked her for its own from the cradle.

Others, surfeited with pious practices, may need to go on strike by spending time in meditation. I have never urged them to go back to their religious practices before they themselves show that they wish to do so. But that time does usually come, and this shows that it is not merely a matter of conditioning, as the followers of Pavlov think. They still yearn for a certain conception of life, a certain dimension and savour which life has only when it is enlightened by the spirit. And they return spontaneously to the discipline and way of life which previously they practised in a constrained and legalistic way, but which they now adopt freely from their heart.

Thus, though St. Paul opposes grace to law, he does not denigrate the law, or depart from its principles: "The law was our custodian until Christ came" (Gal. 3.24). That is the point. The first movement is a guide, a preparation. Whether it be a matter of an imposed morality, at the age when the child still needs it; or self-assertion and revolt at the approach of the age of responsibility; or the testing-time of illness and the questions it raises; or, finally, the self-discovery and self-acceptance which form part of a course of psychotherapy—these are all experiences which prepare the way for another, the experience of abdication, an experience which is much greater, much longer lasting, but which would not be possible if it were not preceded by those other experiences in the first place.

A member of a religious community has been protected in childhood to an exceptional degree. An admirable mother, pious, affectionate, by no means a moralist, awoke in him while he was still a youth a marked interest in the spiritual life. In these circumstances there was no need to forbid him worldly pleasures. They had no attraction for him. His only joy was in communion with God. And so the temptations which beset all young men of his age, and in particular those involving imaginations concerning sex, passed him by without a struggle. In a sense, it was a privilege. He was able to spend several years in the world almost without noticing its dangers, protected as he was by his childish innocence. But it was also a misfortune, because the awakening was terrible. In fact it was only several years later that he felt in himself the awakening of his sexual desires. By then he had risen to be Prior, and it was the confidences of his fellow monks which opened the door, first to his curiosity, then to temptation and defeat.

How tragic it is! It was indeed tragic for him. The harmonious serenity of an abundantly blessed religious life was brusquely shattered for him as if by a raging storm. Everyone looked upon him as a saintly man, but in secret he was engaged in a continuous losing battle. He felt that his life and his position as a priest were a hollow sham. Belatedly he was experiencing the fascination of evil, its terrible power, despite his sincerest resolve and despite his prayers and the help of the sacraments. He had always thought that he hated evil, and now he was finding that he loved it, as we all do. He fell ill. His spiritual director, moved with compassion when he saw that neither confession nor absolution restored his peace of mind, firmly pointed out the medical aspect of the crisis through which he was passing, and said: "You are depressed; you ought to see a doctor." And he sent him to me.

From the start he showed great trust in me, and found no difficulty in confiding in me. Together we analysed many psychological factors in his development. Though it seemed there had been scarcely any emotional shocks in his early childhood, some had occurred during the period of his novitiate. He had looked upon Church and monastery as a mother, full of tender care. And he had been treated harshly. This was probably done in order to counteract his naïve and childish manner. The temptation for a master of novices to do so is understandable. A novice, however, is really a new-born infant—newly born into the religious life. All we have learnt about the intense emotional needs of the first months of life seems to me to be applicable to the novice. I was also able to help the Prior to see that the shame he felt over his defeats was not entirely shame at his sin, but also derived in part from a false shame concerning sex.

None of this, however, brought him any more real relief than had the words of his spiritual director when the latter put his anxieties down to illness. I became more and more convinced that his problem was a religious and not a psychological one. Of course I too could see that the Prior was depressed. But the cause of his depression was the realization of his powerlessness in the face of temptation, and the fact that this powerlessness called in question the whole optimistic moral and religious framework of his life up to then. He knew well that his solitary defeats were sinful. He knew it, just as everybody does, even those who are not religious, even those who try to reassure themselves by saying that it is no more serious than lighting a cigarette. For every one knows that the meaning and purpose of sex is love, not a narcissistic turning in upon oneself. So there we were, in a paradoxical situation: the spiritual director, the priest, saw the disease, whereas I, the doctor, saw the sin—and I called it by its proper name, for it is only in being truthful that we can help people. It was, of course, only apparently paradoxical, since in those matters disease and sin are but two aspects of the same reality. But so long as the Prior tried to look at it as a disease, he found no peace, because there is grace only for sin.

It was not long, I am glad to say, before the Prior was granted a wonderful and healing experience of God's grace, precisely because he had first undergone the experience of being truthful with himself, as well as with me and with God. He recognized that he was responsible for his defeats, that he did not suffer them passively as one does a disease, but that he desired and willed them to take place. He accepted the total humiliation of confessing his struggles and failures in detail, which is easier to do to a psychotherapist than to a priest, because the latter too quickly stops his penitent by assuring him of God's grace.

The Prior already knew all about grace. What he had needed was to make the painful discovery of the true dimensions of sin, so that he could realize also the infinite immensity of grace.

One can clearly see the law of the two movements at work here. I have already emphasized that the first movement is not so much the fact of sin as the conviction that one is sinning, the feeling of guilt and utter powerlessness in face of the enormity of sin and its fascination. And Grace is not, as the Prior had thought, a divine protection safeguarding us against defeat, but the inexhaustible forgiveness of God towards man who recognizes his inexhaustible sin. "Now I understand," he told me, "that I must not only accept that I am a sinner, but also that I shall remain so in this world."

I also was brought up in a Christian home, which was possibly less intensely pious than it would have been had my parents lived. This spared me the necessity of passing through a period of rebellion before finding myself. And I had the benefit of the prayers of many of my parents' friends during my childhood as an orphan. Christianity has been my "place" since my youth. When I was a student I declared myself to be a Christian without fully realizing that the faith I professed was no more than a bundle of philosophical ideas and a personal attachment to Jesus Christ. Nevertheless I was active in the Church and in Christian student societies. I made speeches, led Bible study, and wrote articles about Calvinist theology.

I do not disown all that, but still it was a more theoretical than practical faith. I, too, had always been familiar with the notions of sin and grace, but it was something learned, not lived. Because I had never yet really wept over my sin, never yet been overwhelmed at feeling myself so radically wretched before the holiness of God. It was actually a psychological event which opened for me the door to a deeper and more living faith, when I unburdened myself much more honestly to a certain friend or to my wife.

That is why I never stop fighting for a better understanding between theologians and psychologists, so that psychotherapy may go hand in hand with the cure of souls, instead of going against it. To speak of a reconciliation between the two may seem to some to be going too far. But everyone knows how much opposition psycho-analysis met from theologians in its earliest beginnings, despite the efforts of some of them, such as Pfister, of Zürich. It would be dishonest to close one's eyes to the prejudice and criticism which it still encounters from them, especially in Europe, and among Protestants.

The Roman Church seems to have been quicker to realize the importance in relation to the cure of souls of the work done by the depth psychologists. The American Protestants have also grasped it, for the Americans are a pragmatical people, always on the look-out for anything that will make it easier for them to help others. So one sees American churchmen taking the study of psychology extremely seriously, spending time in psychiatric clinics, and organizing seminars and clubs in order to give themselves a proper psychological training.

In Europe, however, Protestant theologians have a more dogmatic outlook. They are particularly concerned to teach the truth, "the good doctrine" (I Tim. 4.6) as St. Paul recommended Timothy to do. This is above all things a pastoral concern, which we must understand and take seriously. It follows that the contrast which so many people make in their minds between psychology and Christianity, and which I dealt with in my chapter on the two gospels, is one of their chief preoccupations. Is it not, they ask, a doctrine other than that of salvation by Jesus Christ alone that is being preached by psychologists—a humanist doctrine of salvation by oneself, by self-assertion and by naturalist psychological science? That is why I am writing this book, in an attempt to put things in their proper perspective.

In America, on the other hand, I seemed to find a spirit of controversy, particularly among doctors and psychiatrists, who tended to follow Freud's teachings rather than those of Jung and Adler. For example, when I was lecturing in the hospital at Baltimore I told the story of a patient in whom psychological and religious factors were inextricably mixed. One of my fellow-doctors there said to me with an asperity which I rather enjoyed: "But, Dr. Tournier, I have cured such cases without needing to get mixed up with the patients' religious problems, which were no concern of mine!"

Of course! Fortunately I am not trying to question the efficacy of psychoanalysis in the treatment of psychological disturbances. Think of the number of neurotics who have been successfully treated since the beginning of the century by means of techniques which specifically exclude all reference to religious implications. And it must be pointed out that these were patients to whom priests and ministers had for centuries been bringing the charity of their hearts and the encouragement of their faith without at the same time bringing any relief from their anxieties. My Baltimore colleague has a right to be proud and glad of his successes. I only maintain that even if he does not know it he has in this matter been collaborating with God whose will it is that the sick should be healed, and who has therefore called doctors to tend them.

Of course a pure technique can effect a cure. This is what happens when the surgeon sets about the excision of a tumour. It also happens when the psychoanalyst frees his patient from anxieties and inhibitions, making it possible for him to assert himself, to develop, to defend himself, to realize his ambitions, to enjoy life, to work and act—in short, really to live, and also to discover and accept himself as he is, including his sin. As we have seen, all that is the first movement, and it is the proper domain of the psychotherapist. It has been my purpose to show that this prior movement is indispensable if there is to be any genuine validity in the second movement of renunciation, self-forgetfulness, generosity, and faith.

But the real problem goes deeper. Can we doctors keep the two movements rigorously apart, and dismiss the second movement by saying, like my colleague in Baltimore, that it has nothing to do with us, but is a matter for the ecclesiastic, or even the philosopher or the teacher? Can we say that the problem will arise only after the patient has been healed and has left us? I do not think so, because medicine, as the safeguarder of life, necessarily raises, even during the illness, the question of the meaning of life. In so far as we are able we seek to restore to our patients their physical and psychical capacities, so that they may live more fully.

But what will they expect that fuller life to be like? Surely the answer to this depends largely upon what we ourselves think it is, since we will be communicating our ideas to them in proportion to the influence we exert over them. I do not need to tell psychologists that even without a word being said on the subject we each transmit our own concepts to others, and especially to those who trust us. Does the fuller life consist only in self-assertion, enjoyment, developing, acting, winning success, and realizing ambition? If that is what we believe, then we are storing up bitter disappointment for our patients. There are necessary limits to the process of self-fulfilment. However numerous and decisive our successes, we will inevitably encounter obstacles and failures, and at the end of the road is the ultimate obstacle of death, which even the best doctor can only postpone.

Jung[1] and Frankl[2], in company with many other psychoanalysts, have shown us how much these problems of the meaning of life and of death occupy the hearts of all who are ill, even when they carefully disguise the fact, or are not fully aware of it. There takes place a dialectic of life and death between doctor and patient, whether the disease is organic or psychic, even if neither of them mentions it. Finally, to assert oneself does not mean only to defend oneself and impress others, but to assert oneself as a human being—a being who is able to think and to choose, and to formulate a view of what life is.

The second movement, in fact, is also an affirmation of self, but on a much higher plane—a bolder and more adult assertion than revolt can ever be. In the light of it the first movement can be seen to be a necessary but provisional stage, the point of which is that it prepares the ground for the second movement. One must have a place before one can give it up. One must receive before giving, exist before abandoning oneself in faith. We receive a place only so as eventually to leave it, treasure only so as to cast it away, a personal existence only so as to be able to offer it up. Thus, to deprive a man of his place is not only to take that place from him, but also to take away from him the chance of the religious experience of giving it up himself. Simone Weil, who felt so profoundly the alienation of the masses by our impersonal civilization, expressed the point admirably: "When the quality of human personality is

[1] C. G. Jung, *Modern Man in Search of a Soul*, translated by W. S. Dell and C. F. Baynes, Kegan Paul, London, 1933 (reprinted 1961).
[2] Viktor E. Frankl, *Der Unbewusste Gott*, Amandus, Vienna, 1949.

taken from them, the possibility of renouncing it is also taken away ... God has created our independence so that we should have the possibility of renouncing it out of love."³

In the same way, when parents, through their dissensions or their lack of love, deprive a child of his place, they also deprive him of the possibility of leaving it later on, and so enjoying an experience that is no longer only emotional, but spiritual as well. The doctor who is trying to give him a place so as to liberate him from his desertion or vagabond complex restores to him this essentially human prerogative. If he is a Freudian doctor, he will say that he is trying to make his patient adult, independent, and free to give himself. And he will readily point to sex as an example, to show that only those who have evolved to adulthood are capable of real self-giving in love.

If the doctor is a follower of Jung, he will say that he wants to lead his patient towards integration, to liberate all his repressed potentialities, and bring him to accept the totality of himself, so that he may be enabled to give himself fully in answer to that deep-seated urge which Jung called an "archetype". If the doctor is an existentialist, he will say that he is trying to get his patient to face existential problems, to take responsibility for his choices and to commit himself lucidly to what he chooses, since he who is not conscious that he exists cannot feel capable of giving himself.

It is clear that whatever school of psychology is followed, free and loving self-giving always appears as the final objective which the psychotherapeutic treatment aims at making the patient capable of achieving. Simone Weil also expressed her idea by inventing a word: "decreation". The first movement is creation. This is the meaning of psychotherapy: the creation of the person. The second movement will be decreation. The first is enrichment and possession, the second is shedding and detachment. Every religion calls upon its followers to make this act of renunciation. This self-giving is what they call faith.

It is not for me to formulate the theology of this appeal that is proper to each religion. I am concerned with the nature of the psychological phenomenon that is common to all those who answer it. When the Buddha saw his father again, the old Rajah Suddhodana reproached his son for having deserted him. But Gautama replied: "If you want immortality, abandon all idea of possessive

³ *Waiting on God*, p. 134.

love. Desire must die in you, along with the notion of property, for happiness never comes from what one possesses, but from what one gives." It is almost the same, word for word, as what St. Paul reports Jesus as saying: "It is more blessed to give than to receive" (Acts 20.35). There are also ancient Egyptian religious texts which correspond exactly with the teaching of the Gospel.

There is, then, a truth about the meaning of life which is proclaimed by all inspired men. It is a "predogmatic truth", as Dr. Anton de Mol van Otterloo calls it; that is to say that it underlies the more distinctively developed dogma of all religions. This fundamental truth is that human fullness cannot be attained by means of the first movement alone, but by an alternation of the two movements. It cannot result from the satisfaction merely of natural needs, such as receiving, accumulating, possessing, successful self-defence, and enjoyment. It means that we receive only to give, we possess only to dispossess ourselves, we defend ourselves only to be better able to surrender, we enjoy things only in order to share our enjoyment with others.

It means, therefore, that man does not belong only to the order of Nature, but also to that of the Spirit. The latter does not go against the order of Nature, but it transfigures it and gives it its goal. For what happens is that in letting go the treasures that belong to the order of Nature, we discover the treasures of the order of the Spirit, treasures which are not destroyed by death. The first movement always involves gaining something of the order of Nature: self-enlightenment, release from complexes and from the conditioning of our upbringing, independence in respect of other people, the capacity for enjoyment, intellectual knowledge, and material possessions. The second movement always involves letting go of something natural, to which we naturally hold, or which holds us: a grudge, selfish claims, unsatisfied desires, material wealth, and even spiritual riches. The psychological problem which then arises is to know what it is that can make us let go.

The Second Movement

WE HAVE COME to the last chapter of this study of the two movements. I must attempt to sum up what has been said, and to outline the conclusion to be drawn. I have mentioned the two gospels—the gospel of self-assertion suggested implicitly, if not explicitly, by psychology, and the gospel of renunciation taught by the Christian cure of souls. I have said that many of our patients, and we ourselves, are perplexed by the apparent contradiction between them.

Thoughtful people feel that there is some truth in each of the two gospels. The problem is how they are to be synthesized, and their contradictory nature overcome. It is not easy. If we assert and defend ourselves, we feel guilty when we remember Christ's teaching. If we give way and capitulate, we feel guilty towards ourselves, because we feel we have betrayed ourselves. The problem has exercised my mind for a long time. I tried to deal with it in my book *The Strong and the Weak*, relying on the concept of legitimate self-defence. But this has never satisfied me as an answer. After all, when is defence legitimate? When is it in accordance with God's will, and when is it not? The Bible speaks of wars commanded by God, but it also contains his law: "You shall not kill" (Ex. 20.13). Who am I to decide in each case? And if I refer to a spiritual director, will he not himself be influenced by his own past experiences?

That is why my student friend's words aroused such an echo in my heart. They stirred up a painful debate, and set me thinking how I could bring a little more order and light into this old problem. One thing they did was to give me a line to work on: looking for a place and leaving one's place—giving a place to those who have none, and helping those who have one to give up. So there are two successive complementary stages, which must be carefully distinguished if one is not to end up in contradiction and perplexity: there is a time to receive and a time to give.

This is true of the whole of life. Thus the child who has grown up in a favourable home environment will have received the love, the nurture, the protection and health which will make it possible for him to attain to maturity and psychological liberty, and then to pass it all on to his neighbour, quite naturally and spontaneously. But if he has been deprived, or if disease comes and deprives him of his secure environment, the doctor and the psychologist must make every effort to give him what he lacks—health, physical strength, the capacity for enjoyment, the ability to work, to assert himself, to struggle and develop. That is the first movement.

Similarly, he who has received, whose vital needs have been met, is called upon to give what he has received, instead of hoarding it, instead of always claiming more. Because to stop at the first movement is to refuse life, which is change and rhythm; it is to sterilize oneself, to arrest one's development. Many people pass quite spontaneously and naturally to the second movement, simply because they feel the need to give of themselves. But there are some who hold back in an attitude of avarice, selfishness, revendication, and proud independence. The leaders of all religions remind these of the divine laws of life, and seek to help them to share in the experience of generosity, of self-giving, and renunciation. And that is the second movement.

In this way psychology and the cure of souls seem to me to work together. There is a notion which is very familiar to doctors, though less so to philosophers and theologians—it is that of "therapeutic indications". The doctor is a practitioner. He does not often involve himself in argument about principles. He looks at a particular case and tries to see what must be done, what is "indicated". *Hic et nunc*! At this place and at this moment. So when there is a local infection, an abscess in process of formation, the doctor does not at once wield his scalpel. He must wait. This is the moment for antibiotics and plasters.

But when the pocket of pus has collected in liquid form, the indication points to an operation. The abscess must be lanced. And the doctor tents the wound to prevent it from closing up too soon. He must wait once more for all the pus to come out before removing the tent and encouraging scar-formation. Thus each successive therapeutic act is governed by its indications from moment to moment. Similarly there is a time when psychology is "indicated", and a time when soul-healing, "the cure of the souls" is "indicated", a time when the subject must be helped to assert himself, and another when he must be helped to deny himself.

To urge self-denial upon a man who is the victim of deprivation, is to apply a remedy which he may require some day, but which is not indicated at the moment. Every psychologist has seen such cases. I, too, am aware that religion can do harm as well as good. There is the Book of Job in the Bible, in which we see his pious friends striving to make him see that he is responsible for his misfortunes. Fortunately he is better able to defend himself than a neurotic, and he persists in protesting his innocence. I know that one can do a lot of harm quoting isolated biblical texts—for example, by saying to a man weighed down by suffering and injustice that "all things work together for good to them that love God" (Rom. 8.28), a text that the modern translations, fortunately, put somewhat differently: "In everything God works for good with those who love him."

There is a tendency to brush aside even the gravest problems by resorting to religious exhortation. I am treating a woman suffering from anxiety neurosis. It is a terrible and tenacious disease, which calls for a tremendous and painstaking effort on our part. She meets an evangelist whose zeal makes a great impression upon her. "What a mistake it is," he tells her, "to go and see a psychologist! The more you discuss with him, the more insoluble problems you will uncover, and the worse will be your anxiety. All you have to do is to believe! Once you have faith, there are no more problems." Fortunately she had the courage to tell me of the dismay into which this reprimand plunged her. Another patient tells me that a well-intentioned priest had said to her: "You are looking everywhere for a fire to warm yourself at, and you are always disappointed in your search. Why not become yourself a fire to warm others!" Yes, indeed, if only she could! But the fact is that she must first find the real warmth she needs before she can transmit it to others.

However, all we can give our patients to compensate for the things of which they have been deprived will only answer a passing need. For example, when they have given full expression to their repressed rancour, they will necessarily come to feel, eventually, that they cannot leave the matter there. Those who are well find no difficulty in manifesting their aggressiveness. But every attack provokes a riposte. For example, if someone suddenly tells you all the complaints he has against you, you at once discover that you also have complaints against him, which you thought were forgotten and done with. There comes into your mind a host of memories which you in your turn may hurl at your adversary. And this is what happens the world over—men, parties, peoples, endlessly hurling mutual reproaches at each other, in a vicious circle of aggressiveness.

Every defensive gesture provokes a defensive gesture by the adversary, every assault an assault in return. We all feel that there will be no end to this conflict among men until there is a movement in the other direction: until people recognize their faults instead of trying to defend and justify themselves, until we ask for forgiveness instead of returning reproach for reproach, until we give way instead of digging ourselves obstinately in, until we forgive instead of harbouring rancour. The first movement is contagious—aggressiveness arouses aggressiveness. But the second movement can also be contagious—love awakens love in response.

It is never possible, however, to pass from the first movement to the second without a struggle, sometimes a very hard one. Every course of psychological treatment leads sooner or later to a battle of this kind. We remove many of the obstacles that are preventing a patient from developing his full potentialities; but then he sees that there are others that cannot be removed. By means of psychoanalysis we unmask many false forgivenesses, false loves, and false renunciations; but after that the patient finds himself facing real problems which can be solved only through true forgiveness and true renunciation. We help him to win back his capacity for enjoyment and the satisfaction of his desires; but after that he finds that many of his desires will always remain unsatisfied. And perhaps he will realize that the worst obstacle to real self-fulfilment is in himself, in this very resistance against letting go of anything. My colleagues, even the Freudians, are no more indifferent witnesses of these battles than I am, though they may put rather a different interpretation upon them. They know well that a lasting cure will require many renunciations which will be far from easy!

Then, looking back, one has a better understanding of the significance of the first movement: one was concerned, of course, to liberate the patient from a painful symptom or to rescue him from a particularly morbid state, but there was more in it than that. It was

a matter also of preparing the patient to come to the second movement in the most favourable possible conditions. With the aid of
technical medicine we bring him to the threshold of health, to the
frontier, then, of a new domain which is no longer that of Nature
and of medicine, but of the spiritual life and the healing of souls. It
is in our bringing him to this frontier that I see the respective vocations of the theologian and the doctor working together. It is always
the second movement, the movement of love, that is the more
human and the more decisive of the two. We, as doctors, help a
patient to make the first movement, in order to make the second
possible. But what is the use of the first, if the second does not follow it? What is the good of healing if the person does not use his
new health to live fully? I think, therefore, that we can define the
mission of the doctor in the way John the Baptist defined his: to
"make straight the way of the Lord" (John 1.23).

The first movement is not an end in itself; it is a beginning. There
are two sides to every illness, permanently connected with each
other, yet distinct; and each has its unknown element and its risk:
"Will he get better or not?" and "Will he find the answer to the
problem of life, or not?" Health is not the supreme good. I have
already written this elsewhere, but rather tentatively, for fear of
being accused of not being enough of a doctor, or for fear of people
saying that it is easy enough to say when one is young and well.
Now that I am getting old, and have passed through a serious illness,
I can say it more boldly. What, then, is the supreme good?

It cannot be only health, self-fulfilment, satisfaction of one's
desires and instincts, because all these have their limits—the more
so as old age comes on. That is what Jesus explained to the old
teacher Nicodemus. He told him about a new world, of which he
knew nothing, the world of the Spirit into which he must be born.
Nicodemus was no neurotic. He had been able to assert himself; he
had succeeded; he was a man of great influence. He had no need of
a psychotherapist. He was in fact a man of considerable independence of mind; alone among all the important people of the nation
he had been able to recognize the worth of Jesus. After the cruci-
fixion he was to help Joseph of Arimathaea to embalm his body. At
the time of their first meeting he took precautions: he came to see
Jesus by night. But he made his affirmation unambiguously: "We
know that you are a teacher come from God" (John 3.2).

He had, therefore, made his first movement. He had acquired

knowledge and wisdom, maturity and success. He had a place. Jesus, in a manner of speaking, asked him to leave his place, to give up his dependence upon his learning, even his theological learning. He spoke to him about becoming quite naked, fragile, and dependent again, like a new-born-babe, about being "born anew". He forced him to admit that there were some things he did not know or understand, things which were not taught, but could be learned only from experience, and which Jesus called the Kingdom of God: "Are you a teacher of Israel, and yet you do not understand this?" (John 3.10).

Once more we have the alternating rhythm—finding one's place, then leaving it. The rich man was asked by Jesus to give up his riches. The teacher Nicodemus was invited to become a student again. St. Paul, for his part, spoke of putting on the new nature; but he had certainly asserted himself first in the "old nature" (Col. 3.9–10). He had not concealed his convictions, he had fought, he had whole-heartedly persecuted the first Christians. Yes, he had certainly had a place: the sect of the Pharisees, with all their devotion to God. But on the Damascus road Jesus called on him to give up that place *par excellence*, the piety of the Pharisees, a veritable religious fortress, in order to commit him to the extraordinary adventure of liberty, in which he would depend only on the person of Jesus Christ himself (Acts 9.1–9).

What I wish to stress here is that the second movement in St. Paul's case, his self-abandonment to Christ, his identification with Christ (Gal. 2.20), and the preaching of salvation by grace which was to be the chief message of his apostolate, was all the more fruitful because his first movement had been sincere in its fervent attempt to approach God through obedience to the law. He was able to oppose grace to law with all the more conviction because he had once taken the law seriously. There, too, is a double movement. To men like Nicodemus and St. Paul, men of high wisdom and high morality, Jesus reveals that there is something greater than all the wisdom and all the morality that can be acquired in this world. The call to renunciation is addressed to those who are developed and able to defend themselves, not to the weak.

The first movement is receiving something, acquiring something. But no one can go on receiving and acquiring indefinitely. And even if a man receives beyond his expectations, he has not yet had the fundamental experience of life, which is always of the order of the second movement. When he has received much, every man must come some day to the turning-point in his destiny when he must let go of what he has received, on pain of remaining its prisoner and becoming lost in it. This is what Jesus clearly says: "For what will it profit a man, if he gains the whole world and forfeits his life?" (Matt. 16.26); or again: "A man's life does not consist in the abundance of his possessions" (Luke 12.15). It is so obvious that everyone recognizes it, and it is witnessed to by many popular sayings.

The theatre and literature, both serious and humorous, have made great use of the theme of avarice, echoing the words of St. Paul: "The love of the money is the root of all evils" (I Tim. 6.10); echoing also the words of the Preacher, who had experienced all the vanities of this world: "He who loves money will not be satisfied with money ... When goods increase, they increase who eat them; and what gain has their owner ... ?" (Eccles. 5.10–11). Because he who seeks material goods always lacks something. And then anxiety accompanies possession like a shadow, since to possess something is to be fearful of losing it. The truth of this is sometimes confirmed in quite unexpected ways: I was speaking once on this theme of man's "place" in Helsinki, and there was present a Dutchman who had been taken prisoner by the Japanese during the war in Indonesia. I remember his emotion as he told me about it. And I remember too with what feeling he added: "You can't imagine the sense of freedom I had after they had taken from me everything I had."

However, losing a thing is not the same as letting go of it. Only rarely does mere reflection on the vanity of worldly goods lead a man to let them go. Proof of this is the fact that misers speak willingly and eloquently on the subject of this vanity, while at the same time it is extremely difficult to cure them of their avarice. To let go of what one is holding on to is no small matter. A country never lets anything go unless it is forced to do so by military defeat, or at least by powerful political pressure. And the same applies to every man. I myself need only to have fought a long battle in face of a particular renunciation which I felt called upon to make, in order to know how hard it is to let go. I need only to have watched, in my consulting-room or elsewhere, a similar battle being fought by a man who was passionately sincere with himself and in his search for the secret of life, in order to know how hard it is to let go.

Let go! The phrase may seem rather unscientific, but that is precisely why I choose to use it. "Sublimation" belongs to the jargon of psychology, and "renunciation" to that of theology. "Letting go" expresses both these ideas in common terms. It expresses the reality of people's lives. When a man comes to the threshold of the second movement, it always means that he has to let something go. The frustrated man, crushed by complexes, is not free, and we strive to free him. But the man who is full is not free either, if he cannot let go what he has received. We can all see that men and women have very little freedom. Some are the prisoners of their psychological inhibitions (indication: psychology), but the others are the prisoners of what they have received (indication: soul-healing). They are the prisoners of their past, of their upbringing, of their successes, of their ambition, of their prejudices, of their habits.

A certain pious young woman had been admirably brought up by her aged aunts whom she loved dearly. They were women of exemplary character, who returned her love wholeheartedly, and who also protected her, for she was very shy. Basically, she was happy with them, without really realizing that she had remained a child, that she had abdicated. Now her aunts were dead. This was a great grief to her, and also caused her some dismay. She told me of her scruples. Had she any right to depart from the austere way of life of which they had been such a fine example to her? I prepared myself to hear some quite revolutionary idea, as I asked her: "What is it in your life you would like to change?" "Oh," she answered, "I'd like to move some of the furniture round in the flat, and to get rid of some of it, because there's so much of it there you can hardly move."

Many other people are the prisoners of their furniture, even when they have acquired it and arranged it themselves, and of all sorts of other things they have acquired or made. Many are the prisoners of the place they occupy. I try to give my patients a place, to be a place for them. But there is also a risk that they will remain dependent upon me, and upon the place that they have found with me. This was very clear to me from the reaction of some of them when I had to suspend my consultations because of my illness. But several wrote to tell me that the experience had been a salutary one, since they saw that they could do without me, that they could live by themselves and find other supports, without thereby losing the fellowship they had with me.

All our patients, and particularly the more sensitive among them,

are a little afraid of becoming attached to us, for fear of not being
able to break away again. This is one of the effects of the vagabond
complex which I have described. They are vagabonds who, for
that reason, find it difficult to fit in, and who can never do so whole-
heartedly. There are some who struggle within themselves against
their need for attachment, forgetting that the very thing that leads
to successful detachment is successful attachment, and that unsuccessful attachment compromises detachment. These problems are
exacerbated by illness, but they are always present. Poor humans—
they find it so hard to attach themselves, and so hard to detach
themselves, they suffer every way!

That is the very rhythm of life. Every place we find must in the
end be relinquished, if it is not to become our prison. I was, for
example, describing earlier the difficulty through which a patient
passes at the beginning of an illness. For him it is not a matter only
of accepting a whole series of physical and spiritual sufferings, and
the more or less serious threat of death, but also of accepting the
loss of the familiar place represented for him by his life as a healthy
person. Each of us finds it hard to adapt himself to the new place of
sickness or infirmity.

It also happens, however, especially when the illness is prolonged, that the patient gets so used to this new place that he is
afraid to get well. Many are aware of this, and admit it. It is much
more serious when they do not realize it, since it may become an
obstacle to healing. To be healed is to accept another change of
place. It is scarcely less difficult to leave illness than to enter into it;
it is sometimes much harder. To get well is to lose the protection,
care, and support which one received as a sick person. To get well is
once more to face responsibilities, risks, and disappointments from
which one has been excused by illness; it means coming back to
all sorts of difficult problems to which one has been able to close
one's eyes during the illness.

So on the threshold of the second movement we always have to
face the necessity of letting go of something. And we were asking
ourselves, at the end of the last chapter, this question: what is it
that can make us let go? We have seen that merely reflecting on the
vanity of this world's goods rarely suffices, at least in our Western
civilization. An uneasy conscience is scarcely more effective. It can
make us give up a little of our superfluity, but not what we most
cleave to. Many who are rich, who know prosperity, who enjoy

privileges, have a bad conscience as a result—often unconsciously. Professor Baruk has written penetratingly on this subject.[1] This particular malaise has sometimes been termed a "Polycrates complex". Polycrates was Tyrant of the Isle of Samos, in ancient Greece. He was so powerful and wise, so fortunate in his undertakings, that he had given secure peace and prosperity to the island during the forty years of his reign.

Then he began to feel a disquiet: would not the gods be jealous of happiness so exceptional that man had no right to usurp it from them? Would they not punish him with some unforeseen catastrophe, which he wanted to ward off? So he chose his most beautiful jewel, a wonderful ring, and cast it into the sea as an expiatory offering. On the next day, however, he was served a fish to eat. And when he opened the fish, he found his ring inside it. The gods had not accepted his gift. The following year Samos was invaded, conquered, and destroyed, and Polycrates died in the battle. We have here, in this ancient story, a profound intuition of a sort of justice of fate, which implants anxiety in the hearts of those who are privileged, though it does not suffice to make them relinquish their privileges.

In one of his parables Jesus too tells of a man who had succeeded. His affairs had prospered so well that he was planning to demolish his barns and build bigger ones. "But God said to him, 'Fool! This night your soul is required of you; and the things you have prepared, whose will they be?'" (Luke 12.20). "God said to him"— that is specifically biblical. The God of the Bible is the God who speaks, the God who intervenes in the lives of men, who calls men, and sometimes drives them towards renunciation—genuine renunciation. That is what can make men let go: the voice of God. Take away from the story of Abraham the beginning of the sentence: "Now the Lord said to Abram ..." (Gen. 12.1), and Abraham is no more than an obscure adventurer who went back to the nomadic life of his distant ancestors. It is not because he left his place that he is the father of those who believe. It is because his departure was a "Yes!" in answer to God's call. Faced with such facts, the Freudian will talk of sublimation, the Jungian of the power of the archetypes, and an Adlerian of accepting our limitations and our inferiority. I do not contest these notions. I think they are all contained in a much simpler, more personal notion, that of the encounter with God.

[1] *Psychiatrie morale expérimentale.*

People call today for a dynamic psychology. Well, there it is! God is a force that man can encounter, and which can oblige man to let go of that which he would not, or could not let go. It is a force outside himself. It is the encounter with transcendence which Professor Karlfried von Dürckheim calls "the grand experience".[2] It is an opening on to a new dimension of life, in which one relies on the power of God more than on one's own efforts. One of my patients was fond of gliding, and saw in that sport an image of the experience of self-abandonment. For the pilot of a glider cannot send his plane upwards—he has no engine that would pull him up. He can only steer it to where there are ascending currents which will carry it upwards silently and gently.

I spoke above of the patient who, after a long silence, suddenly put a direct and specific question to me: "In your opinion what is the meaning of self-denial?" "It means," I replied, "giving up the directing of one's own life, stopping trying to push it along oneself." That is renunciation, of course, but not impoverishment. It is renunciation for love, and not for fear. It is not denying oneself fulfilment, but giving up depending on oneself to attain it.

As we have just seen, this abandonment brings in its turn a new fulfilment, much greater than that which comes of receiving only, of acquiring and possessing. One thing, however, must be carefully noted: it is only afterwards that one realizes that one has gained more than one has lost in the renunciation that is made in faith. Before the renunciation, we see only what we have to let go: a grudge, security, a possession, a child who has become adult, or who is getting married, or who wants to enter upon the religious life; or perhaps it is a claim, an unsatisfied desire, a disappointed ambition, some little thing we are passionately fond of; or perhaps a jealousy, an impossible or guilty love, an intellectual objection to faith, or one's claim to live one's life as one chooses.

We feel that there is something there that we must let go, and we resist the inner call to do so. I have very often been an observer during moral battles of this sort, and have always been intensely moved by them. What a man may gain by the renunciation facing him is scarcely ever apparent to him. He sees only what he is going to lose by it, something he feels it almost impossible to give up. When the renunciation takes place, one is well aware that it is not

[2] K. von Dürckheim, *Im Zeichen der grossen Erfahrung*, Wilhelm Barth, Weilheim, Upper Bavaria, 1958.

a natural movement, but that a power from outside has intervened, and that it comes neither from that man, nor from the doctor, but from God.

Such a man will say afterwards that he has made a great leap in the dark, that he has let himself go without knowing where he would land, and that he has landed in the arms of God. He will compare his act of self-abandon to the plunge made by the novice swimmer, who suddenly dives in after a long hesitation at the end of the diving-board. An excellent image, I am sure! But we must not forget that it was Satan, and not God, who invited Jesus to throw himself down from the pinnacle of the Temple in Jerusalem, relying upon the angels to bear him up (Luke 4.9–10). Of course, Satan himself can cunningly use this biblical incident to hold back our hesitating diver. Is it really God who is asking him to jump?

How difficult it is to see the way clearly. That man whose confidant I am would very much like me to settle his doubts, and tell him whether he really ought to renounce what he is thinking of renouncing. That may sometimes be the role of the spiritual director, but not that of a doctor. And that is a great relief to me, since it is already difficult enough to judge for myself what I myself ought to give up, and it seems to me to be even more difficult to decide for some one else. The "letting go" therefore seems to me to be a strictly personal matter. A man, for instance, wonders if he ought to give up an improper love affair, "let his mistress go" in order to save his marriage. If I started thinking that he ought to do so, I should be falling into that very sin of judging others which Jesus Christ explicitly urges me to renounce. What do I know about it? Do I know that now is the right moment? Would it perhaps be premature? That man may be only at the first movement, not yet mature enough for an authentic second movement. God alone knows the times he has laid down. There are perhaps very noble motives stopping him from letting go. He would consider it iniquitous, he says, that he should save himself at the cost of his abandoned mistress.

I could also think that the man who hesitates to "let go" of his mistress has remained very childish, that his mistress is a sort of baby's dummy which he cannot do without. In that case I should still be pronouncing a mental judgement upon him, not a moral one this time, but a psychological one. And he would also feel himself to be judged, even if I did not say what I was thinking. You see that the psychotherapist has a problem of "letting go", as well as his patient. His task is to give up all pretension to direct the person who has come to him for help. He must adopt a non-directive attitude towards him. Even more: not only must he renounce telling him what he ought to do and when he ought to do it, but he must also give up thinking it, imagining it, and considering himself capable of forming a judgement about it.

The thing that can free us from any preconceived idea as to the path that others ought to follow, is precisely the conviction that an authentic abandonment can never be imposed from without, that it has value only if it is spontaneous, if it comes from the heart, from an inner conviction, a free decision. This is what I call the power of God. People may, indeed, not attribute it to God. They will say it is their conscience, their moral code, or "being true to themselves". But they always feel it as an imperious inner force which overrules their will. It is indeed, then, a call from the Spirit, a spiritual movement, an intervention by God.

Think, for example, of drunkards who have given up drinking. In the last century a Genevan pastor, Louis Lucien Rochat, founded the Blue Cross organization, which has rescued a large number of these drunkards. They sustained each other in their resolution to abstain, by means of fervent witness borne to the power of Jesus Christ who had snatched them from the slavery of alcoholism. When I was a young houseman at the Policlinique my teacher, who maintained considerable reserve as to his personal beliefs, never failed to send an alcoholic to the Blue Cross, saying that that was his only chance of salvation.

He might also have mentioned the Salvation Army, which has a very great number of successes to its credit, and which achieves them by expressly leading those whom it helps to a personal encounter with Jesus Christ. Today the "Alcoholics Anonymous" movement, which originated in America, is also working wonders in this field. The language is less religious, but the facts remain the same: it is always divine power that helps the victim to overcome a seductive power as strong as that of alcohol. It is the power of God, incarnate in the fraternal, fervent, and welcoming spirit, free of all moral condemnation, which the drunkard finds in such a community.

Nevertheless, I must say that I have sometimes felt uneasy when listening, in the Blue Cross or elsewhere, to people witnessing to the liberation they had experienced twenty or thirty years previously, or even more. Their sincerity is magnificent, and their words may well touch some hearer and bring him to self-examination and a desire to undergo a similar experience. That is of course what matters, and yet the repetition over the years of a particular piece of witness leaves an impression of stagnation. I have felt it sometimes when listening to a "convert". He has made that great leap of faith of which we were speaking just now, as a result of coming into contact with a priest, a pastor, or a friend. He has passed from atheism to faith, or from one church to another, or from one of the traditional churches to a more lively religious movement. Boldly, courageously, and with conviction he has let go of the philosophy of life in which he had been brought up. Often he looks back gratefully upon the time when a powerful impulse of the Holy Spirit snatched him from his past and thrust him into adventure.

He is proud of having found the truth, and would like everybody to find it as well. In his testimony he takes himself as an example as if everyone must travel the same road. But that road, that experience, is really his past; even perhaps a rather distant past. It is not, of course, that he must deny the past, or its truth, but he must not remain, as it were, immobilized in his past, for that would be the opposite of faith. Such a convert is also in danger of remaining dependent upon the person who has helped him to make his great leap, and whose spiritual stature he looks upon as an ideal beyond which it would be impossible to grow. It is, then, even our most precious treasures that we may be called upon to let go, even our most significant religious experiences, so that we may be set free for fresh experiences. I have just met in the street one of my former patients, a lady whom I had not seen for several years. She accosted me eagerly, before I could get a word in: "Ah!" she said, "I have often thought about a remark you once made. You said I was a spiritual glutton. I didn't understand what you meant at the time, but I've realized since then. Life has forced me to let go of a lot of my treasures, and that is what has enabled me to make progress." After a moment's silence she added thoughtfully: "How does one learn to let go?"

It is now possible to see what another of my patients meant when she made this striking observation: "People are always the prisoners of their liberators." Let us look once more at the example of the psychoanalyst whom I mentioned above, who had himself been brought up in a narrow moralism from which he had been liberated by a course of psychoanalysis. That had indeed been a spiritual experience for him, the discovery of a vital truth. That is why he became a psychoanalyst himself, and now devotes himself tirelessly to helping other people to take the same road in their turn. Nevertheless, without realizing it he is now in danger of stopping in his development at the stage he once reached as a result of his experience, he is in danger of being to some extent the prisoner of his psychoanalytical doctrine, that is to say the prisoner of the conception of life it involves. It deals adequately with one aspect of life—but there are many others. Who can tell whether one day he may not be called upon to undergo a new and unexpected experience, an act of faith, which has had no place in his system of thought?

Clearly, whether they have been converted to a religious faith or to psychoanalysis, or to any other dynamic ideology, men and women are always impelled to try and make other people take the same road as they have followed themselves. What was a spontaneous act of life soon becomes a doctrine which is taught as if it were the sole truth. This is the source of all proselytizing, behind which there is always a kind of spiritual imperialism. The ceaseless movement of life is arrested, caught in a past that has gone.

Life and faith always insist on moving forward; and I cannot move forward without leaving something behind. Possibly the most difficult to let go are the treasures of painful experiences. For example, a man has had a wonderful married life. Love, mutual confidence and spiritual fellowship were all one between him and his wife. He could tell her everything, and she had no secrets from him. The relationship of truth stood up to the hard test of the long illness which took his wife from him, whereas in so many other cases husband and wife begin to lie to each other as death approaches. These two were able to face this misfortune, both well aware of the fate that awaited them, and sustained by their faith, more united than ever.

It was an extremely painful experience, but precious too, and one that the widowed husband now treasures. Now he realizes that he must not remain fixed in the past, however wonderful it may have been. That would be to interrupt the movement of life like a stopped clock. He will be really faithful to his departed wife if he keeps going ahead just as she would have done herself if she had been there at his side. Then he meets some friends with whom he shares a common faith. He talks it over with them. One of them has lost a son in the prime of a life full of promise. Another has lost a much loved daughter in tragic circumstances. The grief caused by such losses is never effaced: they must be borne in the heart day by day. But they, too, see that they must turn resolutely towards the future, in spite of everything. It is not that they have to forget the past, and even less to disown it, but to use it as the spring-board for a leap forward towards new experiences. There are so many people who live only on memories! They turn their houses into museums; they interest themselves only in the things that interested the person who has died; they go only to the places they used to visit together; they are the prisoners of a past of which they cannot let go.

PART THREE

Support

11

The Middle of the Way

WE ARE NOT yet done with this psychological study of "letting go". We have just been wondering what can make a man decide to let go of something by which he sets great store. We must now ask what it is that holds him back and stops him letting go. It is something very powerful. I have seen people sitting in my consulting room for a whole hour, as if turned to stone, incapable of action, as they face giving up something they feel they have to give up. Others are plunged into a state of extreme agitation, and some break out into great beads of perspiration.

A woman had an affair with a remarkable man. It lasted for years and was very happy. At first she hoped to marry him, but she soon realized that that would not be possible. It was she who courageously decided to break off the association, after many struggles within herself. She has no illusions about the affair, and would not even want to try to resume a hopeless relationship with him. But she has kept a bundle of letters, and from time to time she reads them again, and weeps over them. She knows very well that it is unhealthy to remain fixed in the past in this way, and that she ought to "let go" of the bundle of letters. She hopes perhaps that I will say to her: "Bring them here, and we'll burn them together," and so spare her a personal decision. What a struggle!

It is never an easy matter to let anything go, even less precious things than those letters. Why is it so hard to "let go"? What makes us hang on to familiar things despite all our aspirations towards freedom? I am willing to accept that this possessive reflex is connected, as the Freudians maintain, with the oral stage of infancy, that it is an infantile inclusion which we have not succeeded in growing out of. But there must be more in it than that.

Once again it was a remark made by one of my patients which set me thinking along certain lines, and I must give you a few details concerning the patient so that you may understand why her remark struck me so forcibly. She suffered from an anxiety neurosis of an agoraphobic type. This is known to be a disease of a particularly distressing and tenacious kind. It can occur suddenly, following an intense emotional shock. It is still more serious when it insidiously grows in a person's mind, when it reveals a more profound underlying anxiety. At first it may be nothing more than a slight feeling of unease when the patient crosses a rather wide open space, and then when he merely crosses a street. He becomes dependent on others, and gradually has to give up entirely going out alone because of his anxiety. He invents various methods of trying to get rid of his feeling, and becomes the prisoner of these procedures. Anxiety, and the fear of anxiety, fill his mind and obsess it.

My patient was a very intelligent woman, of strong character and high moral standards. She had struggled on her own for years trying to overcome her anxiety. This kind of anxiety, however, is quite beyond the reach of will-power and reason. And the humiliating and despairing feeling of impotence that results only aggravates the anxiety. This woman had come to the point of being afraid to venture even to a shop just along the same side of the street as her house. Naturally she was unable to come and see me in Geneva without being driven here by her husband in his car, and not without suffering considerable anxiety on the way.

She knew nothing about me, had read none of my books, and had only heard my name mentioned once before, a long time ago. Nevertheless, my name had suddenly come into her mind one day. She was in Geneva with her husband. After they had done some shopping, her husband asked her: "What would you like to do now?" "I want to see Dr. Tournier." "Who's Dr. Tournier?" "I don't know. I don't even know whether he's still alive, but I'd like to see him." They inquired at a chemist's shop, and arrived at my house. I was very busy just then, but my wife, who has a keen intuition and who had opened the door to them, said to me: "I think you ought to see this woman." And so there we were, committed to a difficult course of treatment.

In the course of this kind of treatment we talk very little with the patient about his feelings of anxiety. What we have to do is by talking with the patient to reveal their original source. We must try to understand the whole development of the patient's life, and especially that of his childhood. Nevertheless, one day when her condition seemed to have improved, I asked her about it. She answered, somewhat vaguely, that she was suffering less anxiety. I tried to get her to be more precise: "On the way here in the car today, were you less anxious?" "Oh," she replied, "at the beginning it's all right; and at the end it's all right; but in the middle I still feel anxiety."

That was the remark that struck me. An apparently ordinary remark, which any agoraphobia sufferer might make. But it is doubtless for that very reason that it struck me, because it expresses a universal truth, which has an application far beyond the case of agoraphobia, as we shall see. My patient, moreover, had made it more concrete by talking about the actual figures in kilometres of the various stages of her journey. I cannot quote the figures here, since some reader could then guess what town she lived in. But let us suppose that it was two hundred and twenty kilometres from Geneva. She would then have said: "The first hundred kilometres are all right; the last hundred are all right; but in between there are twenty kilometres during which the anxiety reappears."

"My husband senses it at once," she added, "and he puts his hand gently on my knee, without slowing down, and holding the steering-wheel with the other hand." An intelligent husband, that! No exhortations, no talk, no humiliating manifestations of sympathy, but just a discreet gesture to show his wife that he had understood, and to bring her a little security. I, too, understood: the hundred kilometres at the start, and the hundred at the end that were all right, and the anxiety in the middle of the journey! I sensed what was happening.

At the start, she was still leaning for support on the place she had just left, her familiar place, the town where she lived and worked. At the end she was leaning on the place she was going to, Geneva, my fireside, my understanding. But in the middle of the journey, there was a period when she was between two supports, having lost the first, and not yet having found the second.

This was, in fact, the case when she had to cross a square or a street. At the beginning she leaned on the security she had just left. At the end, she was already approaching the other side where she would find another security. But in the middle there was a neutral point which had to be crossed without support. You may observe every day, in city traffic, pedestrians who, without being ill, experience an analogous anxiety. The motorist curses the pedestrian who panics half-way across and hesitates instead of continuing calmly on his way. At the beginning he could still have jumped back if the discourteous motorist had been determined to get by; at the end he would quicken his pace in order to reach the footpath on the other side. But in the middle there is a zone where his instinct of self-preservation fails, where it destroys him instead of saving him.

While my patient was describing her anxiety in the middle of the journey, it occurred to me that it was as if the first part had to be covered in a rear-wheel-drive car, and the last part by means of front-wheel-drive. In the middle it would be necessary to alter the car. The back wheels would no longer drive it, and the front ones would not yet be able to pull it, and so the car would remain standing still, paralysed and inert. These things are well known; I certainly knew them already. But that patient's description helped me to grasp them much more clearly, perhaps because it fitted in with the problem of man's place, which was so much in my mind. There is a place that must be left before we can find a new place, and in between there is a place without a place, a place without support, a place which is not a place, since a true place is a support.

This reminds one of course of the well-known experimental neuroses of Pavlov. The famous Russian physiologist brought about a conditioned reflex in a dog, for example, by ringing a bell every time he brought it its food. If one does this for a sufficiently long time, eventually it will only need the ringing of the bell for the dog to start to salivate, even when no food is brought. The conditioned reflex is established. This reflex is extremely specific: if a different bell is rung, no salivation takes place.

But between one bell and another there is a whole gamut of possible bells with intermediate sounds. To one whose sound is very close to that of the first, the dog responds with salivation. To another that is very similar to the second bell, it remains indifferent. But on the boundary half-way between the two there is a zone of uncertainty. The dog's mind does not know whether it ought to order the salivary glands to function or not. And the reaction of the dog in this state of uncertainty is anxiety. It becomes agitated, it barks, it is anxious.

These are classic experiments. They demonstrate quite convincingly that anxiety is the manifestation of hesitation in the mind over what behaviour to adopt. And all our observations of our patients bear this interpretation out. All our patients are people with minds divided and hesitating between two contrary tendencies. So long as a man has only one quite clear rule of conduct, in which he fully believes, to follow, he feels no anxiety, even if the rule of conduct is a false one. But if he comes to doubt, if he is no longer certain that it is right, without being convinced that some other rule is better, then he suffers anxiety.

That, I think, is why so many people show themselves so intransigent in their opinions. They put forward their concept of life as a coherent, absolute, indubitable system, when all the problems of existence are so complex. They rush to refute the slightest objection with an energy that aims to be unanswerable. In this way they protect themselves against the unease of a more moderate, wiser, and more subtly balanced position, which would be charged with middle-of-the-way anxiety.

Conversation between them, too, is usually difficult, since each defends himself against the risk of being shaken in his beliefs. It is a dialogue between deaf people, in which each firmly retains his own position, without there being any possibility of a real exchange of ideas. An anxious, uncertain person feels himself falling between the two stools represented by incompatible points of view. Think of all the dilemmas to which I have referred in my chapter on the two gospels. Ought he to give in and sacrifice himself, as he has been taught to do, forgetting himself and refusing to defend himself? Or ought he to assert himself, defend himself, voice his complaints, as his psychological treatment suggests?

In the middle of the way there is a zone of uncertainty in which the mind is divided between two contradictory suggestions. This explains why in every psychotherapeutic cure there is a critical period during which the anxiety increases, before it diminishes. The patient is shaken in his former views before he has adopted fresh ones, and is more divided than ever within himself. But he will have come to the psychologist because he is already ill, already divided. He was not as firmly installed as he thought in the place where he was brought up—the realm of abnegation and non-resistance. Quite possibly the reason for his anxiety was that, without being fully aware of it, he sensed that the normal demands of life were already calling upon him to defend and assert himself, before the psychologist suggested that he should do so. It is all this latent inner conflict that a course of psychological treatment will bring out into the light of day. Will the patient be able to bear having his outlook on life called in question? If the psychoanalyst has doubts on this score, he will carefully refrain from instituting a too rigorous course of treatment.

So there is always in life a place to leave and a new place to find, and in between a zone of hesitation and uncertainty tinged with more or less intense anxiety. If the division in the mind is violent, it can take on the dimension of a disease, in the form of an anxiety neurosis. But this is only a more dramatic paroxysm of a tension that is inescapably present in all of us, and which shows itself at every critical turning-point in our lives. There is a past security to be lost before we find a new security. No security lasts, however solid, just, or precious. For it is a law of evolution that tomorrow will not be the same as yesterday, and that there results from that difference the anxiety of today, since each moment is a middle zone between the past and the future.

My patient's account of her journey was an illustration of this. I could see in it the universal and perpetual motion of life, in which one place must always be relinquished before another is found. The rhythm of life goes on, carrying us along with it. It does not stop to wait for us. I thought of the trapeze artists, swinging on their trapezes high up under the dome of the circus tent. They must let go of one trapeze just at the right moment, to hover for a moment in the void before catching hold of the other trapeze. As you watch, you identify yourself with them, and experience the anxiety of the middle of the way, when they have let go of their first support and have not yet seized the second.

It seems to me that we have there a picture of life. You see how our problem of places is enlarging now, and also becoming clearer. At bottom it is a problem of support. We cannot live without support, but we must always be letting go of our support under pain of being left behind by the current of life, holding back instead of thrusting forward to grasp a new support. And always, in between, there is a zone of anxiety to be crossed.

I think that is the answer to the question we were asking: what is the force that holds men back, which prevents them from letting go of what they would like to let go? It is the middle-of-the-way anxiety. It is the deprivation, the void in which they are going to find themselves before being able to seize a new support. It is what stops a young woman, for example, from breaking off an unsatisfying amorous association. She says to herself that it is her fear of finding herself alone again. She knows quite well that she must face up to this period of void in order to become free and ready for a new love. But anxiety holds her back, and she hangs on to her disappointing lover.

This is also the explanation of the critical situation I described in Chapter 4. When the environment of our lives changes, when the evolution of society is rapid, we find ourselves in a "middle of the way" between the ideas and customs of the past, and the ideas and customs of the future, and this situation is charged with anxiety. Moreover, the whole of life may be looked upon as a "middle of the way" between antenatal security and the security of heaven, between the maternal bosom and that of God. In between there is necessarily anxiety. The existentialist psychoanalysts, such as Caruso[1] and Daim[2], have emphasized this clearly. Man lives under a constant threat.

However, the law we discovered in regard to man's place remains true: one must first have a place in order to be able to leave it. In the same way, one must first have a support in order to be able to jump. One cannot jump without a spring-board or some solid support from which to take off. One must start from a strong support in order to make a successful jump—even to risk a jump at all. The trapeze artist must first have a firm grip on his trapeze before he lets go of it. He must be able to handle it skilfully and easily; he must be sure of himself. Then he can make the jump. It is obvious, then, how wrong it is to urge the self-abandonment of faith upon a person who has had no human support. One is trying to get him to let go of the precarious support to which he is clinging, and he clings to it just because it is precarious and does not give him the security he needs before he can jump.

The person who has had the benefit of a solid support in childhood from which to launch out into life, will have no difficulty in letting go of that support, and in finding fresh support somewhere else, and living like that, lightly moving from support to support like the trapeze artist flying from trapeze to trapeze. Yes, life is very

[1] Igor Caruso, *Existential Psychology from Analysis to Synthesis*, translated by Eva Krapf, Darton, Longman and Todd, London, 1964.

[2] Wilfried Daim, *Die Umwertung der Psychoanalyse*, Herold, Vienna, 1951.

like a trapeze artist's act. Life never stops. One can never settle down in it. They say that to depart is to die a little. But to stay is also to die a little. It is to remain attached to one's trapeze instead of jumping as life calls us to do.

We must always be letting go what we have acquired, and acquiring what we did not possess, leaving one place in order to find another, abandoning one support in order to reach another, turning our backs on the past in order to thrust wholeheartedly towards the future. I have even seen many people so accustomed to misfortune that they could not believe in good fortune when it came. Suffering was their place, and they could not leave it without experiencing such distress that it spoilt their happiness.

So there is always something to let go, health or sickness, wealth or poverty, good fortune or bad, pride or humility, excitement or monotony, obstinacy or capitulation, fears or whims, solitary inactivity or violent activity. We must even be ready to let go of our good qualities and merits, and that is not easy.

A certain man had suffered much from poverty and social disapproval in his childhood. His father had gone bankrupt. And so he swore to succeed in life. He worked unremittingly. He pursued university studies while at the same time earning his living. He succeeded. He obtained a good post, which allowed him sufficient leisure to enjoy life a little. But he was the prisoner of his success. He did not know how to do anything else but work, and his wife was bored to tears at his side.

And so, when a man hesitates in my consulting-room when he is faced with the need to give something up, I understand what it is that is stopping him: it is not only an instinctive attachment to his old habits, and his fear of losing the familiar place which lent him support. It is also a presentiment of that middle-of-the-way anxiety. Later on he will find a new stability that will be much happier than his present state, as he well knows. But first he must cross that painful supportless zone. In the same way the sufferer from agoraphobia remains fixed to his footway. He could indeed take a few paces, but he feels that half-way across anxiety will appear, more than he can bear.

One patient told me, for example, that she had great trouble in tidying her house, because she could hardly bear to throw anything away. She felt as if she were tearing away a bit of herself and losing it. This is a feeling which may become more acute in the case of a person who is ill, but which is no doubt more widespread than is usually thought. Everybody keeps quantities of useless things. Of course there are some who are more conservative than others, but it is probable that the need to keep everything is a measure of the deep and hidden anxiety in the mind. I am a great hoarder of things. Of course, all the bits of cardboard, leather, iron, electric wire or other hardware that I keep may be useful one day for some little repair job. But there is more behind it than this utilitarian reason. I feel that there is something irrational about it, almost an instinct, a need to retain the support that is constituted by the thousand and one things of our existence.

My patient also experienced the anxiety of the passage of time, the anxiety of knowing that each minute that goes by is swallowed up into a past that will never return. She perceived there, quite consciously, a feeling that I believe is present at the back of every person's mind, but which only just breaks through to the surface of consciousness at certain moments, wrapped in mists into which he may quickly repress it in order to escape the vertigo it causes. But the impression may arise once more in a dream, when he feels he is being rushed along in a mad race that is inescapable and endless.

The analogy of the trapeze artists can teach us something more in our study of "letting go". They set themselves swinging on their trapezes, and you know well that this is essential for the successful performance of their act. Letting go of a motionless trapeze would result in a vertical drop. Only in the full swing of the trapeze can the performer let go of his support and then describe an elegant curve through the air. It is the same with life. It is very dangerous to let go of one's support if life is at a halt, whereas when life is in full swing one can easily let go of it in order to leap forward.

I have just had a letter from an old lady who has suffered a lot. Her husband was persecuted by the Nazis, and died in a concentration-camp. She has no children. Her only support was her flat, where she had all the things that reminded her of her happy years of long ago. In order to be nearer her friends she left her flat, and left the town without suspecting that this exile would plunge her into acute distress. The swing of her life was too weak for her to be able to stand letting go of her support.

An aged relative of mine broke his thigh. Naturally I had him taken to hospital at once. During the first few days there was talk of putting a pin in the femur. But he fell into such a rapid decline that the surgeon soon discreetly withdrew. The patient did not die of the fracture, nor from the immobilization of the leg, which was quickly done. He died because he had been taken out of his usual surroundings; he had been removed from his place at a time when he had not sufficient vital resources to enable him to catch hold of another trapeze.

There are people who have never cast off and launched out into the current of society, but drag along, scarcely moving. Do not ask them to let go of the supoort to which they cling, and launch out into life. They would sink into the depths. This is a problem about which I often have to speak frankly to lonely people who suffer from too much dependence on me. It is evident that I enjoy a liberty which they do not. My life is overflowing, I am made much of by everyone, esteemed, complimented, with friends everywhere, and firm affections. And then I am interested in everything, in science and technology, in history and literature, in painting and music, as much as in medicine, psychology, and theology. I have not only one trapeze. I have hardly let go of one when I find another. I swing from my consulting-room into a lecture-tour or into writing a book. And I have no sooner finished one book than I am thinking about another.

That, at least, was the case a few months ago. I was carried along and upheld by the current of active life which is symbolized by the swinging of the trapezes. But today, I am coming home from convalescing after a long break, and I am beginning to give a few consultations, in small doses. I find myself half-way between sickness and health, and I do indeed feel the unease, not to say the anxiety, of this ambiguous situation. Just a few weeks ago I was convalescing in Malaga. My life was divided, without any problem, between walks with my wife, reading, little games, and the few hours when I settled quietly down to writing this book.

Now I am no longer ill enough to refuse to give consultations, and not yet well enough to give them on the scale I did before, so that each consultation is a disappointment both to my patient and to me. I have to face once more a problem which in general can only be avoided in illness, a problem which faces everybody all the time, and which nobody ever satisfactorily resolves—I mean the problem of the organization and allocation of one's time. But previously, in default of considered choices, I was swept along in the rush of my multiple activity, I leapt from trapeze to trapeze, and scarcely felt the menace of the void. In this way I was able to leap over problems which, now that the flow of activity had been stopped, I must face.

I know, too, that that rather deceptive rush of activity will never come back as it was before. I shall have increasingly to choose, to refuse appointments and the requests I got to give lectures or write articles, which were the trapezes on to which I held as I went along. As it happens, either by nature, or as a result of some complex, I find it more difficult to refuse a request than to grant it. I shall have to get used to a different rhythm of life, in a new place, different from the old one, which will constantly be changing. In between there comes that middle-of-the-way anxiety, and the difficulty one always has to get moving again once one has been stopped. I have seen many people coming to this critical point, when they have suddenly been brought to a halt by illness or by reaching retiring age, or even more gradually, through failing strength, and I know that they have found it much more difficult than they had imagined it would be.

In these circumstances what can I make my support as I start off once more? What can I use as a thread to guide me forward through the darkness of this moment? I need a sort of radar that would enable me to take off and land blind. That radar, I think, is my conviction that God has a purpose for me, a purpose for each one of us, and at every moment of our lives. I believe that God can lead me, even when I cannot yet see the road clearly in front of me. I believe that my illness is not fortuitous, but a part of God's purpose, and that all the problems it raises are opportunities to learn something about him, to undergo new experiences under his guidance.

What I must do, therefore, is to go to him quietly and ask him to speak to me, and show me moment by moment what he expects of me. I know very well that he never asks of us more than one thing at a time, and that it is this simplicity in what God wills that can deliver us from our ambiguity. If I really seek to do his will, I can cast on him all the cares I have about the other things I cannot do.

But God does not want me to remain alone in seeking his will. I must therefore pray in company with my wife; together we must go to him and listen to what he says to us. This is all the more important in view of the fact that when illness touches a man it upsets his whole environment—that is to say, the organization of his family life. It often affects those around him more than the patient himself, whose course of action is dictated by the doctor's instructions. I am well aware, however, that I am not as keen as I ought to be on this search together for God's will. What is it I am afraid of? Is it not that my wife will hold me back too much in the process of taking up my work again, because she is worried about my health? Is it not even more that God himself will demand sacrifices? Which patients am I most loath to give up? Without doubt, those who tire me most! Ah—there we are once more with the problem of "letting go"! It is no easier for me to let go than it is for all those who come to consult me. Is it not very often the fear of having to let go something that holds us back from honest prayer and meditation? God leads us only when we are really ready to let go.

My student friend is going to say now that my book is turning into a sermon about God's purpose, as I told you at the beginning of Chapter 6 he did about my previous book. Other readers will think, like him, that it is annoying to appeal now to a religious idea such as that of God's purpose, in a research that is of interest to all, whether or not they are believers. It is quite necessary, however, for me to say how the matter presents itself to my mind. And I do not see that to present it in a non-religious manner would make any difference. The important thing is to find out what is the right thing to do, the thing that fits in with the universal order of the world. The important thing is to find, not just any place, but my proper place at this moment.

Now at last our problem of man's place, which we have been studying throughout this book, finds its true significance. The important thing for every man is not only to find a place, but to find his own true place, the one God wills for him. I believe that all of us sense that this is so, and that that is what gives our search its importance, its emotional overtones, and even its anxiety. We may well avoid expressing it in religious terms. But we all know from experience that neither instinct nor reason is sufficient to enlighten us.

Consciously or not, we are all seeking, not only a place in the world, but our place before God. Those who hesitate to say so clearly are possibly people who are in fact in between. There are so many in the middle of the way between faith and unbelief. Certain experiences, certain injuries, certain disappointments, have led them to reject the religious formulae they have been taught. But they have no other, unless it is to declare life to be absurd, and all human problems absurd also. So they hold cautiously to the middle of the road. But between faith and unbelief there is necessarily the anxiety of the middle of the way.

That anxiety was expressed in a dream one of my patients had. She had been brought up in a disunited home, and had suffered acutely from the incessant quarrelling of her parents. As the latter belonged to different religious denominations, there were constant arguments about religion between them. Of course this was not the basic cause of the mutual personal hostility, but it was an easy channel of expression for it. The result was that when the daughter reached adolescence she resolutely turned her back on religion, and became a convinced atheist. But doubtless her unconscious was less sure, as the dream in question showed.

In her dream she had an appointment with God. She went to an old and beautiful church. The main door was closed. There were two little doors, one on each side. She went to the right-hand door, and gave her name to a verger who said to her: "Ah! You have an appointment with God? You realize you will have to sing?" She was worried, and asked: "What does one have to sing?" And the verger replied: "Nobody knows what has to be sung." When she told me the dream I was delighted with that reply. It seems to me to express the whole difficulty of the religious problem. Truly, nobody knows what has to be sung! Nobody knows what to do in God's presence; and if one knew, God would not come into it any more! And yet one must sing: our dreamer wanted to go back home so that she could at any rate get a song-book. But the verger pressed her to go in: "Hurry up! You'll be late for your appointment!"

She went in. She saw an immense crowd of people dressed in grey and brown, impassible, impersonal, and sad. She could find no room for herself among them, and none of them offered her a place. Then she heard a voice: "Your place is not here. It is over there in the choir, in that group of people in white dresses singing that fine hymn." The dreamer was worried again: "I haven't a white dress, and I can't sing." But then, suddenly she was somehow in the choir, where there was just one place left for her. She was wearing a white dress and singing heartily. A few weeks after she had that dream, that young woman experienced her Damascus Road. Jesus Christ laid hold upon her, in broad daylight, in the midst of the crowd, at a precise spot which she told me of, and which I know well. Was he not already seeking her at the time of her dream?

12

The Need for Support

Read this chapter.

ALL THIS GOES to show how great is the need of all men for support. It is a long time since it first struck me. That the weak, the lonely, the neurotic, people who have always lacked support, should seek it avidly is obvious and easy to understand. But the strong need it quite as much. It is less noticeable, because they hide it more easily. They can affect a great independence because they have honour and affection lavished upon them. Like them, we can believe ourselves to be strong, we can even imagine that it is we who support others, without realizing the extent to which we are dependent upon them, upon the confidence they have in us. The esteem they hold us in, and the authority they confer upon us. We are always quicker to notice what we have not than what we have. But what should we be without it?

When I lived in the old city I met the pastor of the local church in the street one day, and said to him: "You never come to visit me!" "Oh, you! You don't need it," he answered. "I go and see the lost sheep!" Am I not also a lost sheep? I have seen committed Christians weeping in my consulting-room, "pillars of the church", as we say, people who were meeting their pastors or priests constantly in their Church Councils, people on whom everybody depended, but whom no one troubled to help in their personal difficulties.

And the clergy themselves, always standing in the breach, ready to help others and bring them support—how often they have seemed to me to be without the support they needed themselves. They are usually extremely sensitive people who have chosen a life of service because they were very conscious of the distress of humanity, since they themselves suffered much in their personal lives. Priests have at least one advantage over pastors, in that they have obligatory confessors.

When my sister died, a pastor friend came to see us. He said to us, in praise of her faith: "She was a real pillar of the Church." Ah! If he had known what a fragile, unquiet, tormented, anguished soul she had! I am perhaps a little more solid than she was, at least at certain moments, when I am carried away by a strong conviction. But to others, I am very like her. Thirty years ago a friend came up to me in the street and greeted me, looking me in the eye: "Good morning, Paul, how are you?" It may seem astonishing that I remember such an ordinary question so clearly. But the tone in which it was spoken was not ordinary. I felt that it meant: "You too have your difficulties and problems, you who are always busy with other people's problems. Do you need any help?" I was so moved that I was afraid I was going to cry.

My patients lean on me for support, and I for my part lean on them as well. I lean on my job and my reputation; and it is they who are my job and my reputation. I owe them as much as they owe me. And the confidence they place in me and show me, is a considerable support to me. A book like this one, as I have clearly shown, I owe entirely to them. My thoughts are never anything but an unending reflection upon the human condition. They are born of the experiences I have with my patients, and of all they tell me about their lives. I realize too that I lean upon my readers, and upon all the encouragement they bring me through their letters. I am always very sensitive to them, especially when they touch a personal note, and tell me that I have been a support to them in their own lives and in their development. So I lean for support on the support I try to give them!

When I give a lecture, I know well that I am leaning upon four or five people, sometimes even less, whom I choose intuitively in the audience. I watch out for their reactions on their faces, and in their eyes, and so I go forward, upheld and led by their support. I speak to those few hearers. They, too, lean on me, doubtless, following the thread of my speech rather as if they were being carried along on a moving staircase. But they are also for me a moving staircase which holds me up right to the end. I have often advised performers who suffered from stage-fright to forget the anonymous mass of their audience, and to play or sing in a quite personal manner for just one or two among them.

So in every enterprise and in all the responsibilities of life we lean upon one another. The Rotary Club bases its prestige upon the eminence of its members, and they consolidate their own prestige by belonging to the club. Pupils lean upon their teacher, but the teacher, too, leans upon his pupils. He feels this quite clearly at examination-time, when the inspector will judge the quality of his teaching from their success. But it is already true throughout every lesson. The soldier leans upon his officer, but the officer also leans upon his men.

The policeman leans upon the law, and the law leans upon the policeman. Every American citizen leans upon the President, and he leans upon the loyalty of the citizens. In religious countries the Church leans upon the State, and the State upon the Church; but in others the State leans upon atheism, and atheism upon the State. The communist leans upon Marx or Lenin, or the example of Russia or that of China, on what the party does, or what the leader says; but the party and the leaders lean upon the mass of their supporters.

This is the case with all parties, all social classes, all the groups that face each other in political life or in societies. Those who support the candidature of a new member are those who reckon on his support when he is elected. The civil servant leans upon the State, and the State upon its civil servants; the civil power leans on the army, and the army upon the civil authorities; the press upon public opinion, and public opinion upon the press. The same is true at all levels of national and international politics. The fact is that it is no longer possible to see clearly who is leaning on whom, nor who is only pretending to offer support in order to flatter someone else and obtain his support. In the army the doctor relies upon his badges of rank in giving his support to men against the abuses of others with badges of rank.

Parents hope to derive social support from the family their son is to marry into, and *vice versa*. I have seen cases in which both families were engaged in throwing dust in each other's eyes before their children's marriage, in order to make as much as possible of the support they were bringing, when in reality they were hoping to get more than they were giving. And the young couples, after they were married, found themselves in a much more precarious financial situation than they were ready to face.

Other parents push their children into courses of study. If they fail they consult famous educationists and psychologists. They make them recite their lessons every day. Their aim is to procure for them, as a sort of trump card in the game of life, the support of a diploma, a certificate, a degree, or a doctorate. But their aim is quite as much the support that they will derive themselves from the social success of their children. I am not denying the benefits of learning, nor the intrinsic interest of the studies themselves. But the studies one follows with most enthusiasm are more a luxury than a support in life.

I am speaking here of diplomas. The more organized society becomes, the more diplomas it demands, and the more one feels bereft of social support if all one has to show are one's natural talents. Let some disaster come, and things are different. The officers who enjoy the highest esteem in barracks are not always the best support for their men under fire. There are several plays which have as their theme a shipwreck, and the revolution it causes in the hierarchy of the survivors. All at once it is one of the least honoured who finds himself leading them, and on whom all depend for support. That was what happened to St. Paul when the storm came upon the ship in which he was being taken as a prisoner to Rome (Acts. 27.9–44).

St. Paul leaned upon God and on the assurance God had given him that none of them would perish. His companions did not start any theological arguments on the subject. They were only too glad to lean upon the calm confidence of the apostle. In fact, there is no more effective witness than serenity of that kind in affliction. But we must not exaggerate it by setting the help that God gives over against the support of men. That would run counter to the spirit of the Bible, which unites them, and shows that God upholds us through the ministrations of men. People are well aware that we do not lean for support only on our faith, but also on the comradeship we find in the Church, and also on the authority of the theologians. Roman Catholics lean on the ancient power of their church or on the thought of St. Thomas Aquinas or the charity of St. Francis of Assisi. The Protestants lean on Luther, Calvin, Wesley, or Karl Barth, or perhaps on the Bible, cutting short any discussion even on the most complex problems by quoting some text as if it were an unanswerable argument.

Thus the whole of society, in all its financial, economic, political, juridical, artistic, and intellectual aspects, is seen to be a vast enterprise of mutual support, in which each member tends, from pride, to conceal the fact that he is looking for support, and stresses the support he gives to others. I am not describing this process in order to criticize it. I know how weak men—all men—are. I know that they are all anxiety-ridden, to a greater extent than they realize, or at least than they are willing to reveal. It needs the exceptional atmosphere of the doctor's consulting-room for them to be willing to express it, or even for them to become aware of it.

From his earliest years the child has to learn that art of living which consists in weighing up promptly and surely who are the people he can lean upon. In the family, in school, in a games team, or a gang playing together, he will soon discover the value of a solid friendship, of a loyal comradeship upon which he can count with certainty. He will also be quick to see that the admiration of others, their confidence, and their expectation of his support, provide a tremendous stimulus to his own energy, and so constitute a real support for himself.

Inside the family he soon knows on which of his two parents he can lean. If he thinks his mother will not let him do something he wants to do he first asks his father's permission, and can then say triumphantly to his mother: "Dad says it's all right." If both parents agree in refusing something, he will lean upon the example of his comrades whose parents allow it. The example of others is a very common and powerful support, for good things as well as bad. Contact with a friend who is firm in his beliefs and in his moral conduct will help us to find in ourselves unsuspected strength to be more faithful. But if he permits himself some slight indulgence, we are quick to quote him as an excuse for our own weakness. A man who is thinking of divorce finds the company of divorced persons congenial, their example being a support he can lean on, while his divorce will bring them support against any remorse they themselves may feel.

One often sees families in which all the others lean on one member, and not always the strongest! He may even be one of the children, the most timid and unsure of himself, but still the most willing, the one who suffers from the Cinderella complex which I have already described. When one looks into such families one is astonished to see the extent to which a child can sacrifice himself to his brothers and sisters, while they give him nothing in return, but impudently take advantage of him without his parents noticing, or having the courage to defend him. It even often happens that the parents exploit his willingness to their own advantage. The result is that it is sometimes those whose need for support is greatest who receive least, and who have to give most to others.

It is very far from being the case that all parents give their children, on the threshold of life, all the support they ought to provide for them. This may be due to psychological complexes in the parents, even sometimes unconscious jealousy. Such was one father, in comfortable circumstances, who had not even provided the money that would enable his exceptionally gifted son to study for his matriculation examination. Fortunately a friend of the family secretly advanced the necessary funds without the father affecting to notice. But a stranger cannot take the place of a father, and the son, in spite of having done very well indeed, is still beset by all kinds of psychological difficulties connected with this lack of paternal support.

I myself have been guilty in this respect, and regret it keenly. One of my sons suffers from the organic malformation known as alexia or "word-blindness". When he was at school it was not yet known, and the school medical service which we consulted was not able to help us. We realized well enough that it was not lack of intelligence or of the will to work hard that was holding him back. But one of his teachers did not see it that way. She called him lazy and stupid, scolded him, laughed at him, and encouraged his classmates to do the same. "That is a pitiless age", as La Fontaine said.

I blame myself for not having taken the boy away from that school at once, for not having defended him as I ought to have done. And the reason why I did nothing was the idealism I professed at that time, because I talked of the virtue of acceptance, which bears injustice uncomplainingly, and which forgives. The victim of this particular injustice was not I, but an infirm child, and I could not see it.

Since then I have come across many other cases, and I understand it. We touch here upon the problem of the "two gospels" once more. Parents who are loath to fight, and who take their passiveness for a Christian or a moral virtue, may harm their children by depriving them of the support which is their right while they are still too weak to face life on their own, and especially when they are handicapped physically or by psychological complexes. They may, of course, manage on their own, and do very well, but they will still be subject to a certain uneasy tension, because at the age when they ought to have been protected by their parents, and able to enjoy a carefree childhood, they have had to rely entirely on their own resources. Despite their success, they remain unsure of themselves and are over-zealous, try too hard, and take on more than they can manage. They are exploited by their more cunning workmates, who unload their responsibilities on to them.

The same thing can happen between husband and wife. One of the purposes of marriage is "the mutual society, help, and comfort, that the one ought to have of the other, both in prosperity and adversity". This is what everyone thinks, and the bride and bridegroom promise it to each other. But it is very far from being what happens in every case. I understand very well the suffering of spinsters, who are deprived not only of the joy of a life shared with another person, and of motherhood, but also of the support that a husband can give. They even have to be careful to whom else they look for support, if they wish to safeguard their moral independence, whereas from a husband a woman has a right to expect support without limit.

Expect, indeed! But she does not always get it. A spinster once said to me: "Oh, how I should like to be able to lean on a husband; to set off on a journey, for instance, and be able to leave to him all the worry about plane tickets, hotel reservations, taxis, and luggage!" Afterwards, she got married. She realized that her husband found it very convenient to have a wife who knew how to manage things as well as she did, and that he allowed her to take him round like a baby, leaving everything to her. The husband would perhaps have said to me: "I let her get on with it. She's so pleased to be able to do something for me after having had only herself to do things for."

It is true that women have a greater instinct for service and devotion than men have, and men very often take advantage of the fact. A husband asks for much more support from his wife than he offers her in return. Several women have told me that they felt demeaned by the well-known biblical text: "It is not good that the man should be alone; I will make him a helper fit for him" (Gen. 2.18). It seems to me that it is rather the man who ought to feel humiliated at the thought that God considered him incapable of looking after himself on his own. Personally I think that the divine thought, "It is not good that the man should be alone" concerns woman as well as man, and expresses the immense need for support that every human being feels.

It is quite clear that the man ought to be a support for his wife even more than she for him. There are women who are thought to be too domineering, whose husbands say they "lead them by the nose", or "wear the trousers", to use the common expressions. Looking more closely into it, I have often observed that such wives perform their dominant role unwillingly, because their husbands lack virility. But a more virile husband would also be a more egotistical one! I have seen wives whose trouble is that they have husbands who are too kind, husbands whose rule of life is to please them and, quite sincerely, to approve of everything they do. The result is that all the decisions that they ought to take together rest in reality only on the wife, when she would so much like her husband to be the one to decide.

The problem is a very complicated one. Most women rely more than they realize upon their powers of seduction, and that is one reason why they are afraid of growing old. The man, on the other hand, relies more on his job, which develops as time goes on. But the woman also relies more than she thinks on her husband's position and reputation, or at least upon the social status her marriage gives her. Spinsters know well that however gifted or attractive they are, they not respected as much as married women are, at any rate in Europe. But the husband also leans on the beauty and prestige of his wife, on her success in society, even if he himself feels somewhat humiliated at not being so much at his ease in society as she is.

As soon as married couples start down the slippery slope of trying privately to weigh up how much support each gives and receives from the other, they feel lost and frustrated. The reason why they try to make mental calculations of this kind is that they all have an immense need for support, but pride restrains them—husbands much more than wives—from admitting the fact. They would like to receive the support without having to ask for it.

On the other hand, a woman has a greater emotional need than a man has, consciously at least, whereas the husband finds it more difficult to express his feelings, even though in doing so he would be giving his wife the support she needs. My wife has sometimes said to me, as if it were humiliating to her: "I can't do without you, but you could do without me." What an illusion! I saw well enough, when I was at death's door, the reserves of energy she had to face up to everything. And what should I be, without my wife? And I fully realize that in my job, with all the confidence it gives me, I find more support than she does, and that I ought therefore to be giving her more.

It should be remarked also that a man leans more on ideas, and a woman on persons. A man draws considerable strength from the interest he has in things, while a woman is interested in things to the extent that she feels that a person is interested in her. Thus, a schoolgirl has a passion for geography because she likes her geography teacher, and he likes her. Listen to her as well, as she says to her friends: "My daddy says . . .", or "My daddy does this or that." A boy, on the other hand, talks less about his parents, especially about his mother's love for him. He leans less openly upon them. He wants to be appreciated for himself.

We see many people who delude themselves, many people who do not realize how much support they give to others, to a husband or wife, for instance, nor how much they receive. In fact, husbands and wives depend on each other much more than they realize. They may come to realize it in the evening of life. A widower suddenly discovers how much he leaned for support upon his wife, when he had always thought it was the other way round. Sometimes a wife will say: "I don't know how to help my husband. He is so uncommunicative. If I ask him anything it just irritates him. All I can do is to pray in secret for him." But the husband, for his part, may say to me: "My wife is a much greater help to me than she thinks, and I am very grateful to her." "Have you told her so?" "I don't know how to."

Such misunderstandings are not uncommon. One husband told me at great length about his troubles. When he had finished I asked him: "What does your wife think about it all?" "Oh, she has far too much to worry about, what with her sister being ill, for me to give her more worries." Obviously that is not the real reason. The wife is far more worried at seeing her husband so careworn without being able to help him, or when she learns something indirectly about his affairs without being able to speak about it openly to him.

What, then, is the real reason? A certain reticence, which comes from the shame we all feel at having to admit that we are weaker in face of life than we should like, a reluctance to ask for support, as if to ask for it were a sign of weakness. The tragedy is that this silence weighs upon a husband and wife who love and respect each other, who would each like to help the other, but do not know how to set about it.

It can happen that a man who is greatly respected, a man who un-hesitatingly assumes heavy responsibilities in business and political life, and on whom everyone relies, gives no support whatever to his wife, but leaves her alone, for instance, to deal with the psycholo-gical difficulties of one of their children. But one can never be sure, when a husband abdicates his family responsibilities in this way, that it is not because his wife once refused his help when he offered it. She may be complaining that he leaves everything to her, where-as she may have objected when he tried to take some of the respon-sibility off her shoulders, as if she were afraid of losing the credit for what she did. You can see how delicate and paradoxical all these mutual relationships are.

Another couple married young. The husband was still a student. His wife was the breadwinner, and in addition did all the house-hold chores while he worked at his books. They went through hard times, but were wonderfully happy, really leaning upon one another. They had to wait before having a baby, and the sacrifice was greater for the wife than for her husband. The early years of the husband's professional life were not easy, either, and the wife spent herself unstintingly in order to sustain him.

Then came success, social advancement, wealth. The wife re-mained modest, wrapped up in her work, while the husband associa-ted with all sorts of people who made much of him. Then suddenly the wife realized that they had drifted tragically apart, and she had not noticed it happening. Once, he had leaned upon her. Now he leaned on his money, and on the prestige it gave him in the eyes of a certain pretty woman who could not hold a candle to his wife, but who was nevertheless a socialite in whom he discovered a facile side of life of which he had previously been deprived.

I could give many more examples. Both within the marriage bond, and in social life generally, the problem of support always enters into personal relationships—the universal quest for support, more or less veiled, often unconscious; the pleasure of giving sup-port to others; the disappointment of not receiving it when one ex-pects to have it, or of seeing the support one offers refused by others. Furthermore, the need for support also comes into man's relation-ship with things. Remember the words of Archimedes, the brilliant inventor of the cogged wheel: "Give me a firm spot on which to

stand, and I will move the earth." So the whole advance of the
forces of technology and science may be interpreted as an effort to
find this reinforcement of power, so that man is ever on the look-
out for new and stronger supports. The driving-force behind this
is his immense need for security. And the great paradox is that his
feverish pursuit of support—for example in the unleashing of
atomic energy—further imperils his security. The result is greater
distress than ever.

And so, whatever his material conquests, it is moral support that
he seeks most, someone to help him to win victories over himself
and to achieve what he feels himself called to do. I have just met
one of my former patients, who of course asked me about this book.
I had hardly begun talking to her about this universal need for support when she exclaimed: "Of course everyone of us has some
spring—often a secret one—where he can go and drink, in order to
find strength to face life!" Yes, often secret. How many great artists
would never have become so without an obscure master, whose
name history has forgotten? The confidence shown in them by their
master, quite as much as his teaching, has helped them to give of
their best.

Jesus himself sought support from three of his disciples when he
faced the greatest renunciation in his life, the acceptance of the
Passion and the Cross, in the Garden of Gethsemane (Matt. 26.
36–46). He did not ask for their advice. A few days previously he
had even found it necessary vigorously to reject Peter's advice (Mark
8.32–33). He asked them to watch with him, and pray. And despite
the anguish of that moment—because of the anguish, a psychoanalyst would doubtless say—the disciples fell asleep. The support
that Jesus sought at that supreme moment was not forthcoming.

People in comfortable circumstances, surrounded by supports,
can hardly realize what it is like to be without support, like the
majority of the patients who come to consult us. There are some—
especially French people—who present themselves to me furnished
with a note of recommendation from some eminent personage,
scribbled well-nigh illegibly on the back of an imposing visiting-
card. The personage is unknown to me, and sometimes to the
patient as well. He may have solicited the reference through a third
person. He does not know that in a tiny democratic country like
Switzerland we pay more attention to those who have no one to
recommend them, that we take pleasure in giving support to those

who lack it. And I am often amazed at the progress that can be made by a patient when he finds real support. This is not only a matter of treatment in the conventional meaning of the term. It can sometimes be the result of a quite ordinary approach—a word to an employer, for example. "For the first time in my life," a young woman said to me the other day, "I felt that I had someone behind me."

Even when we have plenty of supports, we go on looking for more. For instance, I am never indifferent to being quoted by an author, especially if it is in a big scientific volume from the pen of some leading light in the university world. But I am also a support for him, for in quoting me and other authors he is demonstrating his erudition. I, too, quote writers and scientists in order to lean on them and on their authority, which I enhance by the very fact of quoting them. I quote my friends, and they quote me. We lean on each other for support in our fight for the same cause. It is the same the world over.

We know that a sufferer from agoraphobia can cross the street provided he is holding someone's hand, even that of a child. We can understand that he should feel secure beside a sure and solid guide. But a little girl? In that case the support is in the responsibility he assumes in leading the child. His attention is diverted from his own anxiety by his desire to give confidence and security to an even weaker person than he is. He is invested with a function which stabilizes him. It is easy to observe how widespread this phenomenon is. People are fortified and reassured by the confidence shown in them by their being given some task to perform. They need to receive a mandate, and this delegation of power is a support to them. Once he has on his badges of rank, an officer who in civilian life is very timid becomes very sure of himself. To be appointed to a position of trust is an effective support to any one of us.

There are ecclesiastics who begin to make converts only after being given an official post by the Church. There are plenty of people who do not dare to undertake anything without being specifically detailed to do it by somebody else. Then they are full of zeal and energy in performing the duty they have had entrusted to them. The incessant manoeuvres of the members of an administrative staff, aimed at climbing the ladder of promotion, are not motivated only by a desire to earn more money, but also by a wish to receive the encouragement that promotion brings with it.

How precious a support it is to feel that one is appreciated! Even just to have someone there. I often feel in regard to my patients that I am playing the part of the little girl with the agoraphobia sufferer. They think that I am taking them by the hand to lead them, but it is they who are taking my hand, and I follow them in the exploration of their minds with the wonder of a child setting off on a journey of discovery. But my presence and my participation in their adventure reassures them and gives them the courage to go on with it. Sometimes, in fact, it is their reintegration into their proper sphere of work that is the eventual fruit of a long and patient effort. There is a woman whom I have been treating for more than twenty years. For the first twelve years at least she was only able to come to see me if she was accompanied by a friend. Long after she had been cured in this respect, and had regained her independence, she was still working at a job that was much inferior to her capabilities. And then quite recently she was appointed to a post of special responsibility in the field of social service. What a joy for her! What a joy—an even greater one, perhaps,—for me!

We all suffer to some extent from agoraphobia. We are all afraid of finding ourselves suddenly in a vacuum, bereft of support. The point of having a job, any job, is not merely that it answers our need to be doing something useful in society. That would not be sufficient to explain the intensity with which each of us seeks a post. Nor the jealousy of those who are unsuccessful. It derives from this fear of being left without support which haunts every human mind—the fear of being out of work, or in those who are more infantile, the fear of losing their parents, even if they do not get on very well with them.

What a tragedy it is, indeed, when a man loses his job, especially if he is no longer young. Only yesterday he was grumbling about his soul-destroying work, his employer, his fellow-workers. But now he has been dismissed. Now at last he sees what he has lost, and he is overcome by a feeling of distress which he never imagined possible. He has lost his place, his support. At the first sign that his applications for work are not likely to succeed, his depression is seriously aggravated. He clings to those who may afford him support, and even there he finds it difficult to accept their help, to believe in their encouragement, to allow himself to put any faith in their assurances. And he is not altogether wrong, for those who generously exhort him to have confidence would be no stronger than he is if the same misfortune were to befall them.

You can guess all that I might say about the constant interplay of support granted, refused, solicited, or withdrawn, like a huge game of chess, in every undertaking, in every office, in every factory, among workers of all kinds. There is the employer who affects to have tremendous authority, but who never makes a decision without first consulting some unknown collaborator who thus exercises the real power behind the throne. There is the one who favours a gifted young employee—which is fair and generous, but which also expresses the employer's need to attach him personally to himself so as to be able to use him for support. There is the comrade on whom one thought one could rely, and who disappears when his support might harm his prospects. There is the one who is more independent-minded than the rest, who does not hesitate to speak his mind to his superiors, and on whom the others lean for support in a way that is not without cowardice.

13

What Support?

IT IS OUR human weakness that must be acknowledged, our immense need for support. If we search for success, or truth, it is not only for the pleasure of success and the contemplation of truth, but also in order to reassure ourselves in our weakness and to lean on the success and on the truths we have discovered. We feel weak, and would all like to be stronger than we are. That is why we imagine other people to be stronger than they really are. It is because we are all weak that both they and we cling to our support, and dare not let go in order to press forward; and it is in this inability to let go that we experience our weakness.

Everyone intuitively feels the truth that was illustrated for us just now by the analogy of the trapeze artists. Everyone realizes that the ideal of personal fulfilment, which is common to psychology, education, and soul-healing, requires continual leaping forward, and that one cannot leap forward without letting go of something behind. You saw that it was true of the trapeze artists, and also of agoraphobia, that one can gain support from behind, or from in front, to say nothing of gaining it from left or right—represented by the other people who are advancing alongside us, and who must themselves be gaining support from behind or in front.

Support from behind includes all I have been talking about—our past, our qualifications, our successes, our forbears. The conservative aristocrat, even if he is penniless, is the type of the man who looks backward for support. The portrait of his illustrious great-grandfather who fought heroically on some foreign field is there, in the place of honour in the drawing-room. Our aristocrat's whole life is lived under the benign and protective eye of the great man, and derives support from him. Even his religion is compounded of veneration for the good old days when men were more religious than they are today.

The revolutionary, for his part, looks forward for support, and in his house is a portrait of Lenin or of Mao Tse Tung that symbolizes for him the great hope on which his life hangs. He looks forward to the great day of world revolution, and is capable of making great sacrifices, of burning all his bridges behind him, and letting go of all the trapezes of his childhood, because he leans solidly on the future for support. Clearly there can be no dialogue between him and the conservative. Neither is leaning for support on the present. One is prolonging the past and the other is anticipating the future.

Christianity seems to me to afford double support: from the past and from the future at one and the same time. So it encourages at the same time the fulfilment of the individual person and his surrender to the person of God. Support from behind is that which relies on what one has done and what one possesses. Christianity does not despise it, since all we possess is given by God and all we do comes from the creative spirit implanted in our hearts by God. Support from in front is that which relies on what we hope and believe in, on the promises of God.

You can see the importance of this conjunction of the two supports, which is like the perfect synchronization of the trapezes, which are each in turn a support for departure and a support for arrival. What complicates the problem of support, as we have seen, is that we must first have solid support for jumping off before we can launch out towards another support ahead of us. It is not right, therefore, to despise the support from behind. There is, however, a further complication—the support from behind, as well as being a springboard for a forward jump, may be a prison, or if you like, an armchair which holds us back with its comfort and its false security.

So many people take pleasure in the armchair! So many people content themselves with the material and spiritual wealth they have inherited from their ancestors, or have accumulated themselves in their own past: their goods, their comfort, their likes, their traditions, their philosophy of life, their scale of values. They are most unwilling for anyone to touch them, to have the armchair removed from under them. They have come to look upon it as a guarantee of security, whereas it is really an excuse for idleness and stagnation.

So many old people talk only of the past, at an age which demands a new development, a revision of values (as C. G. Jung insists[1]). But there are so many in the prime of life who are already like old people in this respect, fossilized in their satisfaction. It is with these satisfied ones that one fails in psychotherapy, since they lack the urge to make progress, and the capacity to recognize their shortcomings. Their misfortunes, they think—for they necessarily have them too—come only through other people. Everything would be all right if only people would listen to them. However, all that is human must be retrograde if it does not advance: they are old, but they are also an example of what psychology calls infantile regression. A hidden nostalgia for the maternal bosom holds them back. One of my patients, frightened by the dimensions of the problems she had to face, expressed this admirably when she exclaimed: "Quick! My mother's two arms to hide in!"

Here again psychology and religion are at one. While psychologists track down infantile regressions in order to help their patients to become adult, the Bible shows us the world and man in perpetual evolution at the call of life and of God. Jesus said: "Woe to you that are rich, for you have received your consolation. Woe to you that are full now, for you shall hunger..." (Luke 6.24–25). True security is always ahead. Those who use support from behind as an armchair forget that it has been given them by God only to help them the better to leap ahead. Even the Church can become an armchair.

God himself is always at work; and in creating man in his own image he has called him to strive and to develop without respite. Dependence on anything other than God is an obstacle to self-realization. What we admire in a thinker like Plato or an artist like Picasso, is this perpetual calling in question of his own thoughts in the former, and of his means of expression in the latter. Life, as God made it, is a ceaseless march forward.

To this must be added the fact that support from behind is always precarious. There is no support that may not collapse. The Tarpeian Rock is close by the Capitol. Reliance for support on social position is basically unsafe. I was brought up by an uncle who was in business, and who was suddenly ruined as a result of acts of serious imprudence on the part of one of his associates. I was a student at the time. I vividly remember a walk we took together

[1] *Psychology of the Unconscious.*

through the town. In the distance we saw one of his closest friends, a man of great influence in the republic and in the business world, and one of those who might have been able to save him. As soon as he saw us he crossed the street and hurried past on the far side, obviously in order to avoid meeting us. It has left me with a certain prejudice against money, capitalism, and the whole fragile system of mutual support in our modern society.

Every one of us in fact distrusts society, even though we all play its game and seek its support. Some one makes us a lot of fine promises—and we wonder if that person will still keep them when it is no longer in his interest to do so. To this mistrust another is added: it is that any support given puts the beneficiary of it more or less in the debt of him who gives it. All men have a sort of instinct which prompts them to avoid relying on the support of anyone who might use it as a handle against them. You see how difficult a problem it is. How can one help those who need support, without humiliating them? Once again experience in the consulting-room throws light on the problem.

No one hesitates to call the doctor for a broken leg, whereas many people feel embarrassed about going to a psychotherapist when they feel they are being handicapped in life. Some even hide it from their own family. Many try for a long time to manage by themselves. As if anyone ever had been able to manage by himself, especially in illness! Nevertheless, in every medical or surgical consultation there exists a more or less humiliating inequality between patient and doctor, if only because one is ill and the other is a doctor. Dr. Armand Vincent makes a perceptive analysis of this situation in his book *Le jardinier des hommes*.[2] The patient is much more conscious of the inequality than the doctor. His feelings of inferiority to the doctor stand in the way of personal contact with him. They are still more acute in psychological consultations, where the contact is vital. But it would be useless to try to bridge the gulf by playing a game of old friends who happened to have met, when the fact is that the patient has come in order to ask for help.

Genuine contact can be established only on a basis of truth. In the same way, for example, children are more conscious than their parents of the gap between the two generations that separates them. Parents are deluding themselves when they imagine they can bridge the gap by pretending to be their children's pals, and they fall all

[2] A. Vincent, *Le jardinier des hommes*, Editions du Seuil, Paris, 1945.

the more heavily when their children rebel. Parents are parents. The doctor, too, must necessarily remain the doctor. However desirous he may be of establishing personal contact with his patient, and however friendly he shows himself, he is still the doctor in the patient's eyes, and the patient always feels that he is a person in need of the doctor's help.

There is, however, an even more delicate side to this problem. The disproportion between my patient and me is not due only to the fact that it is he who is ill and not I, but also to the fact that he has lacked support in his life, whereas I have all I need and more. Apparently, therefore, I have less need of support than he has, though I know myself that such is not the case. But I can scarcely tell him so, at any rate not at first. He thinks me stronger than I am, and he needs to think so, in order to be quite sure that he has not come to the wrong person. He would be put off right at the start if, in order to make him feel that we are nearer to each other than he thinks, I talked to him about my own weakness. That would be like telling him that the piton to which he has attached his rope for the climb is not solid.

The time will come, however, when the truth will be more re-assuring to him than his illusions about me. I shall then be able to talk to him about the doubly paradoxical situation in which I daily find myself. On the one hand, many people come seeking support from me when I feel myself to be so frail; on the other hand, frail though I am, I know that I can afford them effective support. What is the explanation of that? Well, I think it is because the support one can give or receive is not a question of strength at all.

Why is it that so many people, some sick, some well, come to me for support when in fact I feel myself to be so weak? Is it the scientist in me that they are seeking? But I am the least scientific of psychologists. I came to psychotherapy only via practice. Any specialist with a good academic training knows more about it than I do. I do not wish to denigrate his science. On the contrary, I try daily to learn more about it in order to catch up. I know that every therapeutic undertaking has its technical side, in psychology as in surgery, and that it is of prime importance. In an excellent little book *Dialogue avec le médecin*[3], the philosopher Georges Gusdorf describes a country doctor who is extolling the virtues of technical medicine, to which he claims to hold. "A good diagnosis," he says,

[3] G. Gusdorf, *Dialogue avec le médecin*, Labor et Fides, Geneva, 1962.

"and effective therapy. The rest is literature." And he goes on: "A bad doctor full of ideas will still be a bad doctor." I quite agree! That is why I am always trying to become a better doctor. My "weakness" which I mentioned just now has quite a lot to do with the gaps I am aware of in my scientific knowledge. But here I am speaking about support. I know that every patient has a double need: a need for the best possible technical help, and a need for support, for every patient is a person going through a crisis in regard to support. My professional experience has taught me—this is the second paradox—that one can be a support to others despite one's technical insufficiencies, and that the best specialist has not finished his task if all he has done is to provide the support of his scientific knowledge.

Then do people come to me looking for a man of faith, as they so often tell me? Quite frankly, I feel my gaps in this respect much more acutely than in technical matters! How many patients might I have been able to help effectively instead of failing, if I had had sufficient faith? And I ought to say, equally frankly, that there are, I believe, men who have much more faith than I have, but who nevertheless give no real support to other people, simply because people feel inferior to them in faith. Do people come to me in search of a man of prayer? Alas! Here too I can only reproach myself most keenly, and say that I am ashamed of having written so many true things about the value of prayer and meditation, and of being so bad at them in practice.

I think after all that the reason why people come to me for support is because I am weak, and not strong. A sort of instinct prompts them to look for someone who is like them, but who tries to follow his vocation in spite of his weakness, relying on God rather than on his own efforts. When I have the joy of seeing someone regaining courage and confidence, conquering himself, resolving his problems, I know well that there is not much that I have done, but that it is the work of God. I am only a catalyst, and what enables me to be so is simply the fact that, for myself as well, I count on God more than on myself to make up for my weakness. And when I have formed a sufficiently close relationship with a patient to be able to talk to him about it sincerely, it is that which helps and sustains him, rather than the mirage of the strong man which he may have imagined he saw in me before.

There are so many people who seem to us to be very strong,

people who have come out on top in the social, political, or cultural game! They crush us rather than support us, because we feel inferior to them. But in the privacy of the consulting-room, or to anybody with a more percipient eye, they are seen to be strangely dependent upon others, on their wives, or on some friend who has assumed a magical role in their lives.

On the other hand I see anxiety-ridden people, conscious of their own weakness, on whom everybody leans for support like a rock, in their families, in their offices, or in the society or Church to which they belong. They even feel guilty about coming to me for help: "If my friends found out, they would be astonished!" One of my patients told me quite recently of an incident of this kind: "Whatever can you be going to look for in Geneva?" exclaimed one of her closest friends. "You are so strong, you are our leader, you are the one we all depend on."

Another, as she talked to me, recognized the psychological difficulties that had been standing in the way of her making contact with members of the opposite sex, had made her shy and withdrawn, and had kept her away from any possible admirer, so that she was condemned to a spinsterhood which she hated. Her virtue was due to her psychological complexes rather than to her high moral standards, real though these were. And yet numbers of girls were in the habit of confiding in her and looking to her for support. They would tell her all about their sexual adventures, and even say how disappointing they were, and how ashamed they were at not having the courage to break off these improper associations. It was the courage to break them off that they came to find in her because they felt that she had the moral stamina they lacked. Many others have had a similar experience: we can be a support to others, not only in spite of, but even because of our own complexes, when we ourselves are in just as much need of support.

No, true support is not a matter of strength. The more one thinks about this, the more one realizes its truth. When we go for support to a strong man, it is generally in order to ask him for a limited service. We need his authority in order to be successful in a course of action whose outcome is uncertain; we use him as an armoured tank to attack a strong-point. It is short-term help in a matter which is, after all, external to ourselves. About our inner questionings, our hesitations and defeats, we are generally less inclined to talk to him. He seems too strong to understand us. We are afraid he will find our poor scruples ridiculous. And if he is strong-willed, we are afraid he will want to impose his will on us. Either we should give in to him and become a mere satellite in orbit around him, or else we should try to retain our independence, and risk a conflict, for he is always sure he is right.

I have nothing against the strong. Who could take their place? Life is hard! What a relief it is when a strong man takes in hand an affair that has become muddled and spoilt, and one is sure that he will fight to the end and without running away. In any case our fear that they will play the tyrant may be unfounded. There are plenty of strong men who are most particular about respecting the liberty of others; whereas there are many weak people who are tyrannical in an attempt to compensate for their weakness. Gentlemen reflect smugly that there are more women than men in the psycho-therapists' consulting-rooms. But we often have the impression that it is the husband who ought to be consulting us, because the wife is not finding in him the support she needs, and that is what is making her ill.

I merely maintain that the problem of support is more complex than it at first appears to be, and that though the support of the strong may be useful to us, it is not the only support we need. The risk in depending on a strong man is that we may delude ourselves into thinking that we are stronger simply because he sustains us with his strength—like a trapeze artist who thought he was flying through the air without support because he was safely swinging on his firm trapeze. The support we need most is not that which carries us, but that which enables us to leap forwards on our own—not the support that pushes and pulls us, like a locomotive pulling a waggon, but one which helps us to advance ourselves. A support of that kind is very difficult to define.

What we are looking for is not someone who will cut through our dilemmas for us, but someone who will try to understand them. Not someone who will impose his will upon us, but someone who will help us to use our own will. Someone who, instead of dictating to us what we must do, will listen to us with respect. Not someone who will reduce everything to an academic argument, but someone who will understand our personal motives, our feelings, and even our weakness and our mistakes. Someone who will give us confidence in ourselves because he has unshakeable confidence in us, who will take an interest in our struggles without prejudging their outcome, who will not allow himself to be discouraged if we take a different road from the one he would have taken.

Theologians, and even psychologists, seem sometimes to be too sure of what line we ought to follow. They all have their theories and their principles. They are so ready to lay down what would be the right course of action. What can we say to them if we do not agree? They are always right! And so we are afraid they will tire of us if we cannot follow them. We may find one who is liberal-minded enough not to compel us, but is he not going to lose interest in us, and say: "Do as you like, but don't go on asking for my advice and support"? It is the same with all those who come to us. They, too, are very often torn between two contradictory fears, between the fear that we shall push them too hard, and the fear that we shall not push them enough.

The majority of those who consult us are not primarily seeking advice. They have already said to themselves, over and over again, all that can be said about their problem. They may even have an idea of how it can be solved, but they have not dared, or have not been able, to follow it out. The support they want is a support to counter their own weakness. They need to express themselves, not to have an arbitration award pronounced against them. They need a place where they can be completely sincere, and feel themselves completely free. That is so rare in this world! Freedom is a wonderful support to have. They need to be able to say what is holding them back, before they can manage to overcome their inner resistance. You see, we have come back to the struggle to "let go" which we were considering earlier. The support that is essential to us is the support that will help us to win that battle, to be more faithful to ourselves, to dare to grow, to dare to let go what we must let go if we are to grow.

The ideal support, then, is a presence, a vigilant, unshakeable, indefectible presence, but one that is discreet, gentle, silent, and respectful. We want help in our struggle, but do not want our personal responsibility to be taken from us. A look, a smile, an intense emotion—these are the things that can help us to win our victories over ourselves.

Some of my readers may have thought that the idea of "letting go" which I have stressed with such insistence is too negative. Life is made up not of what we let go, but of what we achieve. There is nothing that helps me to make the leap into action more than stating my conviction that I am called to make it—nothing commits me more surely to following out that conviction and turning it into action. It was, in fact, to avoid committing myself in that way that I myself hesitated so long to say what it was I felt called to do. But what that actually meant was that I had to let go of my hesitations and all the pretexts that I had been using in order to avoid making the decision.

It is not possible, alas, to cure all those who are ill! One may be tempted to abandon them when all hope of real healing vanishes. Is it even honest to go on giving them consultations and taking their money? Dr. Balint has made a shrewd analysis of the scruples which some doctors may feel in such circumstances.[4] But this patient who must come to terms with his illness or infirmity and go on through life without any hope of final relief—does he not need our support even more than any other? This is the case with many organic diseases for which science can afford only temporary alleviation. It is also the case with a large number of neurotics, to whom prolonged analytical treatment has failed to bring any radical liberation. One has then to be content with "support psychotherapy"—an expression which is often given a slightly pejorative sense. Of course, in such cases I always wonder if it is not my fault that I have been unable to heal the patient, because of my technical inadequacy. But I know that even the most technically skilled practitioners all have their failures. And it sometimes happens that when they see that their skill is unable to effect a cure, they say to the patient: "I can do nothing more for you." I admire their honesty and humility. They are also quite properly concerned that their time should not be wasted when it might be spent on other patients with whom their technique may be more effective.

It is, however, a thing I have never been able to bring myself to say. Is it my pride? Without doubt. At all events it is my keenness to succeed. But it is also, I think, because I am interested not only in the disease, but also in the person. It is for the same reason that I go on receiving visits from several of my former patients, although they have long since been cured, or at least their condition has been improved as far as that seems possible. I want to support them in their still difficult lives. I have just been jotting down a few names: more than twenty have come into my mind straight away, whom I

4 Michael Balint, *The Doctor, his Patient and the Illness*, Pitman Medical Publishing Co., London, 1957.

have been seeing regularly for more than ten years, twenty years, and even more than thirty in some cases. There are some who bring my wife and me flowers on the occasion of the tenth or the twentieth anniversary of their first visit, for my wife has always encouraged me in this faithfulness.

As I read through the list of names I am immensely thankful. There is not one of them that has not brought me some satisfaction. With some of them, I am quite sure that it is my unflagging patience which has made it possible for us to gather fruit which at one time it seemed our labours would never bring to maturity. Patience, however, is the wrong word, since it suggests an effort to overcome impatience, which is not at all applicable in my case. Those who come to us for help are always afraid that they are going to exhaust our patience, and it is just when that fear disappears that they can really accept the support we offer them. Doctors have very varying temperaments, and it is well that that should be so, for in this way we complement each other. There are some who like nothing better than quick and complete success. Of course I appreciate it when that happens, but I am most interested in going deeply into cases, and I learn much more from the careful study of one person's life than from seeing a large number of others passing by.

The doctor's task is not merely to prescribe therapeutic agents, but to give those who have been injured by life the support they need. I imagine that every doctor feels this. And there are many who practise it without pretending to be psychotherapists. A few years ago a young woman who was the victim of serious family conflicts came to see me in the absence of her neurologist. The latter was well known to me—a follower of the classical, "organicist" school, as it is called. That is to say one who believes only in the physical causes of disease, and firmly denies any psychological interpretation of them. He even adopts a somewhat aggressive attitude towards psychoanalysts, as he does also, moreover, towards the Christian faith. He would be hurt, I imagine, if one were to describe him as a psychotherapist and not a neurologist.

I asked the patient whether she visited her neurologist frequently. "Oh, yes!" she replied. "I've been seeing him almost daily for more than ten years. He always gives me courage! And I often 'phone him between visits!" Now that is a means which is not available to me. I am incapable of giving my support by telephone. I need the exchange of glances, and the communication of silence, which soon turns to unease on the telephone. Nevertheless it occurred to me that the neurologist, far removed as he was from us in the matter of doctrine, was very close to us in practice. I also know a surgeon who, though a rough-mannered man, used often to go and visit a young crippled girl for whom his art could do nothing further, simply to support her in her affliction. There is a saying which often figures in the closing addresses of conferences: "Sometimes to heal—often to relieve—always to console." We may paraphrase it by saying: "Always to give support."

Of course all doctors cannot devote as much time to all their patients as a psychotherapist does to a small number, or as the admirable surgeon no doubt did to that one cripple girl! But what we are considering here is not so much a matter of the quantity of time as the quality of commitment. It is a matter of one's fundamental attitude. Reassuring remarks are not enough. If I say: "You can always count on me," the patient will sense at once whether they are empty words, or express a faithful promise. Whether I tell him to come back tomorrow, next week, or next month, is not important. What does matter is that he should know that I am continuing to give him my attention. "The nail has held!" a young woman says to me as she comes in. "What nail?"—"The nail I am hanging on. I feel like a picture hanging on a wall. If the nail comes out, the picture falls. My nail was this appointment that you gave me for just after my holidays." It is, in fact, the holidays that she fears most, alone, or alone with her husband. Not that she is in conflict with him. Rather the contrary, for she feels herself to be a stranger to him, incapable of spontaneity. She is constantly afraid that her anxiety will show, that she will behave oddly and that her husband will think her silly. "All the time during the holidays," she says, "I have been watching the nail so as to hold on, and everything went all right." She added: "I don't feel at all that I am hanging on you emotionally; I hang on you existentially."

The problem of support is in fact an existential problem. No one can truly exist without support, more especially if he suffers from anxiety. A person who is afraid of himself—and there are plenty— is reassured because he feels that I am not afraid for him. He knows that he can tell me anything, and I shall not judge him. He can pour out all his discouragements, and I shall not be discouraged. I am a silent man. I do not need to say much. It is my existence that counts, my real presence. A short while ago alluding to a well-known French children's picture-book, a patient said to me: "You remind me of the old elephant, Babar's teacher, with Babar dancing round him, playing on his pipe."

Attention, a presence, a loving presence, a trusting presence. "I have no aim in life yet," a patient says to me. An aim in life is one kind of support. But it cannot be invented out of nothing: it must come of itself. Nor can I invent an aim for my patient's life; to suggest one would be unreal. So I answer: "In the meantime, I'm here." —"You sound as if you were waiting for something. Are you?" She replies excitedly. She seems surprised by my almost involuntary remark, though she has sensed its sincerity. Fancy someone actually waiting for something for her! That is a real support for her in her dim search. But what am I waiting for? What is it that even far better psychological technicians than I, even orthodox Freudians, wait for? Is it not nature, the spontaneous evolution of life, life thrusting upward? We cannot manufacture life, growth, evolution— we can only wait for it. It is because the patient feels that his doctor is waiting like that, trustingly, that he feels his support.

And where does life come from? Where does the force that is active in Nature come from? From God. I am indeed waiting for something, something new, something still unknown, for every man as well as for myself. I am waiting for it to come, not from that man, nor from myself, but from God. Then the support, in the last analysis, is not only a human presence, but a prayer, even if it is made in secret. Prayer is the sign that one is not alone. True support, to use Simone Weil's great phrase, is "waiting on God".

14

Divine Support

ALL MEN ARE looking, in fact, for God's support. Some are quite aware of the fact; in others it is only a vague nostalgic longing. Some seek it openly, seriously and humbly; others hide what they are doing behind a façade of pleasantries or oaths. It is the only support that measures up to their infinite need for security. At the beginning of this book we were talking about the "Paradise Lost" complex which seems to affect the whole of the human race. This "Paradise Lost" complex is at the same time a "lost support" complex, an anguished feeling experienced by all men, that they have lost the support they needed in order to live. They all know from experience how precious are the various kinds of support they may, with tremendous effort, provide for themselves. The exploitation of the forces of Nature, the great progress that has been made in science and technology, in medicine and psychology, in social organization—none of these things can give them any certain or durable guarantee. What about reliance on people, then—on friendship, love, loyalty? Even the happiest of lovers, who surely have got what they were waiting for, let fall the same anxious question: "Will you always love me?"

It is an absolute support that men and women are looking for, a support without limit—and it obviously can come only from God. A patient is leaving after her first consultation. She had hesitated for several years before coming to see me. We made good contact straight away. But the time has gone, and she must leave. She lives a long way away, and it will be a long time before she can come back. She pauses a moment at the door, turns round, and then after a silence she asks me: "Can I at any rate write to you?"—"Of course!" There is a further silence. She looks at me and adds: "May

I write often?" I reply, a little pompously: "There is no limit!" Neither she nor I can delude ourselves, and it is to mark the extravagance of the remark that I said it in the way I did. Fortunately she understands. She might have been hurt that I should make a little joke about a matter that is so loaded with anxiety.

I am rather proud of the fact that I read with care all the letters I get, however voluminous, and that I answer them all, as far as I can. I carry in my mind the "archetype of the Saviour" that Dr. Maeder talks about.[1] I should like to be able to give without limit to men and women the security they need. My pride comes into it, of course, as witness my keen—too keen—sense of hurt when I disappoint some one. At bottom, I find it as difficult as my patients do to accept that everything should be so limited and relative in this world. Obviously, those who suffer from anxiety feel and express their need for support more pressingly, and we may be tempted to think that they expect too much. But if they did not, they would not be ill, and would not need a doctor. Like the rest of us, they could keep up appearances, and pretend to be reasonable and accommodating. For is it not a fact that all those who are well have, hidden in their hearts, the same longing for support?

This universal desire for support is quite natural, since man is the most vulnerable of living creatures, and the only one who knows his own frailty. The plant is protected by the incredible superabundance of its seeds, the tiger by its claws and its teeth, the elephant by the thickness of its skin, the tortoise by its shell, the hare by its fleetness, the eagle by its wings, and all animals by instincts that are much more reliable than those of man. In man intelligence can compensate to some extent for the lack of instinct. But we are all aware that it is a two-edged weapon, that it can be man's destruction as well as his salvation. The safety measures he takes in order to guard against the new dangers that come with progress are always a half-century or more late.

Man is also the creature most conscious of the dangers that threaten him, the only one who knows he must die. He tries in vain to shut his eyes—events are constantly giving him brutal warnings of how precarious his position is. No natural disaster takes place anywhere on earth without the news reaching him with all its horrible details. But things nearer home affect him more directly—a

[1] Alphonse Maeder, *La personne du médecin, un agent psychothérapeutique*, Delachaux and Niestlé, Neuchâtel and Paris, 1953.

husband or wife whose health seemed so sound is suddenly found
to have a cancer which proves on operation to be in such an advanced state that the surgeon can do nothing but sew up the
patient's belly; a brilliant friend, wise and intelligent, is senselessly
killed in a road accident; a child is run over by a lorry; a growing
son, just starting out on a life full of promises, sinks into neurosis
or alcoholism.

Fate, however, is not the only factor at work. There is also man's
wickedness, which is like the opposite side of the coin to his moral
superiority. Dr. Baruk has clearly shown this in his book,[2] as well
as the fact that man is capable of more refined and more brutal
hate than any animal. This is a tendency to perversion in him which
is absent in the animals, except perhaps when they are in captivity.
Man is afraid of man. He passionately denounces the evil in other
men's hearts, because he fears it as a threat against himself. And
in his fear he threatens them in his turn. He looks all the more for
support so as to be strong and able to defend himself, and the
stronger he is, the more enemies he has.

As his conscience becomes more sensitive he discovers in himself, in his own heart, the evil he has been denouncing in others—
aggressiveness, jealousy, and falsehood. The more he tries sincerely
to understand himself, the more discouraged he becomes over his
own weaknesses, and his own powerlessness in the face of temptation. Feelings of guilt poison his life, and far from stimulating him
to do good, they handicap him still more in his moral battle with
himself, and drive him into dissimulation. The support he needs,
therefore, is not only protection against the threats from outside,
but protection against himself, to conquer himself, to overcome the
fear or the emotion which paralyses him just when he ought to act,
and to overcome the insatiable desires which hold him prisoner.
So he looks for such supports as he can find—fragile they are, but
he clings to them. They are the symbols of a more complete support
which he is always waiting for.

Yes, the limitless support which men so painfully lack is to be
found only in God. Everybody knows that, even the atheists, who,
whether or not they realize it, are just a little jealous of the believers, who have in God a last resort through which they can sometimes win victories which would have been impossible for them on
their own, and to console them when they are disappointed in other

[2] *Psychiatrie morale expérimentale.*

people and with themselves. God is always there, always available, and for everyone, both small and great, unbelievers as well as believers, rebels as well as those who obey him. He is the only support on which we may always rely.

We were saying that the supreme support we are all looking for is a faithful presence, an unfailing presence, but one that is discreet, gentle and respectful of our liberty and even our weakness; an ever-watchful presence, always ready for action, but never forcing us. That is what we find in God. Unwearyingly he awaits our obedience, but he never imposes his will. We even complain about his silence when we question him. He lets us grope after him. "He will not break a bruised reed or quench a smouldering wick" (Matt. 12.20).

His patience is inexhaustible. The more personal experience I have, and the more I hear of the experiences of others, the more do I wonder at God's unimaginable patience. He would never make the remark I quoted above: "I can do nothing more for you." God practises, in a manner of speaking, and in regard to all men, an inexhaustible "support psychotherapy". He is a vital support, existential in the proper meaning of the word, "for in him we live and move and have our being" (Acts 17.28), as St. Paul put it to the Athenians in the Areopagus. And then, morally, he alone is absolutely faithful, as no man can ever be.

We find in all men's hearts, like an archetype, this longing for a sure support, free of all risk of disappointment or failure. In dreams, an enclosed space often does not signify the anxiety of imprisonment at all, but on the contrary the total peace of complete protection. In German it is expressed by a word that is almost untranslatable: *Geborgenheit*, the feeling of being in safety, surrounded and protected as if by one's mother's arms. It is perhaps also a vague reminiscence of our intra-uterine life, before we were cast forth into the great risk of life in the sunlight. There is an excellent little book by Dr. Théo Bovet on this fundamental human need.[3]

This need for total protection is none other than the need for God. The psalmist, who has found it, exclaims: "Thou dost beset me behind and before, and layest thy hand upon me" (Ps. 139.5). The words admirably express the experience of the believer, his sense of being enfolded in God's protective care. Faith is a double support

[3] Théo Bovet, *Angst und Geborgenheit. Das Problem des heutigen Menschen*, Haupt, Berne, 1956.

—in front and behind. In front are God's promises on which faith is founded. But the believer is not limited, like the revolutionary, to counting on the future. He also gets support from behind, from a solid historical reality, from what God has done in the past, in which we see the manifestation of his love and the pledge of what he will do in the future. Our analogy of the trapeze artists comes in again here. There is no strength greater than that of God to help us to let go of the past, and to escape from its bonds. But that past was in fact the strong support that God gave us to help us to leap forward towards him.

You will realize how many more Bible passages I might quote to illustrate this divine succour and support; how much testimony as well, from believers in every age and of every religion. I had already filled up several pages with them, but I have just torn them up, because though they might please pious souls, there are others who might be put off by them, feeling that I had allowed myself to be carried away by my conditioning as a churchman. I read them to my wife, and we both saw that they were tending to turn into a sermon, as my student friend had said. I see now that he was right.

How easy it is for us to fall into the habit of using texts which mean something to us, because they correspond with our actual experience, but which to others seem to be nothing but insipid and wearisome formulae.

I have nothing to teach those believers who know by heart the biblical passages in which God's support is pictured as a refuge, as a buckler, as an immovable rock, and in which the Christian life is compared to a house built upon a rock, or to the sheep that is safely led by a sure shepherd. These images seem banal today, but in times of persecution the martyrs drew from them an indomitable strength which well illustrates the power of God's support. And whenever persecution reappears in our own day, these old testimonies take on their glory once again.

But I am always more interested in the faith of those who are unbelievers. Their faith is revealed in their untiring search for real support, and their rebellion when those on which they have been counting betray them. For divine support is not reserved exclusively for believers, as the latter are only too ready to think. Jesus' teaching is categorical in this respect. He speaks movingly of the providence of God, who feeds the birds of the air, and feeds men too—all men, without discrimination. He speaks also of the special grace which God bestows according to his good pleasure, and with an obvious predilection for sinners—as, for example, for the "prodigal son" in the parable, who had behaved very badly, so that the elder son thought it quite unfair.

But it is not only a matter of parables, this one or any of the others I could quote. It is a matter of the incidents of which the Bible and the history of the Church are full, from which it is clear that God is pleased to grant his support to the weak rather than to the strong, to those who are conscious of their weakness, of their failures, of their faults and of their powerlessness to overcome them, rather than to those who are self-satisfied and proud of their victories over themselves and of their social success and their faith. God offers his support to the sick, to those who are in affliction, to all the despised, the despairing, to little David rather than to Goliath the giant, to the adulterous woman rather than to her virtuous accusers, to the humble members of the church of Corinth rather than to the clever arguers of the Areopagus.

The whole of the Mosaic legislation is aimed at the protection of the weak, the orphan, the widow, the workman, the slave, the debtor, the leper, the stranger and the refugee—even the criminal, and domestic animals. This special care of God for the unfortunate stands out even more in the New Testament, in which we see Jesus going to meet the sick, bringing them the help of his healing presence; seeking out the lonely, like the man at the pool of Bethzatha (John 5.2–9), or officials such as Levi (Mark 2.14) or Zacchaeus (Luke 19.2), who have drawn upon themselves the hate of the people for having enriched themselves at their expense. We see Jesus taking pleasure in the company of poor Galilean fishermen, prostitutes and questionable characters, and of a foreign woman drawing water, whom he honoured with very great revelations (John 4.5–30), whereas he was silent before Pilate, invested as the latter was with all the power of Rome (Mark 15.5). It was to his handful of obscure disciples that he promised the help of the Holy Spirit. "I will not leave you desolate" (John 14.18), he told them; and again: "When they deliver you up, do not be anxious how you are to speak or what you are to say; for what you are to say will be given to you in that hour; for it is not you who speak, but the Spirit of your Father speaking through you" (Matt. 10.19–20).

There is a universal truth in that. When men think they are

strong or virtuous, they rely upon themselves, upon the strength of their muscles or their guns, upon their intelligence and experience, on their own certainty that they are right. That is why it is so dangerous for men to be strong, or for a nation to be powerful. But when affliction comes upon him, whether he is a believer or not, a man looks instinctively for help and support. He feels a little awkward, perhaps, as he stammers out a prayer—he who looks upon himself as an unbeliever—or even when he heaves a sigh that has the accent of a prayer. Nevertheless, it is such a man as he who may have the experience of having his prayer answered, of receiving unexpected strength and assistance.

In a lecture on the experiences underlying all religions, Professor Karlfried von Dürckheim has described[4] the spiritual events which unbelievers may experience with astonishment. Under heavy bombardment, for instance, or in the course of a serious illness, a man suddenly feels that he has gone beyond fear, and that this feeling does not come from himself, but that it is something given to him. Without his knowing why, he has penetrated a different world, the world of transcendence. He has achieved a break-through into that unknown world where he discovers, says Prof. Dürckheim, strange realities: a life which is lived beyond the natural phenomena of life and death, a meaning of things that is beyond the rational categories of sense and nonsense, a love that is beyond the emotional experiences of sympathy and antipathy, and a "yes" which transcends the logical contradictions of "yes" and "no".

Perhaps that man had formulated for himself a view of life and of the world in which there was no room for such things. He may afterwards begin to question the experiences he has just had, wondering whether he may not have been the victim of an illusion. He may deny the experience because he cannot fit it into his old system of thought, especially if he has at some time turned his back on the Church and on religion, as a result of serious disappointments. And yet he did experience an unknown force then. That force is God's help, the divine support which is not reserved for believers, but is offered to all men, and which can sustain them in the most desperate situations, and rescue them from despair. What distinguishes the believer is thus solely the fact that he knows that

[4] K. von Dürckheim, *Religious Experience beyond Religions. Modern Trends in World Religions*, The Open Court Publishing Co., La Salle, Ill., 1959.

that support comes from God, whereas the unbeliever sees it only
as an insoluble mystery.

The difference between them, however, has far-reaching implications. Consider! That same God, all-powerful and perfect, who
reigns supreme over the immensities of time and infinite space; that
same God who invented universal gravitation, atomic power, and
the human brain which is capable of discovering their laws so as to
be able to use them; that same God who invented physics and
chemistry, life and all the phenomena we observe in the tiniest cell—
that same God is interested in men. He has implanted in their
hearts an aspiration to know him; he speaks to them, reveals himself, loves them and wants their love. Much more, he is personally
interested in me, in every detail of my life, rejoicing in my joys and
grieving over my sorrows. We say all this as if it were quite simple,
but there are times when I think it seems incredible!

And he calls me, he entrusts me with a task, he sends me sick
people to care for and readers to write for. What a support for me!
We have already seen that to receive a mandate, to be invested
with a function is always a powerful support to a person. How much
more so when we are conscious that the mandate comes from God!
Then even timid people find themselves possessed of indomitable
energy. Such a one was Jeremiah, who received a tremendous task
from God. God made him a prophet "to pluck up and to break
down, to destroy and to overthrow, to build and to plant" (Jer.
1.10). Yes, to destroy, to let go of all the concepts on which the
faith of his people was founded; and to build, through the very
persecution which he drew down upon himself, a quite new faith,
dependent upon God alone.

And God sustains me in my task. My friends sometimes tell me
that I am too pessimistic. But though I am pessimistic about man-
kind, I am optimistic about God. I depend on him and on his
astonishing resources. I am not persecuted as Jeremiah was, but
like him I was timid, hesitant, uncertain, and I am well aware of
my weakness. I do not know what to say to all the people who bring
me their dilemmas, for they seem to me generally to be insoluble.
But I become quite different the moment I believe I can see what
God's will is. I can face any obstacle. Of course I am often mistaken, I can never be certain. There is such a disproportion between
God and me! But it is the same God who will afterwards be able to
make me understand where I went wrong, and who has taught me

that it is better to make a mistake with conviction than to remain always in doubt.

There is one point in this connection which it is important to emphasize. It is that the divine support on which we rely is not only, as is often thought, some supernatural intervention, exceptional and miraculous, outside the laws of nature, but also the ordinary, quite simple and everyday help which God gives us through Nature and her physical and chemical laws; through medicines, for instance, and through our natural capacities, our intelligence and all the scientific and technological discoveries that man has made.

Many people, believers as well as unbelievers, make a false distinction between the two forms of divine support, supernatural and natural. This is completely contrary to the spirit of the Bible, which always presents the visible, natural, and mediate realities as being the image and witness of the invisible, supernatural, and immediate realities. It is the same God who comes to man's assistance directly through the Word he speaks to him, and indirectly through the forces of nature and through the intelligence he has given him in order to subdue them.

Take, for example, the problem of the healing of disease. There are scientists, even sometimes very learned ones, but worshippers of science, who believe only in technical medicine, and who do not recognize the resources of religion. Christian witness on the subject of "spiritual healing" irritates them. They answer it by pointing proudly to the progress made by science, as if this were not one of God's gifts, equally with the miraculous healings recounted in the New Testament. On the other hand, we find in reverent religious circles doctrinaire believers in spiritual healing who condemn all recourse to doctors and to scientific medicine. For them, to take a medicine, to submit to a surgical operation, or to consult a psychoanalyst is to show lack of faith. So there is no real communication between these two schools of thought, which nevertheless have one thing in common—the false distinction they both make between natural and supernatural divine support.

In reality, all healing comes from God. If you break your arm, the surgeon will apply himself to setting the broken ends of bone in the correct position. But it is not he who unites the bone again. For that he waits upon Nature, and so upon God, just as much as the religious person does when he prays to God about it. There is no reason, moreover, why the two should not be joined in one, why the surgeon should not assume that his technical task is the special work that God has entrusted to him, and recommend his patient to God's grace in prayer. What matters is not doctrinaire argument, but that sick people should be healed, that every effort should be made to that end, and that God should be praised if the efforts are successful.

It must be said that the public are not always taken in by these doctrinal distinctions. One sees unbelievers who go into religious meetings to ask for the laying-on of hands, and religious people who are wise enough to go to a good doctor when they are seriously ill themselves, or even highly-skilled doctors using quack remedies on some well-loved patient for whom science can do no more. Can one ever be sure, they wonder? Were not many of our time-honoured techniques first discovered by quacks? Viktor von Weizsäcker once rightly said[5] that in times of distress men will turn to any one, provided that they can hope for some help from him. In Jesus Christ's day the help that could be expected from scientific medicine was very uncertain. It remained so for many centuries, as is shown by the racy tirades of Molière's characters. Today, it is the help that religion can give which is too little recognized. I am quite sure that if I had had more faith I should have been able to cure patients whom I did not cure. Let us therefore try to unite science and faith, instead of setting them one against another.

There is a double danger in advocating spiritual healing as opposed to natural healing. First there is the possibility that the patient will be turned away from medicine, of which Calvin said that it is one of God's gifts. But there is also the danger of the demoralization of the patient if he is not cured. He has been told: "God loves you, and he will heal you if you ask him with faith." Then if he is not healed he concludes either that God does not love him or else that the fault lies in his own lack of faith.

These harmful suggestions are contrary to the message of the Bible, which always looks upon the natural and the supernatural as one. Jesus can walk on the sea (Matt. 14.25), borne up by God's direct support. But more often he quite naturally uses a boat, and sees it as a place where God is, a place where God's support and protection are to be found, as is proved by the fact that he sleeps

---

[5] V. von Weizsäcker, "Zur Frage der 'christlichen Medizin' ", in *Tutzinger Aerztebrief*, No. II, Tutzinger am Starnberger See.

peacefully amidst the tempest (Matt. 8.24). Similarly God gives
manna to the Israelites in the desert, thus affording direct and
miraculous assistance (Ex. 16.31); he makes water come forth from
the rock which he has commanded Moses to strike with his staff
(Ex. 17.6); and this support is being given to a nation in full
rebellion against him! But when Jesus tells us to ask God for our
daily bread, he is no doubt talking about bread from the baker's. He
frequently points to the wonderful prodigality of Nature as a sign
of divine support (Matt. 6.25–34).

Nature might be described as Jesus' text-book of theology, and
that is a method of teaching which a doctor can well appreciate!
Nature is for him, as for the psalmist, much more than a creation
—it is a revelation and an incarnation of God. As we saw in
Chapter 3, God is universal, invisible, and outside time; but he
chooses places of incarnation in which to reveal himself in this world
of space and time in which we live. The whole of Nature, then, is to
be seen as the true answer to the problem of man's place which we
have been studying in this book. Nature is the place given by God,
the place where he is found. There are many who feel this keenly,
and find it easier to meet God in Nature than in a church. But here
again we must beware of putting asunder what God has joined
together. The desert was not sufficient in itself for the Desert Fathers,
the anchorites and hermits: they built chapels there.

All the places God gives us are supports which he knows we need.
This explains why a place can exercise the mysterious, and even
spell-binding, influence over us of which we spoke at the beginning
of this book, and be such a powerful support to us. The place
which God gives us is there, silent, discreet, but present, like his
support. It does not slip away from us; it bears us as the ground
bears us, without constraint. Like Nature, it is a manifestation of
the presence of God. A women poet, a sensitive, ardent, and restless
soul, once told me of a dream she had had when she was pregnant.
The whole world seemed to her to be an immense divine matrix in
which she was safely hidden. It was the image of the perfect place.

Is not the perfect place one where security is total, but where full
growth is possible? The support that God gives us is given for our
growth. It is time for us to return to the problem of development,
about which so many people think that there is a contradiction between psychology and the Christian ethic. It is time to say that that
idea is false. God wills for every man that growth and development

which the psychologist tries to bring to those who come to consult him because they have been deprived of it by the misfortunes of their lives.

God wills the development of all men. When from time to time he makes them hear his call to self-denial, to renunciation, and even self-sacrifice, it is not for their impoverishment but for their enrichment. Christianity is in full accord with psychology. Like psychology, it sees man in continual evolution from a lesser condition to a greater one, from limited freedom to greater freedom, from poor wealth to truer wealth. The Gospel of Jesus Christ is nothing if not a gospel of growth. It sets our eyes on a development more complete than any that can be conceived by a psychology confined within the limits of nature. All Christ's calls to detachment are accompanied by promises which point to their real meaning. In answer to the apostle Peter's question, he says: "Every one who has left houses or brothers or sisters or father or mother or children or lands, for my name's sake, will receive a hundredfold, and inherit eternal life" (Mat. 19.29).

This conversation takes place after the story of the rich young man whom Jesus had invited to sell all his possessions. To him also he had said: "You will have treasure in heaven" (Matt. 19.21). "Treasure . . . an hundredfold . , . life"—a gospel of growth indeed! In other passages Jesus contrasts insecure early treasures with treasures laid up in heaven, "where neither moth nor rust consumes and thieves do not break in and steal. For where your treasure is, there will your heart be also" (Matt. 6.20–21).

Psychology, too, is well aware that it is only by means of renunciation and sacrifice that greater riches can be attained. That is one of the laws of life. In order to attain his maturity, a man must cast off what remains of the child in him. In order to attain autonomy he must cast off many prejudices. The hard experience of a course of psychoanalysis itself, which can witness the collapse of so many false treasures, is a school of renunciation! Dr. Nodet compares it to the "narrow gate" of which Jesus speaks (Matt. 7.13–14), and which "leads to life".

Dr. Balint, in the book I have referred to, is careful to avoid any religious reference. But he writes of "a limited though considerable change in the personality of the doctor", which will make him conscious of his own problems. It sounds remarkably like the change in attitude which is meant by the New Testament term "repentance" (in Greek, μετάνοια, "a change of mind and purpose"). What, after all, is repentance but this recognition of our own problems and faults? Dr. Balvet, of Lyons, also refers[6] to this overwhelming experience of the psychiatrist, and calls it "lucidity" concerning oneself. Moreover, he adds that this lucidity is "the technical form of renunciation." You see, we come back to this word "renunciation" which psychologists have often complained about in Christian teaching.

So our two movements—receiving and giving—form part both of the Christian life and of the practice of psychology. They correspond to an inevitable rhythm of life itself, which evolves through a constant alternation between enrichment and relinquishment. This is what we expressed by the analogy of the trapeze artists. But we must not carry that analogy too far: the trapeze artists are engaged only in a game, whereas life is a serious matter, in which we are concerned with successful living rather than random leaping. When God gives us riches and then takes them away, it is so that he can give us more valuable riches still and bring us to true life through both of these movements. Psychology is aimed at helping men and women to follow this difficult road. Faith sees it as a divine law, and allows itself to be led by God, and relies on his support. The aim of psychology is the moral autonomy which men strive so hard to achieve, and the revelation of faith is that it is when one abandons oneself to Jesus Christ that one attains inner freedom.

[6] Paul Balvet, "Problèmes de vie du psychiatre", in *Présences*, No. 87, 2nd term 1964 (Prieuré de St. Jean, Champrosay, Seine-et-Oise).

15

The Problem is still Difficult

WE HAVE COME to the end of our study. I have attempted to see
how we can reconcile in our minds, and then combine in our practice, scientific psychology and Christian ministry, which seem so
often to be in opposition to each other. Men and women have a
vital need of a place and support. Psychology concerns itself with
those who have been deprived of them, in an attempt to give them
what they have lacked, because it is necessary to receive before one
can give.

One cannot, however, go on receiving indefinitely. To attach oneself to what one has received, both materially and morally, is to
opt out of the current of life, which demands a continual leaping
forward, and it means that one is ill-prepared for the supreme renunciation of death. So the theologian concerns himself with those
who have received, in order to announce to them the laws of life
and to urge them to renunciation, to help them to grasp the only
support that never fails—eternal life. Men still need a solid support
from which to start, if they are to accomplish this leap forward, and
doctors and psychologists have laboured to furnish this for them.

So doctors and theologians need each other. They must necessarily collaborate to help men and women to develop, and to fulfil
their destiny. The doctor tries to remove the physical obstacles to
their development. The psychologist tries to remove their psychic
handicaps, and the theologian such spiritual obstacles as sin,
selfishness, guilt-feelings, and ignorance of God. They all require
similar qualities: knowing how to listen, to understand, love, give,
comfort, sustain the weak, and lead men without ever dominating
them.

Nevertheless, I am well aware that all this is too academic and theoretical. We make intellectual distinctions between things which are inextricably mixed in practice, and every day brings us new difficulties which leave us perplexed and powerless. This is what I must deal with before I close. The necessary collaboration between doctors and theologians is far from being as easy, lively, and real as it ought to be.

Can we see it as a rigorous division of labour between distinct fields of activity? All that I have written in this book shows that that is impossible. Yet there are many who think it ought to be done. In the United States I met Professor Westberg, the author of an excellent book, *Minister and Doctor Meet*[1]. He told me of the incident that decided him to strive from then on to bring about a real dialogue between our two disciplines. He was a hospital chaplain at the time. He went to see the medical superintendent and asked him: "Ought we not to talk together about the patients? We are both concerned with them, in our respective spheres, and we never exchanges our views about them." The doctor had said to him: "You do your job and I'll do mine. We have nothing to say to each other." He had an admirable frankness, that doctor, a quality that is not to be found in all those (and they are many) who think as he did.

It was still possible to conceive of a watertight bulkhead between our vocations in the days when doctors treated only the body, and when physics and metaphysics were still strictly separated, as Aristotle had taught. But since then psychology has come along unexpectedly and claimed a place between physics and metaphysics. It pertains to physics in so far as it is one of the natural sciences, governed by their objective methods. But it raises metaphysical questions, and increasingly so as it develops; witness the later writings of Freud, in which he attempted a psychological interpretation of religion. Witness also the new depth-psychology, which addresses itself to existential questions, the nature of man, the meaning of his life, his feelings of guilt, and his death. This ambiguous interpolation of psychology in the scheme of things is awkward to many theologians and doctors. The former think it has trespassed upon their preserve, and the latter, in still considerable numbers, either attack it openly or oppose it with passive resistance.[2]

[1] Granger E. Westberg, *Minister and Doctor Meet*, Harper and Row, New York, and Hamish Hamilton, London, 1961.
[2] See Jacques Sarano, "Psychologie? pour quoi faire?", in *Présences*, No. 91, 2nd term 1965, Prieuré de St. Jean, Champrosay, Seine-et-Oise.

It is no longer possible nowadays to think in distinct categories, to leave metaphysics to the theologians and philosophers, as if it were no concern of doctors, and scientific medicine to doctors as if it were of no interest to theologians or philosophers. We see Paul Ricoeur, Professor of Metaphysics at the Sorbonne, turning to the study of Freud.[3] Dr. Klaus Thomas, of Berlin, was a doctor of theology. He realized that one could not be a complete theologian without studying philosophy, and so he did a doctorate in philosophy. Then he saw that it was not possible to be a philosopher knowing nothing about psychology, so he became a doctor of psychology. Finally he saw that he could not master psychology without being a doctor, and so he did a doctorate of medicine.

Nor is it possible to say that psychology is reserved for the sick and soul-healing for those who are well. There is no frontier between health and sickness, and the psychologists have taught us more about normal human nature than all the philosophers managed to do over many centuries. All doctors have a spiritual influence over their patients, even without trying, simply because of their personal contact with them, even if it is the most cursory glance. All psychotherapists are engaged in soul-healing, even if they try not to be. All ministers of religion, as they exercise their function of the cure of souls, are thereby having a psychotherapeutic effect upon their parishioners. Moreover, everybody is constantly acting psychotherapeutically, in so far as the essence of psychotherapy is dialogue, the effort to understand, and affective transference. And everybody practises soul-healing, in so far as soul-healing consists in witnessing to one's convictions, and giving comfort and advice to others.

Close collaboration is all the more necessary at the bedside between doctors and chaplains. For example, any doctor knows how a patient's inner attitude to his sickness can influence its course. Scientific medicine, however—psychoanalysis excepted—tends to reduce the patient to a passive attitude. The patient undergoes his sickness as if it were an event foreign to himself, and he passively submits to the treatments which the doctor prescribes—too often without explanation. The chaplain can arouse him to an attitude of active collaboration in his treatment through his becoming aware of his own responsibility for himself and for his health.

[3] P. Ricoeur, *De l'interprétation. Essai sur Freud*, Editions du Seuil, Paris, 1965.

That is why Dr. William McLendon, who was responsible for my last lecture-tour in the United States, organized at the Moses H. Cone Memorial Hospital, Grensboro, N.C., a symposium at which three clergymen spoke: one was a rabbi, the Rev. Joseph Asher, another a Roman Catholic priest, Mgr. Hugh Dolan, and the third a Protestant minister, the Rev. Fred W. Reid. Two doctors also spoke—Dr. McLendon and myself—and all on the same theme: the medicine of the person in the hospital. He had carefully prepared for the symposium by holding meetings at which doctors and chaplains came together. You can imagine how interested I was in the symposium. Nevertheless, it must be admitted that it was an introduction to dialogue, rather than a dialogue properly so-called. Among mutual congratulations we exchanged, with admirable unanimity, general ideas on the unity of the human person and on the need for a dialogue between our respective disciplines.

A really concrete dialogue begins only when it is possible to discuss together, without reticence, the case of each patient, as I have seen happening, for instance, in Dr. Gordon Johnsen's hospital in Norway. I have myself had some very happy experiences of such conversations with priests or pastors who have been exercising their ministry in regard to some of my patients. We have been able to agree on the advice to be given in cases where the caution of the Church has not always been in accord with the boldness of psychology! We have been able to pray together for our patients. But I must point out that sincere and profound contact of this sort is quite rare. The confrontation of differing points of view is not easy. We do not speak the same language, except in the case of clergymen who have made a study of psychology. But in that case what takes place is more in the nature of an argument between psychologists than a dialogue between our respective disciplines.

The obstacle is, I believe, much deeper and less conscious. I feel that doctors and clergy are a little afraid of each other. Handshakes and cordial smiles, mutual deference and praise serve to hide a cautious reserve. On both sides they are held back by feelings of inferiority. The theologians are too afraid of showing themselves ignorant of medical matters, and the doctors of religious matters. Both are at home in their own domains, and hesitate to venture outside them to face a real dialogue. The minister of religion is afraid of being thought a naïve idealist or a narrow moralist if he states his convictions to the doctor, and the doctor is afraid of being thought

a shocking materialist if he revels his views, or an infidel if he
voices his doubts.

The fact is that each is secretly critical of the other, and each sus-
pects that the other is critical of him. I leave aside the personal
criticisms which would exist between two doctors, or two ministers.
But between the two vocations there is a vaguely-defined area of con-
tentious mutual criticism of a general nature, and this must be brought
out into the open and liquidated before real dialogue can begin.

I remember Dr. Kütemeyer, of Heidelberg, saying to the Evangelical Academy at Bad Boll: "We must see things as they are; all
our patients are worse after the chaplain's visit." I have been told of
a remark made by Prof. Ajuriaguerra, of Geneva, about Pastor
Bernard Martin: "He is the only chaplain who does not do damage
to the patients." The remark is expressed in more courteous terms,
but it says practically the same thing. I happen to know Pastor
Martin very well: basically he has the mind of a doctor—and I know
he will take that as a compliment!

Doctors complain that chaplains give their patients feelings of
guilt rather than freeing them from them, that they weary them with
lengthy religious disquisitions that are too complicated and abstract, that they talk too much, and do not know how to listen. They
find them too dogmatic and accuse them of claiming, each for himself, a monopoly of truth, of not recognizing the faith of others, of
other denominations, of other religions, and even of all those who
"only err, seeking God, and desirous to find him" as the author of
the Book of the Wisdom of Solomon says (Wisd. 13.6). They
accuse them, too, of not recognizing the part played by delirium in
the things said by some patients, and of taking as a genuine conversion the over-optimistic testimony of a cycloid at the moment when
he is passing from depression to excitement.

In addition there is a background of somewhat banal complaints
against the churches on account of their conservative and formal-
istic outlook, and of the constraint they impose on men's minds—
or else on account of their coldness and of the spiritual solitude in
which they often leave their followers. This last criticism is doubtless one of the most important today, because of the individualistic
spirit of the West which permeates our churches. Even missionaries
recognize, for example, that a Moslem finds in his community a
support which Christians sometimes look for in vain from their own
Church.

Doctors have, however, a more fundamental complaint. It is that priests and pastors teach an inapplicable morality, and that they leave their people without an answer and without help when they realize that it is inapplicable. This teaching involves the commandments about non-resistance against the wicked, and systematic self-denial, which I referred to in Chapter 6. These commandments, in certain circumstances, may well be a proper call to a "second movement" in particular cases, though not a general rule of conduct. I have seen several converts whose anxiety-state has been considerably aggravated by their conversion. This, however, was not a psychological problem, but fairly and squarely a moral and religious one, for they had found themselves in an impasse through trying desperately to follow an impracticable moral code.

There are theologians who are well aware of this. I have heard Mlle. Suzanne de Diétrich maintaining that the Sermon on the Mount is not a moral code at all, but a simple discourse in which Jesus was trying to convince his hearers, imbued as they were with a sense of their own righteousness, that it is impossible to live without committing sin. If this is the case, why are the faithful unreservedly urged to apply it? There are of course many other criticisms. I wish only to refer to Job's profound remark, which André Neher quotes to explain Jeremiah: "God is either too far away or too near." Too far away, he seems to be deaf to man's cry for help; too near, he crushes him with his grandeur.

On the other hand, the clergy nurse plenty of grievances against doctors. There are criticisms *ad personam* aimed at the conduct of individuals, the mercenary spirit of one, the touchiness or the authoritarian attitude of another, or his lack of respect for the human person, his religious convictions, or his conscientious scruples. But the more serious complaints, in my view, are those that relate to the things I have been dealing with in this book. There is the denial of the fact of sin, either expressly, as in the case of certain psychologists who see it only as a myth born of a projection of the super-ego, or implicitly, as in the case of the numerous doctors who profess a naturalistic philosophy, either through disillusionment or cynicism, which treats moral problems as of no importance and encourages people to pander to their instincts. As for those doctors who take life seriously, they are criticized for advocating a limitless self-fulfilment which is as utopian as the moral code of which we were speaking just now.

These are all serious differences of opinion between men who assume weighty responsibilities as the confidants and advisers of others. And yet we are so afraid of creating an uneasy atmosphere that we scarcely ever touch upon them at meetings between theologians and doctors. We really need each other's help in trying to define a right attitude at a time when psychology has shaken the foundations of traditional morality. One cannot go from one extreme to another, from moralistic severity to the moral licence which has been characteristic of decadent civilizations. One cannot with impunity consign men and women to disaster on the excuse of liberating them from improper constraints. There has been only one love in my life, but I know very well that I owe the fact to my psychological complexes more than to my virtue, to say nothing of the grace of God! But I still congratulate myself for it, for it has spared me endless unhappiness.

Nevertheless, a true dialogue must consist of someming more than a frank exchange of ideas about conceptions of life and morality. It must include our personal problems and our intimate difficulties. This kind of dialogue is even rarer. Hospital chaplains are ready to look upon their duties as extending at need beyond the patients, to the nurses and cooks, and to the nuns in a church hospital, but not to the doctors. Yet it is these last who need it most, since it is they who are morally the most isolated, who find it most difficult to step out of their prestige role and show themselves as they are, with all their secret anxieties, failures, and rebellions.

When one thinks of the spiritual responsibilities—and I use the word "spiritual" advisedly—which devolve upon the innumerable psychotherapists who are consulted daily by people both sick and well, one trembles when one realizes that they are for the most part practically abandoned by the churches. Who is concerned with them? Who helps them to help others? Only their teacher, the psychotherapist who has directed their analytical training; and the sessions and seminars they hold together. But clearly all this is within a closed circle, confined to psychologists. Ministers of religion are rarely bold enough to exercise the cure of souls among psychotherapists. There is also the problem of the attachment of our patients to the Church. It is quite clear that when one of them has had, as a result of his cure, a spiritual experience, he ought not to remain dependent only on us. He ought to be able to integrate himself into a community. And that is by no means easy.

But it is in our hearts and minds that the union is difficult to make—the union which I have referred to throughout this book, between the two gospels, between the life of nature and the life of grace. "Action and prayer are equally necessary," one of my patients said to me. But she went on: "How are they to be combined? Either I act, and forget to pray, or I pray, and forget to act!" Of course, it is a matter of nothing less than the reconciliation of the finite and the infinite, the visible and the invisible, objectivity and subjectivity, the two worlds, temporal and spiritual, to both of which we belong. It is time to say that they all meet in God, who created both heaven and earth, but that is only a general maxim, and leaves us still facing our practical difficulties in the details of everyday life.

There is one of Jesus' sayings which haunts me: his instructions to his disciples when he sent them into the world: "Be wise as serpents and innocent as doves" (Matt. 10.16). Ah, it is not easy to be both at once! Sometimes I am as suspicious as a serpent. That is the scientific and realistic attitude, which sets up controls at every point in order to track down every cause of error, constantly calls everything in question, and in which scientific doubt is supreme. Sometimes I have the innocence of the dove—and its wings as well, believing everything I am told and deluding myself. Thus I am the serpent when I am the doctor, and the dove when I am the be- liever. Jesus, however, does not set these two attitudes over against one another. He requires us to have them both together. He is not entirely on the side of the dove, rejecting the serpent. On the con- trary, he compared himself to the serpent which Moses lifted up in the wilderness (John 3.14).

For example, we almost all make an analogous distinction be- tween Good Friday and Easter, between the preaching of sacrifice and that of resurrection. What Christian is there who flatters him- self that he unites them harmoniously? I shall be told that Good Friday and Easter are celebrated on different days, that they rep- resent an alternating rhythm; and that it is those believers who are able to identify themselves most closely with the suffering crucified Christ who also experience with him most intensely the joy of the Resurrection. That is true in theory, but very rare in practice. The Eastern Orthodox churches put greater emphasis on the Resurrec- tion, it seems to me, and those of the West, both Catholic and Pro- testant, on the Cross. It is not without astonishment that one sees

Louis Evely[4] inviting Christians to follow the "way of joy" with as much fervour as the "way of the Cross".

There are plenty of gloomy Christians, who delight in the contemplation of the Passion, for whom Christianity means essentially sacrifice, renunciation, and pain. They do not find themselves altogether at ease in the triumphant joy of Easter because they feel that the Cross is no longer being taken seriously if it is looked upon only as a stage in the road to the Resurrection. Other preachers, I am glad to say, stress the incomparable power of the Gospel as a source of life, of victories, and of fulfilment. One of the best known is Pastor Norman Peale, of New York.[5] There is something to restore the courage of those neurotics who always insist on turning to the severe and pessimistic parts of the Bible. Finally, there are yet others who have such an optimistic view that it seems utopian, in that it fails to reckon with the harsh reality of failures, disappointments, and sacrifices, from which none of us can escape.

It is true that all living things are subject to rhythmic alternations. Thus there is the systole and diastole of the heart, its contraction and dilatation. In the systole phase it is incapable of dilating, and in the diastole phase it is incapable of contracting. But we can do something, by means of thought, will, or emotion, to interfere with the normal rhythm of respiration. We can cut short an uncompleted inspiration with a premature expiration. So the rhythms of nature are pure only in the unconscious state, and are disturbed by the intervention of conscious thought. This is the explanation of the peculiar difficulty of the human condition. It is the heavy price we pay for the privilege of consciousness, a price we cannot avoid paying, because we cannot prevent ourselves from thinking, analysing intellectually, separating and opposing things which in living reality are complementary.

So it is with the "two movements" which I have distinguished and described in this book, in order to comprehend in its apparently contradictory totality the picture of man as seen at the same time in the light of scientific psychology and in that of the Bible. I may rightly be taken to task for having adopted an over-simplified picture, too abstract and intellectual a picture, which is not justified by

[4] L. Evely, *Le chemin de joie*, Causeries aux Fraternités de Charles de Foucauld, Presto-Print, Brussels.

[5] See his review, *Guideposts*, New York, N.Y., and his book *The Power of Positive Thinking*, Prentice-Hall, New York, 1952; The World's Work, Tadworth, Surrey, 1953.

the complexities of everyday life. Are we ever exclusively in one or other of the two movements? Are we not always to some degree in both at once?

For instance, I talk about this theory of the two movements to a young woman who has come for my help as a Christian and also as a psychologist. Having been brought up in another religion, she experienced at the age of adolescence a most decisive conversion to Christianity, a sudden and total adherence to the truth of the Gospel. Then, long after, she suffered from psychological disturbances the pain of which formed a remarkable contrast with the joy of her early years of life in the faith. It is not to be wondered at that she began to harbour doubts about the doctrines she professes. Such cases are not rare, but they are difficult to deal with. In order to sort things out a thorough psychological analysis is necessary.

That young woman recognized then that serious emotional repressions were involved in her conversion. Then there took place in her what psychologists call "short-circuiting"—that is to say that in the euphoria of conversion many problems had been pushed into the background, problems which ought first to have been resolved. The dynamism of her conversion had made it possible for her to by-pass these problems, and now, long afterwards, she was discovering that they were still tenaciously there. These discoveries are liberating on the one hand, but very disturbing on the other. What, for instance, was the part played in her conversion by the true divine call, and how much of it was psychoanalytical determinism? Possibly an evangelist would see only the former, and a psychoanalyst only the latter. As for me, I can see both!

Fortunately she too can see them both. She cannot deny what she saw to be true at the time of her conversion, nor what she can now see to be true concerning the psychological mechanisms from which she is suffering. She accepts my theory of the two successive movements, but it is of little help to her. Now she wonders perplexedly every day whether this or that act of renunciation in the conduct of her life is really demanded by God or suggested by her psychological complexes. "How can I tell whether my renunciation is genuine or not?" she exclaims.

You see how difficult the problem still is—the very problem which I have been trying to throw light upon in this book. We all find ourselves, moment by moment, faced with the need to choose between self-assertion and self-denial. Jesus says that he has power to lay down his life, and to take it again (John 10.18). But where does the frontier lie between "laying down one's life" and "allowing oneself to be used as a door-mat", between "taking one's life again" and refusing the sacrifice demanded? Of course, in the passage quoted, Jesus was speaking explicitly of his total dependence on God. We are to give our lives when God requires us to do so, and to take them again when God prescribes that we should do so, to defend ourselves or not to defend ourselves in accordance with his will, and precisely when he wills it. But our psychological mechanisms are always intervening between God and ourselves, and darkening our perception of his will.

Take another case, a woman who is not a convert. On the contrary, she has grown up in the hothouse atmosphere of an exceptionally religious family, frequenting church societies and solemn retreats. She has undergone intense "conditioning", as the Pavlovians say. She suffered a dramatic awakening when she realized that serious troubles affecting her physical health were connected with this conditioning. Whereas her friends followed the teaching about self-denial only so far as they wished, and followed their instincts which led them to look for a husband and for success in life, she had taken it so seriously that she had sacrificed herself to such an extent that she now found herself, twenty years later, right outside the realities of life. Illness came and filled the agonizing void.

She did not lose her faith, but she held aloof from the Church, and for years did not attend Mass or use the sacraments. This struck me as being a healthy reaction, and her spiritual director, who came to see me, understood it. Now her health is already improved, and she realizes that she still longs for the great fervours of her childhood. She therefore agreed to take part in a great rally of Catholic youth in which the atmosphere was fraternal but less conformist than the traditional Church.

There, after innumerable conversations with priests and lay people, she suddenly decided to go back to the way of the confessional and communion. When I see her again, she is in an ambivalent state of mind, happy freely to have taken the step she has, and also anxious. Was it premature? Had she passed through the first movement completely enough to be able to enter healthily into the second? And when can one be sure of having completed the first? And yet she cannot hold off the second indefinitely, she who has known since childhood that the true meaning of life cannot be found in egotistical self-fulfilment!

A foreign priest to whom she had unburdened herself is as concerned as I am with all these questions. He writes to me at great length, seeking to know my opinion. But really neither he nor I can provide the answers. They relate to events that are so subjective that it is impossible to find solutions from outside. Only the way she develops subsequently will show whether her return to the sacraments has been beneficial or harmful from the psychological point of view. It is certainly beneficial from the religious point of view, but nevertheless it could bring on new health difficulties. The important thing is that both the priest and I should be free of all preconceived ideas if we are to help that woman to find her way, without putting any constraint upon her, whatever happens.

One serious complication in the discrimination that we should like to make between the phases of the two movements is that we can never be sure when a complex has really been liquidated. To put it more exactly, there is no definitive cure for a complex. The more intelligent psychoanalysts recognize this openly. They speak only of becoming sufficiently conscious of our complexes to be able to hold our own against them. This judicious attitude is in marked contrast with the over-simplifications of the fanatical proselytes of psychoanalysis who pronounce themselves to be completely liberated from their complexes. The winning of a few victories over them is in itself to have made considerable progress. Our life is made up of a few victories and a lot of defeats; it is still a mixture of a little liberty and a lot of determinism. Scientific psychology and Christian soul-healing can combine to lead us to greater liberty—but liberty will never be complete in this world.

There is a further analogy here between the psychological and the religious experience. Through faith it is possible to win a victory over a sin which has seemed tenacious. But afterwards one finds one is still a sinner, and still capable even of slipping back into the old elementary sin which one thought was liquidated. It is rather dangerous, therefore, to talk about being saved, since believers who experience this kind of disappointment are sometimes led to doubt the authenticity of their conversion and the reality of their salvation. My answer to them is in the words of St. Paul: "In this hope we were saved" (Rom. 8.24). So we may say also that in this hope we have been psychologically healed.

When a course of psychoanalytical treatment is prolonged indefinitely without definite result, it is usually because the patient is still expecting the total self-enlightenment which he has naïvely thought possible, and which he hoped would remove all division of mind and all hesitation as to the right course to take. He is incapable of making up his mind to give what Dr. Alphonse Maeder calls[6] the "little shove", that is to say an act of self-commitment undertaken with a certain boldness in spite of all the obscurities that remain, and about which one might go on arguing for ever. A firm act of obedience, even if mistaken, provided it is done in good faith, is worth a thousand sincere hesitations. To procure for our patients just enough liberty for them to be able to give that little shove, is, I believe, all the help we can hope to give them, through both our psychological and our spiritual care.

I am well aware of this, having suffered in childhood from turning far too much in upon myself. Thanks to the help of others, and to God's grace, I was able gradually to overcome this tendency to secretiveness, to the point that now people come to me in large numbers to find personal contact. But my complex is still there at the back of my mind, and I always have to surmount a strong inner resistance before I am able to speak openly about myself to another person, and especially before I can take part in any communal life. It has meant that I have great discretion, which is quite useful in my profession, but it has also meant that some of my patients have been disappointed in me, and have complained that I am too secretive.

So one has to be shy to understand shy people and to help them to overcome their shyness. One has to be weak to understand the weak and to help them to overcome their weakness. One has to have known what it is to lack a place to understand those who cannot find a place for themselves, and to help them to discover one. Yet one must not be too shy, too weak, too much of a wanderer. One needs to have been helped oneself to win some victories over one's natural complexes. It has been said that no one can lead another person further than he has gone himself. I have often said so myself, but I am not sure that it is altogether true.

Some of those who have helped me most have been severely handicapped themselves—some of them psychologically ill. It can

---

[6] A. Maeder, *Ways to Psychic Health*, translated by Theodore Lit, Hodder and Stoughton, London, 1954.

happen that some one who is submerged in his own difficulties chances to say something that strikes us to the point of liberating us from blockages which he has not yet been able to cope with in himself. Many people cannot come to terms with this relative quality of our moral and psychological victories, and of those which we can procure for others. Many people are unable to accept that the lucidity which we seek to acquire is so limited. What do we really know about our underlying motivations? At one moment we can interpret our behaviour in one way, and a moment later in quite another. We can decide that we have been too generous or extremely selfish, quite courageous or thorough cowards, that we have really asserted ourselves or, on the contrary, merely been concealing a capitulation.

All human problems remain without any satisfying solution. All of us who are fighting in our various ways against evil and suffering, must admit, with Dr. Sarano, in his fine book on pain,[7] that the problem of evil and suffering remains insoluble to our sincerest efforts to unravel it, even when enlightened by faith. But is it not a consolation to find that despite our limitations—doubtless because of them—we can sometimes bring effective help to others? Is this not a sign that God can use us, that we can be the channels of his grace, either through our psychological science or through our faith?

We cannot stop ourselves wondering, asking ourselves all sorts of questions, looking for solutions, but we are soon out of breath. The more I study people—and myself—the more do I put my faith in God alone. God upsets all our neat intellectual formulae. He always has surprises in store for us. There was, for example, an intelligent and sensitive woman whom psychological disturbances had once brought to me. She had been brought up in a strict religious environment, from which she had withdrawn after our consultations. Her cure seemed to be linked with this liberation from a too rigorous religious constraint. It is a case, therefore, that I might well have quoted in support of my theory of the two movements. Then I suddenly received a letter from her. I was pleased, for I had not heard from her for some years. She told me that she had gone back to the Church she had left, and that her return had given her more happiness and peace than she had known at the time of her healing. I think this is only apparently contradictory—it is the same God who led her once to free herself from the onerous tutelage of

[7] Jacques Sarano, *La douleur*, l'Epi, Paris, 1965.

her Church so that she could become adult and be healed, and who had now called her back to the Church so that she could recover all the religious fervour she had lost during her spiritual isolation. Every person has his own road to follow, and we cannot know what it is beforehand. What counts in the end of the day is what God does, not what we do. The only really important thing is that each of us should come to know him, whatever the unforeseen detours we have to make.